THE MAKING OF A COUNTER CULTURE

Theodore Roszak was born in Chicago in 1933, attended the University of California at Los Angeles, and received his Ph.D. from Princeton in 1958. He is a member of the history department of California State College at Hayward, and was editor of and contributor to *The Dissenting Academy* (1968). He has had articles and reviews in many magazines, among them *The Nation, Liberation, New Politics,* and *The New American Review.*

THE MAKING OF A COUNTER CULTURE

Reflections on the Technocratic Society and Its Youthful Opposition

THEODORE ROSZAK

ANCHOR BOOKS

Doubleday & Company, Inc.

GARDEN CITY, NEW YORK

1969

The Making of a Counter Culture was published simultaneously in a hardcover edition in 1969 by Doubleday & Company, Inc.

Portions of chapters I, II, IV, V and VI originally appeared in *The Nation* in March and April 1968, and have been revised for publication in this volume.

Anchor Books edition: 1969

Grateful acknowledgment is made to the following for permission to reprint their material:

American Sociological Association and John T. Gullahorn
Excerpt from "Some Computer Applications in Social Science," by J. T. and J. E. Gullahorn. *American Sociological Review*, vol. 30, June, 1965.

Dr. Harvey Bluestone and The American Journal of Psychiatry
Excerpts from "Reaction to Extreme Stress: Impending Death by Execution," by Harvey Bluestone, M.D., and Carl L. McGahee, M.D. The *American Journal of Psychiatry*, volume 119, pages 393–96.

City Lights Books
Lines of "Wichita Vortex Sutra" from *Planet News*, by Allen Ginsberg. Copyright © 1968 by Allen Ginsberg.

Corinth Books, Inc.
Lines from *Empty Mirror: Early Poems*, by Allen Ginsberg. Copyright © 1961 by Allen Ginsberg; excerpt from Introduction by William Carlos Williams to *Empty Mirror*.

Harcourt, Brace & World, Inc.
Excerpt from *Poems 1923–1954*, by e. e. cummings.

International Times
Excerpt from "Paradise Now," by Julian Beck. IT, July 12–25, 1968.

The Julian Press, Inc.
Excerpt from *Gestalt Therapy*, by Frederick Perls, Ralph Hefferline and Paul Goodman

University of Oklahoma Press
Excerpt from *The Social Impact of Bomb Destruction*, by Fred Charles Ikle. Copyright © 1958 by the University of Oklahoma Press.

University of Chicago Press and Ure Smith PTY, LTD.
"The Lightning Snakes," from *World of the First Australians*, by R. M. and C. H. Berndt.

CONTENTS

CONTENTS

Art Degraded, Imagination Denied:
War Governed the Nations

* * * *

Rouse up, O Young Men of the New Age! set your foreheads against the ignorant Hirelings! For we have Hirelings in the Camp, the Court & the University, who would, if they could, for ever depress Mental & prolong Corporeal War.

—WILLIAM BLAKE

PREFACE

As a subject of study, the counter culture with which this book deals possesses all the liabilities which a decent sense of intellectual caution would persuade one to avoid like the plague. I have colleagues in the academy who have come within an ace of convincing me that no such things as "The Romantic Movement" or "The Renaissance" ever existed— not if one gets down to scrutinizing the microscopic phenomena of history. At that level, one tends only to see many different people doing many different things and thinking many different thoughts. How much more vulnerable such broad-gauged categorizations become when they are meant to corral elements of the stormy contemporary scene and hold them steady for comment! And yet that elusive conception called "the spirit of the times" continues to nag at the mind and demand recognition, since it seems to be the only way available in which one can make even provisional sense of the world one lives in. It would surely be convenient if these perversely ectoplasmic *Zeitgeists* were card-carrying movements, with a headquarters, an executive board, and a file of official manifestoes. But of course they aren't. One is therefore forced to take hold of them with a certain trepidation, allowing exceptions to slip through the sieve of one's generalizations in great numbers, but hoping always that more that is solid and valuable will finally remain behind than filters away.

All this is by way of admitting openly that much of what is said here regarding our contemporary youth culture is subject to any number of qualifications. It strikes me as obvious

beyond dispute that the interests of our college-age and adolescent young in the psychology of alienation, oriental mysticism, psychedelic drugs, and communitarian experiments
comprise a cultural constellation that radically diverges from
values and assumptions that have been in the mainstream of
our society at least since the Scientific Revolution of the
seventeenth century. But I am quite aware that this constellation has much maturing to do before its priorities fall into
place and before any well-developed social cohesion grows
up around it.

At this point, the counter culture I speak of embraces only
a strict minority of the young and a handful of their adult
mentors. It excludes our more conservative young, for whom
a bit less Social Security and a bit more of that old-time religion (plus more police on the beat) would be sufficient to
make the Great Society a thing of beauty. It excludes our
more liberal youth, for whom the alpha and omega of politics is no doubt still that Kennedy style. It excludes the
scattering of old-line Marxist youth groups whose members,
like their fathers before them, continue to tend the ashes of
the proletarian revolution, watching for a spark to leap forth.
More importantly, it excludes in large measure the militant
black young, whose political project has become so narrowly
defined in ethnic terms that, despite its urgency, it has become for the time being as culturally old-fashioned as the na-
tionalist mythopoesis of the nineteenth century. In any
event, the situation of black youth requires such special treatment as would run to book length in its own right.

If there is any justification for such exceptions in a discussion of youth, it must be that the counter cultural young
are significant enough both in numbers and in critical force
to merit independent attention. But from my own point of
view, the counter culture, far more than merely "meriting"
attention, desperately requires it, since I am at a loss to know

where, besides among these dissenting young people and their heirs of the next few generations, the radical discontent and innovation can be found that might transform this disoriented civilization of ours into something a human being can identify as home. They are the matrix in which an alternative, but still excessively fragile future is taking shape. Granted that alternative comes dressed in a garish motley, its costume borrowed from many and exotic sources—from depth psychiatry, from the mellowed remnants of left-wing ideology, from the oriental religions, from Romantic *Weltschmerz*, from anarchist social theory, from Dada and American Indian lore, and, I suppose, the perennial wisdom. Still it looks to me like all we have to hold against the final consolidation of a technocratic totalitarianism in which we shall find ourselves ingeniously adapted to an existence wholly estranged from everything that has ever made the life of man an interesting adventure.

If the resistance of the counter culture fails, I think there will be nothing in store for us but what anti-utopians like Huxley and Orwell have forecast—though I have no doubt that these dismal despotisms will be far more stable and effective than their prophets have foreseen. For they will be equipped with techniques of inner-manipulation as unobtrusively fine as gossamer. Above all, the capacity of our emerging technocratic paradise to denature the imagination by appropriating to itself the whole meaning of Reason, Reality, Progress, and Knowledge will render it impossible for men to give any name to their bothersomely unfulfilled potentialities but that of madness. And for such madness, humanitarian therapies will be generously provided.

There may be many readers for whom the issues raised in this book will seem meaningless as gibberish. It is not easy to question the thoroughly sensible, thoroughly well-intentioned, but nevertheless reductive humanism with which the technocracy surrounds itself without seeming to speak a dead and discredited language. Especially so if one admits—as I do (*pace* the doctrinaire eschatology of old and new left)—that it may well lie within the capability of the technocracy to utilize its industrial prowess, its social engineering, its sheer affluence, and its well-developed diversionary tactics, to reduce, in ways that most people will find perfectly acceptable, all the tensions born of disorganization, privation, and injustice which currently unsettle our lives. (Note that I do not say it will *solve* the problems; but rather, like adjustive psychotherapy, it will cunningly soothe the neurotic hurt.) The technocracy is not simply a power structure wielding vast material influence; it is the expression of a grand cultural imperative, a veritable mystique that is deeply endorsed by the populace. It is therefore a capacious sponge able to soak up prodigious quantities of discontent and agitation, often well before they look like anything but amusing eccentricities or uncalled-for aberrations. The question therefore arises: "If the technocracy in its grand procession through history is indeed pursuing to the satisfaction of so many such universally ratified values as The Quest for Truth, The Conquest of Nature, The Abundant Society, The Creative Leisure, The Well-Adjusted Life, why not settle back and enjoy the trip?"

The answer is, I guess, that I find myself unable to see anything at the end of the road we are following with such self-assured momentum but Samuel Beckett's two sad tramps forever waiting under that wilted tree for their lives to begin. Except that I think the tree isn't even going to be real, but a plastic counterfeit. In fact, even the tramps may turn out to be automatons . . . though of course there will be great, programmed grins on their faces.

THE MAKING OF A COUNTER CULTURE

Chapter I

TECHNOCRACY'S CHILDREN

The struggle of the generations is one of the obvious constants of human affairs. One stands in peril of some presumption, therefore, to suggest that the rivalry between young and adult in Western society during the current decade is uniquely critical. And yet it is necessary to risk such presumption if one is not to lose sight of our most important contemporary source of radical dissent and cultural innovation. For better or worse, most of what is presently happening that is new, provocative, and engaging in politics, education, the arts, social relations (love, courtship, family, community), is the creation either of youth who are profoundly, even fanatically, alienated from the parental generation, or of those who address themselves primarily to the young. It is at the level of youth that significant social criticism now looks for a responsive hearing as, more and more, it grows to be the common expectation that the young should be those who act, who make things happen, who take the risks, who generally provide the ginger. It would be of interest in its own right that the age-old process of generational disaffiliation should now be transformed from a peripheral experience in the life of the individual and the family into a major lever of radical social change. But if one believes, as I do, that the alienated young are giving shape to something that looks like the saving vision our endangered civilization requires, then there is no avoiding the need to understand and to educate them in what they are about.

The reference of this book is primarily to America, but it is headline news that generational antagonism has achieved international dimensions. Throughout the West (as well as in Japan and parts of Latin America) it is the young who find themselves cast as the only effective radical opposition within their societies. Not all the young, of course: perhaps only a minority of the university campus population. Yet no analysis seems to make sense of the major political upheavals of the decade other than that which pits a militant minority of dissenting youth against the sluggish consensus-and-coalition politics of their middle-class elders. This generational dichotomy is a new fact of political life, one which the European young have been more reluctant to accept than their American counterparts. The heirs of an institutionalized left-wing legacy, the young radicals of Europe still tend to see themselves as the champions of "the people" (meaning the working class) against the oppression of the bourgeoisie (meaning, in most cases, their own parents). Accordingly, they try valiantly to adapt themselves to the familiar patterns of the past. They reach out automatically along time-honored ideological lines to find allies—to the workers, the trade unions, the parties of the left . . . only to discover that these expected alliances strangely fail to materialize and that they stand alone and isolated, a vanguard without a following.

In Germany and Italy the major parties of the left opposition have allowed themselves to be co-opted into the mainstream of respectable politicking—perhaps even to the point of joining governing coalitions. Despite the fact that German students (less than 5 per cent of whom come from working-class families) risk the wrath of the police to crusade beneath banners bearing the names of Rosa Luxemburg and Karl Liebknecht, the backlash their street politics produces is as sharp among the workers as the bourgeoisie. When Berlin students demonstrate against the war in Vietnam, the trade unions respond (as in February 1968) with counter-demonstrations supporting Washington's version of "peace and freedom" in Southeast Asia.

In Britain, the Aldermaston generation and its disillusioned successors have long since had to admit that the Labour Party, angling always for the now decisive middle-class vote, is little more than Tweedledum to the Tories' Tweedledee. As for the British working class, the only cause that has inspired a show of fighting spirit on its part during the sixties (other than the standard run of wages and demarcation grievances) is the bloody-minded cry to drive the colored immigrants from the land.

In France, the battle-scarred students of the May 1968 Rebellion have had to watch the much-mellowed CGT and PC conniving to function as President de Gaulle's labor lieutenants in the maintenance of responsible, orderly government against the menace of "anarchy" in the streets. If the students march by rebellious thousands to the barricades, their cautious parents march in behalf of the status quo by the tens of thousands and vote by the millions for the general and the managerial elite he has recruited from the *Ecole polytechnique* for the purpose of masterminding the new French affluence. Even the factory workers who swelled the students' ranks from thousands to millions during the early stages of the May 1968 General Strike seem to have decided that the essence of revolution is a bulkier pay envelope.

Over and again it is the same story throughout Western Europe: the students may rock their societies; but without the support of adult social forces, they cannot overturn the established order. And that support would seem to be nowhere in sight. On the contrary, the adult social forces—including those of the traditional left—are the lead-bottomed ballast of the status quo. The students march to the Internationale, they run up the red flag, they plaster the barricades with pictures of Marxist heroes old and new . . . but the situation they confront stubbornly refuses to yield to a conventional left-right analysis. Is it any wonder that, in despair, some French students begin to chalk up the disgruntled slogan *"Je suis marxiste, tendance Groucho"* ("I'm a Marxist of the Groucho variety")? At last they are forced to admit that the entrenched consensus which repels their dissent is the generational phenomenon which the French and German young have begun to call "daddy's politics."

If the experience of the American young has anything to contribute to our understanding of this dilemma, it stems precisely from the fact that the left-wing of our political spectrum has always been so pathetically foreshortened. Our young are therefore far less adept at wielding the vintage rhetoric of radicalism than their European counterparts. But where the old categories of social analysis have so little to tell us (or so I will argue here), it becomes a positive advantage to confront the novelty of daddy's politics free of outmoded ideological preconceptions. The result may then be a more flexible, more experimental, though perhaps also a more seemingly bizarre approach to our situation. Ironically, it is the American young, with their underdeveloped radical background, who seem to have grasped most clearly the fact that, while such immediate emergencies as the Vietnam war, racial injustice, and hard-core poverty demand a deal of old-style politicking, the paramount struggle of our day is against a far more formidable, because far less obvious, opponent, to which I will give the name "the technocracy"—a social form more highly developed in America than in any other society. The American young have been somewhat quicker to sense that in the struggle against *this* enemy, the conventional tactics of political resistance have only a marginal place, largely limited to meeting immediate life-and-death crises. Beyond such front-line issues, however, there lies the greater task of altering the total cultural context within which our daily politics takes place.[1]

* * * *

By the technocracy, I mean that social form in which an industrial society reaches the peak of its organizational integration. It is the ideal men usually have in mind when they speak of modernizing, up-dating, rationalizing, planning. Drawing upon such unquestionable imperatives as the demand for efficiency, for social security, for large-scale co-ordination of men and resources, for ever higher levels of affluence and ever more impressive manifestations of collective human power, the technocracy works to knit together the anachronistic gaps and fissures of the industrial society. The meticulous systematization Adam Smith once celebrated in his well-

[1] For a comparison of American and European student radicalism along the lines drawn here, see Gianfranco Corsini, "A Generation Up in Arms," *The Nation*, June 10, 1968.

Daniel Cohn-Bendit and his spontaneous revolutionaries in France are something of an exception to what I say here about the young European radicals. Cohn-Bendit's anarchist instincts (which greatly riled the old-line leftist student groups during the May 1968 troubles) provide him with a healthy awareness of "the bureaucratic phenomenon" in modern industrial society and of the way in which it has subtly eroded the revolutionary potential of the working class and of its official left-wing leadership. He therefore warns strongly against "hero-worshiping" the workers. But even so, he continues to conceive of "the people" as the workers, and of the workers as the decisive revolutionary element, the students functioning only as their allies and sparkplugs. This leads him to the conclusion that the subversion of the status quo need not await a total cultural transformation, but can be pulled off by "insurrectional cells" and "nuclei of confrontation" whose purpose is to set an example for the working class. See Daniel and Gabriel Cohn-Bendit, *Obsolete Communism: The Left-Wing Alternative* (New York: McGraw-Hill, 1969), especially the keen analysis of the working partnership between "empiricist-positivist" sociology and technocratic manipulation, pp. 35–40.

known pin factory now extends to all areas of life, giving us human organization that matches the precision of our mechanistic organization. So we arrive at the era of social engineering in which entrepreneurial talent broadens its province to orchestrate the total human context which surrounds the industrial complex. Politics, education, leisure, entertainment, culture as a whole, the unconscious drives, and even, as we shall see, protest against the technocracy itself: all these become the subjects of purely technical scrutiny and of purely technical manipulation. The effort is to create a new social organism whose health depends upon its capacity to keep the technological heart beating regularly. In the words of Jacques Ellul:

Technique requires predictability and, no less, exactness of prediction. It is necessary, then, that technique prevail over the human being. For technique, this is a matter of life and death. Technique must reduce man to a technical animal, the king of the slaves of technique. Human caprice crumbles before this necessity; there can be no human autonomy in the face of technical autonomy. The individual must be fashioned by techniques, either negatively (by the techniques of understanding man) or positively (by the adaptation of man to the technical framework), in order to wipe out the blots his personal determination introduces into the perfect design of the organization.[2]

In the technocracy, nothing is any longer small or simple or readily apparent to the non-technical man. Instead, the scale and intricacy of all human activities—political, economic, cultural—transcends the competence of the amateurish citizen and inexorably demands the attention of specially trained

[2] Jacques Ellul, *The Technological Society*, trans. John W. Wilkinson (New York: A. A. Knopf, 1964), p. 138. This outrageously pessimistic book is thus far the most global effort to depict the technocracy in full operation.

experts. Further, around this central core of experts who deal with large-scale public necessities, there grows up a circle of subsidiary experts who, battening on the general social prestige of technical skill in the technocracy, assume authoritative influence over even the most seemingly personal aspects of life: sexual behavior, child-rearing, mental health, recreation, etc. In the technocracy everything aspires to become purely technical, the subject of professional attention. The technocracy is therefore the regime of experts—or of those who can employ the experts. Among its key institutions we find the "think-tank," in which is housed a multi-billion-dollar brainstorming industry that seeks to anticipate and integrate into the social planning quite simply everything on the scene. Thus, even before the general public has become fully aware of new developments, the technocracy has doped them out and laid its plans for adopting or rejecting, promoting or disparaging.[3]

Within such a society, the citizen, confronted by bewildering bigness and complexity, finds it necessary to defer on all matters to those who know better. Indeed, it would be a violation of reason to do otherwise, since it is universally agreed that the prime goal of the society is to keep the productive apparatus turning over efficiently. In the absence of expertise, the great mechanism would surely bog down, leaving us in the midst of chaos and poverty. As we will see in later chapters, the roots of the technocracy reach deep into our cultural past and are ultimately entangled in the scientific world-view of the Western tradition. But for our purposes here it will be enough to define the technocracy as

[3] For a report on the activities of a typical technocratic brain trust, Herman Kahn's Hudson Institute, see Bowen Northrup's "They Think For Pay" in *The Wall Street Journal*, September 20, 1967. Currently, the Institute is developing strategies to integrate hippies and to exploit the new possibilities of programmed dreams.

that society in which those who govern justify themselves by appeal to technical experts who, in turn, justify themselves by appeal to scientific forms of knowledge. And beyond the authority of science, there is no appeal.

Understood in these terms, as the mature product of technological progress and the scientific ethos, the technocracy easily eludes all traditional political categories. Indeed, it is characteristic of the technocracy to render itself ideologically invisible. Its assumptions about reality and its values become as unobtrusively pervasive as the air we breathe. While daily political argument continues within and between the capitalist and collectivist societies of the world, the technocracy increases and consolidates its power in both as a trans-political phenomenon following the dictates of industrial efficiency, rationality, and necessity. In all these arguments, the technocracy assumes a position similar to that of the purely neutral umpire in an athletic contest. The umpire is normally the least obtrusive person on the scene. Why? Because we give our attention and passionate allegiance to the teams, who compete within the rules; we tend to ignore the man who stands above the contest and who simply interprets and enforces the rules. Yet, in a sense, the umpire is the most significant figure in the game, since he alone sets the limits and goals of the competition and judges the contenders.

The technocracy grows without resistance, even despite its most appalling failures and criminalities, primarily because its potential critics continue trying to cope with these breakdowns in terms of antiquated categories. This or that disaster is blamed by Republicans on Democrats (or vice versa), by Tories on Labourites (or vice versa), by French Communists on Gaullists (or vice versa), by socialists on capitalists (or vice versa), by Maoists on Revisionists (or vice versa). But left, right, and center, these are quarrels between technocrats or between factions who subscribe to technocratic values from first to last. The angry debates of conservative and liberal, radical and reactionary touch everything except the technocracy, because the technocracy is not generally perceived as a political phenomenon in our advanced industrial societies. It holds the place, rather, of a grand cultural imperative which is beyond question, beyond discussion.

When any system of politics devours the surrounding culture, we have totalitarianism, the attempt to bring the whole of life under authoritarian control. We are bitterly familiar with totalitarian politics in the form of brutal regimes which achieve their integration by bludgeon and bayonet. But in the case of the technocracy, totalitarianism is perfected because its techniques become progressively more subliminal. The distinctive feature of the regime of experts lies in the fact that, while possessing ample power to coerce, it prefers to charm conformity from us by exploiting our deep-seated commitment to the scientific world-view and by manipulating the securities and creature comforts of the industrial affluence which science has given us.

So subtle and so well rationalized have the arts of technocratic domination become in our advanced industrial societies that even those in the state and/or corporate structure who dominate our lives must find it impossible to conceive of themselves as the agents of a totalitarian control. Rather, they easily see themselves as the conscientious managers of a munificent social system which is, by the very fact of its broadcast affluence, incompatible with any form of exploitation. At worst, the system may contain some distributive inefficiencies. But these are bound to be repaired . . . in time. And no doubt they will be. Those who gamble that either capitalism or collectivism is, by its very nature, incompatible with a totally efficient technocracy, one which will finally eliminate material poverty and gross physical exploitation, are making a risky wager. It is certainly one of the oldest, but one of the weakest radical arguments which insists stubbornly that capitalism is *inherently* incapable of laying golden eggs for everyone.

The great secret of the technocracy lies, then, in its capacity to convince us of three interlocking premises. They are:

1. That the vital needs of man are (contrary to everything the great souls of history have told us) purely technical in character. Meaning: the requirements of our humanity yield wholly to some manner of formal analysis which can be carried out by specialists possessing certain impenetrable skills and which can then be translated by them directly into a congeries of social and economic programs, personnel management procedures, merchandise, and mechanical gadgetry. If a problem does not have such a technical solution, it must not be a *real* problem. It is but an illusion . . . a figment born of some regressive cultural tendency.

2. That this formal (and highly esoteric) analysis of our needs has now achieved 99 per cent completion. Thus, with minor hitches and snags on the part of irrational elements in our midst, the prerequisites of human fulfillment have all but been satisfied. It is this assumption which leads to the conclusion that wherever social friction appears in the technocracy, it must be due to what is called a "breakdown in communication." For where human happiness has been so precisely calibrated and where the powers that be are so utterly well intentioned, controversy could not possibly derive from a substantive issue, but only from misunderstanding. Thus we need only sit down and reason together and all will be well.

3. That the experts who have fathomed our heart's desires and who alone can continue providing for our needs, the experts who *really* know what they're talking about, all happen to be on the official payroll of the state and/or corporate structure. The experts who count are the certified experts. And the certified experts belong to headquarters.

One need not strain to hear the voice of the technocrat in our society. It speaks strong and clear, and from high places. For example:

Today these old sweeping issues have largely disappeared. The central domestic problems of our time are more subtle and less simple. They relate not to basic clashes of philosophy or ideology, but to ways and means of reaching common goals—to research for sophisticated solutions to complex and obstinate issues. . . .

What is at stake in our economic decisions today is not some grand warfare of rival ideologies which will sweep the country with passion, but the practical management of a modern economy. What we need are not labels and clichés but more basic discussion of the sophisticated and technical questions involved in keeping a great economic machinery moving ahead. . . .

I am suggesting that the problems of fiscal and monetary policy in the Sixties as opposed to the kinds of problems we faced in the Thirties demand subtle challenges for which technical answers—not political answers—must be provided.[4]

Or, to offer one more example, which neatly identifies elitist managerialism with reason itself:

Some critics today worry that our democratic, free societies are becoming overmanaged. I would argue that the opposite

[4] John F. Kennedy, "Yale University Commencement Speech," New York *Times*, June 12, 1962, p. 20.

is true. As paradoxical as it may sound, the real threat to democracy comes, not from overmanagement, but from undermanagement. To undermanage reality is not to keep free. It is simply to let some force other than reason shape reality. That force may be unbridled emotion; it may be greed; it may be aggressiveness; it may be hatred; it may be ignorance; it may be inertia; it may be anything other than reason. But whatever it is, if it is not reason that rules man, then man falls short of his potential.

Vital decision-making, particularly in policy matters, must remain at the top. This is partly, though not completely, what the top is for. But rational decision-making depends on having a full range of rational options from which to choose, and successful management organizes the enterprise so that process can best take place. It is a mechanism whereby free men can most efficiently exercise their reason, initiative, creativity and personal responsibility. The adventurous and immensely satisfying task of an efficient organization is to formulate and analyze these options.[5]

Such statements, uttered by obviously competent, obviously enlightened leadership, make abundantly clear the prime strategy of the technocracy. It is to level life down to a standard of so-called living that technical expertise can cope with —and then, on that false and exclusive basis, to claim an intimidating omnicompetence over us by its monopoly of the experts. Such is the politics of our mature industrial societies,

[5] From Robert S. McNamara's recent book *The Essence of Security* (New York: Harper & Row, 1968) pp. 109–10. In the present generation, it is second- and third-level figures like McNamara who are apt to be the technocrats par excellence: the men who stand behind the official facade of leadership and who continue their work despite all superficial changes of government. McNamara's career is almost a paradigm of our new elitist managerialism: from head of Ford to head of the Defense Department to head of the World Bank. The final step will surely be the presidency of one of our larger universities or foundations. Clearly it no longer matters *what* a manager manages; it is all a matter of juggling vast magnitudes of things: money, missiles, students . . .

our truly *modern* societies, where two centuries of aggressive secular skepticism, after ruthlessly eroding the traditionally transcendent ends of life, has concomitantly given us a proficiency of technical means that now oscillates absurdly between the production of frivolous abundance and the production of genocidal munitions. Under the technocracy we become the most scientific of societies; yet, like Kafka's K., men throughout the "developed world" become more and more the bewildered dependents of inaccessible castles wherein inscrutable technicians conjure with their fate. True, the foolproof system again and again bogs down in riot or apathetic rot or the miscalculations of overextended centralization; true, the chronic obscenity of thermonuclear war hovers over it like a gargantuan bird of prey feeding off the bulk of our affluence and intelligence. But the members of the parental generation, storm-tossed by depression, war, and protracted warscare, cling fast to the technocracy for the myopic sense of prosperous security it allows. By what right would they complain against those who intend only the best, who purport to be the agents of democratic consensus, and who invoke the high rhetorical sanction of the scientific world view, our most unimpeachable mythology? How does one take issue with the paternal beneficence of such technocratic Grand Inquisitors? Not only do they provide bread aplenty, but the bread is soft as floss: it takes no effort to chew, and yet is vitamin-enriched.

To be sure, there are those who have not yet been cut in on the material advantages, such as the "other Americans" of our own country. Where this is the case, the result is, inevitably and justifiably, a forceful, indignant campaign fixated on the issue of integrating the excluded into the general affluence. Perhaps there is an exhausting struggle, in the course of which all other values are lost sight of. But, at last (why should we doubt it?), all the disadvantaged minorities are accommodated. And so the base of the technocracy is broadened as it assimilates its wearied challengers. It might almost be a trick, the way such politics works. It is rather like the ruse of inveigling someone you wish to capture to lean all his weight on a door you hold closed . . . and then, all of a sudden, throwing it open. He not only winds up inside, where you want him, but he comes crashing in full tilt.

In his analysis of this "new authoritarianism," Herbert Marcuse calls our attention especially to the technocracy's "absorbent power": its capacity to provide "satisfaction in a way which generates submission and weakens the rationality of protest." As it approaches maturity, the technocracy does indeed seem capable of anabolizing every form of discontent into its system.

Let us take the time to consider one significant example of such "repressive desublimation" (as Marcuse calls it). The problem is sexuality, traditionally one of the most potent sources of civilized man's discontent. To liberate sexuality would be to create a society in which technocratic discipline would be impossible. But to thwart sexuality outright would create a widespread, explosive resentment that required constant policing; and, besides, this would associate the technocracy with various puritanical traditions that enlightened men cannot but regard as superstitious. The strategy chosen, therefore, is not harsh repression, but rather the *Playboy* version of total permissiveness which now imposes its image upon us in every slick movie and posh magazine that comes along. In the affluent society, we have sex and sex galore—or so we are to believe. But when we look more closely we see that this sybaritic promiscuity wears a special social coloring. It has been assimilated to an income level and social status available only to our well-heeled junior executives and the jet set. After all, what does it cost to rent these yachts full of nymphomaniacal young things in which our playboys sail off for orgiastic swimming parties in the Bahamas? *Real* sex, we are led to believe, is something that goes with the best scotch, twenty-seven-dollar sunglasses, and platinum-tipped shoelaces. Anything less is a shabby substitute. Yes, there is permissiveness in the technocratic society; but it is only for the swingers and the big spenders. It is the reward that goes to reliable, politically safe henchmen of the status quo. Before our would-be playboy can be an assembly-line seducer, he must be a loyal employee.

Moreover, *Playboy* sexuality is, ideally, casual, frolicsome, and vastly promiscuous. It is the anonymous sex of the harem. It creates no binding loyalties, no personal attachments, no distractions from one's primary responsibilities—which are to the company, to one's career and social position, and to the system generally. The perfect playboy practices a career enveloped by noncommittal trivialities: there is no home, no family, no romance that divides the heart painfully. Life off the job exhausts itself in a constant run of imbecile affluence and impersonal orgasms.

Finally, as a neat little dividend, the ideal of the swinging life we find in *Playboy* gives us a conception of femininity which is indistinguishable from social idiocy. The woman becomes a mere playmate, a submissive bunny, a mindless decoration. At a stroke, half the population is reduced to being the inconsequential entertainment of the technocracy's pampered elite.

As with sexuality, so with every other aspect of life. The business of inventing and flourishing treacherous parodies of freedom, joy, and fulfillment becomes an indispensable form of social control under the technocracy. In all walks of life, image makers and public relations specialists assume greater and greater prominence. The regime of experts relies on a lieutenancy of counterfeiters who seek to integrate the discontent born of thwarted aspiration by way of clever falsification.

Thus:

We call it "education," the "life of the mind," the "pursuit of the truth." But it is a matter of machine-tooling the young to the needs of our various baroque bureaucracies: corporate, governmental, military, trade union, educational.

We call it "free enterprise." But it is a vastly restrictive system of oligopolistic market manipulation, tied by institutionalized corruption to the greatest munitions boondoggle in history and dedicated to infantilizing the public by turning it into a herd of compulsive consumers.

We call it "creative leisure": finger painting and ceramics in the university extension, tropic holidays, grand athletic excursions to the far mountains and the sunny beaches of the earth. But it is, like our sexual longings, an expensive adjunct of careerist high-achievement: the prize that goes to the dependable hireling.

We call it "pluralism." But it is a matter of the public authorities solemnly affirming everybody's right to his own opinion as an excuse for ignoring anybody's troubling challenge. In such a pluralism, critical viewpoints become mere private prayers offered at the altar of an inconsequential conception of free speech.

We call it "democracy." But it is a matter of public opinion polling in which a "random sample" is asked to nod or wag the head in response to a set of prefabricated alternatives, usually related to the *faits accompli* of decision makers, who can always construe the polls to serve their own ends. Thus, if 80 per cent think it is a "mistake" that we ever "went into" Vietnam, but 51 per cent think we would "lose prestige" if we "pulled out now," then the "people" have been "consulted" and the war goes on with their "approval."

We call it "debate." But it is a matter of arranging staged encounters between equally noncommittal candidates neatly tailored to fit thirty minutes of prime network time, the object of the exercise being to establish an "image" of competence. If there are interrogators present, they have been hand-picked and their questions rehearsed.

We call it "government by the consent of the governed." But even now, somewhere in the labyrinth of the paramilitary agencies an "area specialist" neither you nor I elected is dispatching "special advisors" to a distant "trouble spot" which will be the next Vietnam. And somewhere in the depths of the oceans a submarine commander neither you nor I elected is piloting a craft equipped with firepower capable of cataclysmic devastation and perhaps trying to decide if—for reasons neither you nor I know—the time has come to push the button.

It is all called being "free," being "happy," being the Great Society.

From the standpoint of the traditional left, the vices of contemporary America we mention here are easily explained —and indeed too easily. The evils stem simply from the unrestricted pursuit of profit. Behind the manipulative deceptions there are capitalist desperados holding up the society for all the loot they can lay hands on.

To be sure, the desperados are there, and they are a plague of the society. For a capitalist technocracy, profiteering will always be a central incentive and major corrupting influence. Yet even in our society, profit taking no longer holds its primacy as an evidence of organizational success, as one might suspect if for no other reason than that our largest industrial enterprises can now safely count on an uninterrupted stream of comfortably high earnings. At this point, considerations of an entirely different order come into play among the managers, as Seymour Melman reminds us when he observes:

The "fixed" nature of industrial investment represented by machinery and structures means that large parts of the costs of any accounting period must be assigned in an arbitrary way. Hence, the magnitude of profits shown in any accounting period varies entirely according to the regulations made by the management itself for assigning its "fixed" charges. Hence, profit has ceased to be the economists' independent measure of success or failure of the enterprise. We can define the systematic quality in the behavior and management of large industrial enterprises not in terms of profits, but in terms of their acting to maintain or to extend the production decision power they wield. Production decision power can be gauged by the number of people employed, or whose work is directed, by the proportion of given markets that a management dominates, by the size of the capital investment that is controlled, by the number of other managements whose decisions are controlled. Toward these ends profits are an instrumental device—subordinated in given accounting periods to the extension of decision power.[6]

Which is to say that capitalist enterprise now enters the stage at which large-scale social integration and control become paramount interests in and of themselves: the corporations begin to behave like public authorities concerned with rationalizing the total economy. If profit remains an important lubricant of the system, we should recognize that other systems may very well use different lubricants to achieve the same end of perfected, centralized organization. But in so doing they still constitute *technocratic* systems drawing upon their own inducements.

In the example given above of *Playboy* permissiveness, the instruments used to integrate sexuality into industrial

[6] Seymour Melman, "Priorities and the State Machine," *New University Thought*, Winter 1966–67, pp. 17–18.

rationality have to do with high income and extravagant mer-
chandizing. Under the Nazis, however, youth camps and
party courtesans were used for the same integrative purpose
—as were the concentration camps, where the kinkier members of the elite were rewarded by being allowed free exercise
of their tastes. In this case, sexual freedom was not assimilated
to income level or prestige consumption, but to party privilege. If the communist regimes of the world have not yet
found ways to institutionalize sexual permissiveness, it is because the party organizations are still under the control of
grim old men whose puritanism dates back to the days of
primitive accumulation. But can we doubt that once these
dismal characters pass from the scene—say, when we have a
Soviet version of Kennedy-generation leadership—we shall hear
of topless bathing parties at the Black Sea resorts and of orgiastic goings-on in the *duchas?* By then, the good apparatchiks and industrial commissars will also acquire the per-
quisite of admission to the swinging life.

It is essential to realize that the technocracy is not the exclusive product of that old devil capitalism. Rather, it is the
product of a mature and accelerating industrialism. The profiteering could be eliminated; the technocracy would remain
in force. The key problem we have to deal with is the
paternalism of expertise within a socioeconomic system which
is so organized that it is inextricably beholden to expertise.
And, moreover, to an expertise which has learned a thousand
ways to manipulate our acquiescence with an imperceptible
subtlety.

Perhaps the clearest way to illustrate the point, before we
finish with this brief characterization of the technocracy,
is to take an example of such technician-paternalism from a
non-capitalist institution of impeccable idealism: the British
National Health Service. Whatever its shortcomings, the NHS
is one of the most highly principled achievements of British

socialism, a brave effort to make medical science the efficient servant of its society. But of course, as time goes on, the NHS will have to grow and adapt to the needs of a maturing industrial order. In June 1968, the BBC (TV) produced a documentary study of the NHS which gave special emphasis to some of the "forward thinking" that now transpires among the experts who contemplate the future responsibilities of the service. Among them, the feeling was unmistakably marked that the NHS is presently burdened with too much lay interference, and that the service will never achieve its full potential until it is placed in the hands of professionally competent administrators.

What might one expect from these professionals, then? For one thing, better designed and equipped—notably, more automated—hospitals. Sensible enough, one might think. But beyond this point, the brainstorming surveyed by the documentary became really ambitious—and, mind, what follows are perfectly straight, perfectly serious proposals set forth by respected specialists in their fields. No put-ons and no dire warnings these, but hard-nosed attempts to be practical about the future on the part of men who talked in terms of "realities" and "necessities."

The NHS, it was suggested, would have to look forward to the day when its psychiatric facilities would take on the job of certifying "normal" behavior and of adjusting the "abnormal"—meaning those who were "unhappy and ineffectual"—to the exacting demands of modern society. Thus the NHS would become a "Ministry of Well-Being," and psychiatric manipulation would probably become its largest single duty.

Further: the NHS would have to take greater responsibility for population planning—which would include administration of a program of "voluntary euthanasia" for the unproductive and incompetent elderly. The NHS might have to enforce a program of compulsory contraception upon all adolescents, who would, in later life, have to apply to the Service for permission to produce children. It would then be the job of the NHS to evaluate the genetic qualities of prospective parents before granting clearance to beget.[7]

How are we to describe thinking of this kind? Is it "left-wing" or "right-wing"? Is it liberal or reactionary? Is it a vice of capitalism or socialism? The answer is: it is none of these. The experts who think this way are no longer part of such political dichotomies. Their stance is that of men who have risen above ideology—and so they have, insofar as the traditional ideologies are concerned. They are simply . . . the experts. They talk of facts and probabilities and practical solutions. Their politics *is* the technocracy: the relentless quest for efficiency, for order, for ever more extensive rational control. Parties and governments may come and go, but the experts stay on forever. Because without them, the system does not work. The machine stops. And *then* where are we?

How do the traditional left-wing ideologies equip us to protest against such well-intentioned use of up-to-date technical expertise for the purpose of making our lives more comfortable and secure? The answer is: they don't. After all, locked into this leviathan industrial apparatus as we are, where shall we turn for solutions to our dilemmas if not to the experts? Or are we, at this late stage of the game, to

[7] The program referred to is the documentary "Something for Nothing," produced for BBC-1 by James Burke and shown in London on June 27, 1968. In a 1968 symposium on euthanasia, Dr. Eliot Slater, editor of the *British Journal of Psychiatry*, was of the opinion that even if the elderly retain their vigor, they suffer from the defect of an innate conservatism. "Just as in the mechanical world, advances occur most rapidly where new models are being constantly produced, with consequent rapid obsolescence of the old, so too it is in the world of nature." Quoted in "Times Diary," *The Times* (London), July 5, 1968, p. 10.

relinquish our trust in science? in reason? in the technical intelligence that built the system in the first place?

It is precisely to questions of this order that the dissenting young address themselves in manifestoes like this one pinned to the main entrance of the embattled Sorbonne in May 1968:

The revolution which is beginning will call in question not only capitalist society but industrial society. The consumer's society must perish of a violent death. The society of alienation must disappear from history. We are inventing a new and original world. Imagination is seizing power.[8]

*   *   *   *

Why should it be the young who rise most noticeably in protest against the expansion of the technocracy?

There is no way around the most obvious answer of all: the young stand forth so prominently because they act against a background of nearly pathological passivity on the part of the adult generation. It would only be by reducing our conception of citizenship to absolute zero that we could get our senior generation off the hook for its astonishing default. The adults of the World War II period, trapped as they have been in the frozen posture of befuddled docility—the condition Paul Goodman has called "the nothing can be done disease"—have in effect divested themselves of their adulthood, if that term means anything more than being tall and debt-worried and capable of buying liquor without having to show one's driver's license. Which is to say: they have surrendered their responsibility for making morally demanding decisions, for generating ideals, for controlling public authority, for safeguarding the society against its despoilers.

[8] From *The Times* (London), May 17, 1968: Edward Mortimer's report from Paris.

Why and how this generation lost control of the institutions that hold sway over its life is more than we can go into here. The remembered background of economic collapse in the thirties, the grand distraction and fatigue of the war, the pathetic if understandable search for security and relaxation afterwards, the bedazzlement of the new prosperity, a sheer defensive numbness in the face of thermonuclear terror and the protracted state of international emergency during the late forties and fifties, the red-baiting and witch-hunting and out-and-out barbarism of the McCarthy years . . . no doubt all these played their part. And there is also the rapidity and momentum with which technocratic totalitarianism came rolling out of the war years and the early cold war era, drawing on heavy wartime industrial investments, the emergency centralization of decision making, and the awe-stricken public reverence for science. The situation descended swiftly and ponderously. Perhaps no society could have kept its presence of mind; certainly ours didn't. And the failure was not only American. Nicola Chiaromonte, seeking to explain the restiveness of Italian youth, observes,

. . . the young—those born after 1940—find themselves living in a society that neither commands nor deserves respect. . . . For has modern man, in his collective existence, laid claim to any god or ideal but the god of possession and enjoyment and the limitless satisfaction of material needs? Has he put forward any reason for working but the reward of pleasure and prosperity? Has he, in fact, evolved anything but this "consumer society" that is so easily and falsely repudiated?[9]

[9] The "falsely" in this quotation relates to Chiaromonte's very astute analysis of a doctrinaire blind spot in the outlook of Italian youth—namely their tendency to identify the technocracy with capitalism, which, as I have suggested, is a general failing of European youth movements. This very shrewd article appears in *Encounter*, July 1968, pp. 25–27. Chiaromonte does not mention the factor of fascism in Italy, but certainly in Germany the cleavage between young

On the American scene, this was the parental generation whose god Allen Ginsberg identified back in the mid-fifties as the sterile and omnivorous "Moloch." It is the generation whose premature senility Dwight Eisenhower so marvelously incarnated and the disease of whose soul shone so lugubriously through the public obscenities that men like John Foster Dulles and Herman Kahn and Edward Teller were prepared to call "policy." There are never many clear landmarks in affairs of the spirit, but Ginsberg's *Howl* may serve as the most public report announcing the war of the generations. It can be coupled with a few other significant phenomena. One of them would be the appearance of *MAD* magazine, which has since become standard reading material for the junior high school population. True, the dissent of *MAD* often sticks at about the Katzenjammer Kids level: but nevertheless the nasty cynicism *MAD* began applying to the American way of life—politics, advertising, mass media, education—has had its effect. *MAD* brought into the malt shops the same angry abuse of middle-class America which comics like Mort Sahl and Lenny Bruce were to begin bringing into the night clubs of the mid-fifties. The kids who were twelve when *MAD* first appeared are in their early twenties now—and they have had a decade's experience in treating the stuff of their parents' lives as contemptible laughing stock.

At a more significant intellectual level, Ginsberg and the beatniks can be associated chronologically with the aggressively activist sociology of C. Wright Mills—let us say with the publication of Mills' *Causes of World War III* (1957), which is about the point at which Mills' writing turned from scholarship to first-class pamphleteering. Mills was by no means the first postwar figure who sought to tell it like it is about the state of American public life and culture; the

and old has been driven deeper than anything we know in America by the older generation's complicity with Nazism.

valiant groups that maintained radical journals like *Liberation* and *Dissent* had been filling the wilderness with their cries for quite as long. And as far back as the end of the war, Paul Goodman and Dwight Macdonald were doing an even shrewder job of analyzing technocratic America than Mills was ever to do—and without relinquishing their humanitarian tone. But it was Mills who caught on. His tone was more blatant; his rhetoric, catchier. He was the successful academic who suddenly began to cry for action in a lethargic profession, in a lethargic society. He was prepared to step forth and brazenly pin his indictment like a target to the enemy's chest. And by the time he finished playing Emile Zola he had marked out just about everybody in sight for accusation.

Most important, Mills was lucky enough to discover ears that would hear: his indignation found an audience. But the New Left he was looking for when he died in 1961 did not appear among his peers. It appeared among the students —and just about nowhere else. If Mills were alive today, his following would still be among the under thirties (though the Vietnam war has brought a marvelous number of his academic colleagues out into open dissent—but will they stay out when the war finally grinds to its ambiguous finish?).

Admittedly, the dissent that began to simmer in the mid-fifties was not confined to the young. The year 1957 saw the creation at the adult level of resistance efforts like SANE and, a bit later, Turn Toward Peace. But precisely what do groups like SANE and TTP tell us about adult America, even where we are dealing with politically conscious elements? Looking back, one is struck by their absurd shallowness and conformism, their total unwillingness to raise fundamental issues about the quality of American life, their fastidious anti-communism, and above all their incapacity to sustain any significant initiative on the political landscape. Even the Committee of Correspondence, a promising effort on the part of senior academics (formed around 1961) quickly settled for publishing a new journal. Currently the diminishing remnants of SANE and TTP seem to have been reduced to the role of carping (often with a deal of justice) at the impetuous extremes and leftist flirtations of far more dynamic youth groups like the Students for a Democratic Society, or the Berkeley Vietnam Day Committee, or the 1967 Spring Mobilization. But avuncular carping is not initiative. And it is a bore, even if a well-intentioned bore, when it becomes a major preoccupation. Similarly, it is the younger Negro groups that have begun to steal the fire from adult organizations—but in this case with results that I feel are apt to be disastrous.

The fact is, it is the young who have in their own amateurish, even grotesque way, gotten dissent off the adult drawing board. They have torn it out of the books and journals an older generation of radicals authored, and they have fashioned it into a style of life. They have turned the hypotheses of disgruntled elders into experiments, though often without the willingness to admit that one may have to concede failure at the end of any true experiment.

When all is said and done, however, one cannot help being ambivalent toward this compensatory dynamism of the young. For it is, at last, symptomatic of a thoroughly diseased state of affairs. It is not ideal, it is probably not even good that the young should bear so great a responsibility for inventing or initiating for their society as a whole. It is too big a job for them to do successfully. It is indeed tragic that in a crisis that demands the tact and wisdom of maturity, everything that looks most hopeful in our culture should be building from scratch—as must be the case when the builders are absolute beginners.

Beyond the parental default, there are a number of social and psychic facts of life that help explain the prominence of the dissenting young in our culture. In a number of ways, this new generation happens to be particularly well placed and primed for action.

Most obviously, the society is getting younger—to the extent that in America, as in a number of European countries, a bit more than 50 per cent of the population is under twenty-five years of age. Even if one grants that people in their mid-twenties have no business claiming, or letting themselves be claimed for the status of "youth," there still remains among the authentically young in the thirteen to nineteen bracket a small nation of twenty-five million people. (As we shall see below, however, there is good reason to group the mid-twenties with their adolescent juniors.)

But numbers alone do not account for the aggressive prominence of contemporary youth. More important, the young seem to *feel* the potential power of their numbers as never before. No doubt to a great extent this is because the market apparatus of our consumer society has devoted a deal of wit to cultivating the age-consciousness of old and young alike. Teen-agers alone control a stupendous amount of money and enjoy much leisure; so, inevitably, they have been turned into a self-conscious market. They have been pampered, exploited, idolized, and made almost nauseatingly much of. With the result that whatever the young have fashioned for themselves has rapidly been rendered grist for the commercial mill and cynically merchandised by assorted hucksters—*including* the new ethos of dissent, a fact that creates an agonizing disorientation for the dissenting young (and their critics) and to which we will return presently.

The force of the market has not been the only factor in intensifying age-consciousness, however. The expansion of higher education has done even more in this direction. In the United States we have a college population of nearly six million, an increase of more than double over 1950. And the expansion continues as college falls more and more into the standard educational pattern of the middle-class young.[10] Just as the dark satanic mills of early industrialism concentrated labor and helped create the class-consciousness of the proletariat, so the university campus, where up to thirty thousand students may be gathered, has served to crystallize the group identity of the young—with the important effect of mingling freshmen of seventeen and eighteen with graduate students well away in their twenties. On the major campuses, it is often enough the graduates who assume positions of leadership, contributing to student movements a degree of competence that the younger students could not muster. When one includes in this alliance that significant new entity, the non-student—the campus roustabout who may be in his late twenties—one sees why "youth" has become such a long-term career these days. The grads and the non-students easily come to identify their interests and allegiance with a distinctly younger age group. In previous generations, they would long since have left these youngsters behind. But now they and the freshmen just out of high school find themselves all together in one campus community.

[10] The rapid growth of the college population is an international phenomenon, with Germany, Russia, France, Japan, and Czechoslovakia (among the developed countries) equaling or surpassing the increase of the United States. UNESCO statistics for the period 1950–64 are as follows:

	1950	1964	Increase
U.S.A.	2.3 million	5 million	2.2x
U.K.	133,000	211,000	1.6x
U.S.S.R.	1.2 million	3.6 million	3.0x
Italy	192,000	262,000	1.3x
France	140,000	455,000	3.3x
W. Germany	123,000	343,000	2.8x
W. Berlin	12,000	31,000	2.6x
Czechoslovakia	44,000	142,000	3.2x
Japan	391,000	917,000	2.3x
India	404,000	1.1 million	2.2x

The role of these campus elders is crucial, for they tend to be those who have the most vivid realization of the new economic role of the university. Being closer to the technocratic careers for which higher education is supposed to be grooming them in the Great Society, they have a delicate sensitivity to the social regimentation that imminently confronts them, and a stronger sense of the potential power with which the society's need for trained personnel endows them. In some cases their restiveness springs from a bread-and-butter awareness of the basic facts of educational life these days, for in England, Germany, and France the most troublesome students are those who have swelled the numbers in the humanities and social studies only to discover that what the society really wants out of its schools is technicians, not philosophers. In Britain, this strong trend away from the sciences over the past four years continues to provoke annoyed concern from public figures who are not the least bit embarrassed to reveal their good bourgeois philistinism by loudly observing that the country is not spending its money to produce poets and Egyptologists—and then demanding a sharp cut in university grants and stipends.[11]

Yet at the same time, these non-technicians know that the society cannot do without its universities, that it cannot shut them down or brutalize the students without limit. The universities produce the brains the technocracy needs; therefore, making trouble on the campus is making trouble in one of the economy's vital sectors. And once the graduate students—many of whom may be serving as low-level teaching assistants—have been infected with qualms and aggressive

[11] In his 1967 Reith Lectures, Dr. Edmund Leach seeks to account for the steady swing from the sciences. See his *Runaway World*, British Broadcasting Company, 1968. For reflections on the same phenomenon in Germany, see Max Beloff's article in *Encounter*, July 1968, pp. 28–33.

discontents, the junior faculty, with whom they overlap, may soon catch the fevers of dissent and find themselves drawn into the orbit of "youth."

The troubles at Berkeley in late 1966 illustrate the expansiveness of youthful protest. To begin with, a group of undergraduates stages a sit-in against naval recruiters at the Student Union. They are soon joined by a contingent of non-students, whom the administration then martyrs by selective arrest. A non-student of nearly thirty—Mario Savio, already married and a father—is quickly adopted as spokesman for the protest. Finally, the teaching assistants call a strike in support of the menaced demonstration. When at last the agitation comes to its ambiguous conclusion, a rally of thousands gathers outside Sproul Hall, the central administration building, to sing the Beatles' "Yellow Submarine"—which happens to be the current hit on all the local high-school campuses. If "youth" is not the word we are going to use to cover this obstreperous population, then we may have to coin another. But undeniably the social grouping exists with a self-conscious solidarity.

If we ask who is to blame for such troublesome children, there can be only one answer: it is the parents who have equipped them with an anemic superego. The current generation of students is the beneficiary of the particularly permissive child-rearing habits that have been a feature of our postwar society. Dr. Spock's endearing latitudinarianism (go easy on the toilet training, don't panic over masturbation, avoid the heavy discipline) is much more a reflection than a cause of the new (and wise) conception of proper parent-child relations that prevails in our middle class. A high-consumption, leisure-wealthy society simply doesn't need contingents of rigidly trained, "responsible" young workers. It cannot employ more than a fraction of untrained youngsters fresh out of high school. The middle class can therefore afford to prolong the ease and drift of childhood, and so it does. Since nobody expects a child to learn any marketable skills until he gets to college, high school becomes a country club for which the family pays one's dues. Thus the young are "spoiled," meaning they are influenced to believe that being human has something to do with pleasure and freedom. But unlike their parents, who are also avid for the plenty and leisure of the consumer society, the young have not had to sell themselves for their comforts or to accept them on a part-time basis. Economic security is something they can take for granted—and on it they build a new, uncompromised personality, flawed perhaps by irresponsible ease, but also touched with some outspoken spirit. Unlike their parents, who must kowtow to the organizations from which they win their bread, the youngsters can talk back at home with little fear of being thrown out in the cold. One of the pathetic, but, now we see, promising characteristics of postwar America has been the uppityness of adolescents and the concomitant reduction of the paterfamilias to the general ineffectuality of a Dagwood Bumstead. In every family comedy of the last twenty years, dad has been the buffoon.

The permissiveness of postwar child-rearing has probably seldom met A. S. Neill's standards—but it has been sufficient to arouse expectations. As babies, the middle-class young got picked up when they bawled. As children, they got their kindergarten finger paintings thumbtacked on the living room wall by mothers who knew better than to discourage incipient artistry. As adolescents, they perhaps even got a car of their own (or control of the family's), with all of the sexual privileges attending. They passed through school systems which, dismal as they all are in so many respects, have nevertheless prided themselves since World War II on the introduction of "progressive" classes having to do with "creativity" and "self-expression." These are also the years that saw the proliferation of all the mickey mouse courses which take the self-indulgence of adolescent "life problems" so seriously. Such scholastic pap mixes easily with the commercial world's effort to elaborate a total culture of adolescence based on nothing but fun and games. (What else could a culture of adolescence be based on?) The result has been to make of adolescence, not the beginning of adulthood, but a status in its own right: a limbo that is nothing so much as the prolongation of an already permissive infancy.

To be sure, such an infantization of the middle-class young has a corrupting effect. It ill prepares them for the real world and its unrelenting if ever more subtle disciplines. It allows them to nurse childish fantasies until too late in life; until there comes the inevitable crunch. For as life in the multiversity wears on for these pampered youngsters, the technocratic reality principle begins grimly to demand its concessions. The young get told they are now officially "grown up," but they have been left too long without any taste for the rigidities and hypocrisies that adulthood is supposed to be all about. General Motors all of a sudden wants barbered hair, punctuality, and an appropriate reverence for the conformities of the organizational hierarchy. Washington wants patriotic cannon fodder with no questions asked. Such prospects do not look like fun from the vantage point of between eighteen and twenty years of relatively carefree drifting.[12]

Some of the young (most of them, in fact) summon up the proper sense of responsibility to adjust to the prescribed

[12] Even the Young Americans for Freedom, who staunchly champion the disciplined virtues of the corporate structure, have become too restive to put up with the indignity of conscription. With full support from Ayn Rand, they have set the draft down as "selective slavery." How long will it be before a conservatism that perceptive recognizes that the ideal of free enterprise has nothing to do with technocratic capitalism?

patterns of adulthood; others, being incorrigibly childish, do not. They continue to assert pleasure and freedom as human rights and begin to ask aggressive questions of those forces that insist, amid obvious affluence, on the continued necessity of discipline, no matter how subliminal. This is why, for example, university administrators are forced to play such a false game with their students, insisting on the one hand that the students are "grown-up, responsible men and women," but on the other hand knowing full well that they dare not entrust such erratic children with any power over their own education. For what can one rely upon them to do that will suit the needs of technocratic regimentation?

The incorrigibles either turn political or drop out. Or perhaps they fluctuate between the two, restless, bewildered, hungry for better ideas about grown-upness than GM or IBM or LBJ seem able to offer. Since they are improvising their own ideal of adulthood—a task akin to lifting oneself by one's bootstraps—it is all too easy to go pathetically wrong. Some become ne'er-do-well dependents, bumming about the bohemias of America and Europe on money from home; others simply bolt. The FBI reports the arrest of over ninety thousand juvenile runaways in 1966; most of those who flee well-off middle-class homes get picked up by the thousands each current year in the big-city bohemias, fending off malnutrition and venereal disease. The immigration departments of Europe record a constant level over the past few years of something like ten thousand disheveled "flower children" (mostly American, British, German, and Scandinavian) migrating to the Near East and India—usually toward Katmandu (where drugs are cheap and legal) and a deal of hard knocks along the way. The influx has been sufficient to force Iran and Afghanistan to substantially boost the "cash in hand" requirements of prospective tourists. And the British consul-general in Istanbul officially requested Parliament in late

1967 to grant him increased accommodations for the "swarm" of penniless young Englishmen who have been cropping up at the consulate on their way east, seeking temporary lodgings or perhaps shelter from Turkish narcotics authorities.[13]

One can flippantly construe this exodus as the contemporary version of running off with the circus; but the more apt parallel might be with the quest of third-century Christians (a similarly scruffy, uncouth, and often half-mad lot) for escape from the corruptions of Hellenistic society: it is much more a flight *from* than *toward*. Certainly for a youngster of seventeen, clearing out of the comfortable bosom of the middle-class family to become a beggar is a formidable gesture of dissent. One makes light of it at the expense of ignoring a significant measure of our social health.

So, by way of a dialectic Marx could never have imagined, technocratic America produces a potentially revolutionary element among its own youth. The bourgeoisie, instead of discovering the class enemy in its factories, finds it across the breakfast table in the person of its own pampered children. To be sure, by themselves the young might drift into hopeless confusion and despair. But now we must add one final ingredient to this ebullient culture of youthful dissent, which gives it some chance of achieving form and direction. This is the adult radical who finds himself in a plight which much resembles that of the bourgeois intellectual in Marxist theory. In despair for the timidity and lethargy of his own class, Marx's middle-class revolutionary was supposed at last to turn renegade and defect to the proletariat. So in postwar America, the adult radical, confronted with a diminishing public among the "cheerful robots" of his own generation, naturally gravitates to the restless middle-class young. Where else is

[13] For the statistics mentioned, see *Time*, September 15, 1967, pp. 47–49; *The Observer* (London), September 24, 1967; and *The Guardian* (London), November 18, 1967.

he to find an audience? The working class, which provided the traditional following for radical ideology, now neither leads nor follows, but sits tight and plays safe: the stoutest prop of the established order. If the adult radical is white, the ideal of Black Power progressively seals off his entrée to Negro organizations. As for the exploited masses of the Third World, they have as little use for white Western ideologues as our native blacks—and in any case they are far distant. Unless he follows the strenuous example of a Regis Debray, the white American radical can do little more than sympathize from afar with the revolutionary movements of Asia, Africa, and Latin America.

On the other hand, the disaffected middle-class young are at hand, suffering a strange new kind of "immiserization" that comes of being stranded between a permissive childhood and an obnoxiously conformist adulthood, experimenting desperately with new ways of growing up self-respectfully into a world they despise, calling for help. So the radical adults bid to become gurus to the alienated young or perhaps the young draft them into service.

Of course, the young do not win over all the liberal and radical adults in sight. From more than a few their readiness to experiment with a variety of dissenting life styles comes in for severe stricture—which is bound to be exasperating for the young. What are they to think? For generations, left-wing intellectuals have lambasted the bad habits of bourgeois society. "The bourgeoisie" they have insisted, "is obsessed by greed; its sex life is insipid and prudish; its family patterns are debased; its slavish conformities of dress and grooming are degrading; its mercenary routinization of existence is intolerable; its vision of life is drab and joyless; etc., etc." So the restive young, believing what they hear, begin to try this and that, and one by one they discard the vices of their parents, preferring the less structured ways of their own childhood and adolescence—only to discover many an old-line dissenter, embarrassed by the brazen sexuality and unwashed feet, the disheveled dress and playful ways, taking up the chorus, "No, that is not what I meant. That is not what I meant at all."

For example, a good liberal like Hans Toch invokes the Protestant work ethic to give the hippies a fatherly tongue-lashing for their "consuming but noncontributing" ways. They are being "parasitic," Professor Toch observes, for "the hippies, after all accept—even demand—social services, while rejecting the desirability of making a contribution to the economy."[14] But *of course* they do. Because we have an economy of cybernated abundance that does not need their labor, that is rapidly severing the tie between work and wages, that suffers from hard-core poverty due to maldistribution, not scarcity. From this point of view, why is the voluntary dropping-out of the hip young any more "parasitic" than the enforced dropping-out of impoverished ghetto dwellers? The economy can do abundantly without all this labor. How better, then, to spend our affluence than on those minimal goods and services that will support leisure for as many of us as possible? Or are these hippies reprehensible because they seem to enjoy their mendicant idleness, rather than feeling, as the poor apparently should, indignant and fighting mad to get a good respectable forty-hour-week job? There are criticisms to be made of the beat-hip bohemian fringe of our youth culture—but this is surely not one of them.

It would be a better general criticism to make of the young that they have done a miserably bad job of dealing with the

14 Hans Toch, "The Last Word on the Hippies," *The Nation*, December 4, 1967. See also the jaundiced remarks of Eric Hoffer in the New York *Post Magazine*, September 23, 1967, pp. 32–33; Milton Mayer writing in *The Progressive*, October 1967; and Arnold Wesker's "Delusions of Floral Grandeur" in the English magazine *Envoy*, December 1967.

distortive publicity with which the mass media have burdened their embryonic experiments. Too often they fall into the trap of reacting narcissistically or defensively to their own image in the fun-house mirror of the media. Whatever these things called "beatniks" and "hippies" originally were, or still are, may have nothing to do with what *Time, Esquire, Cheeta,* CBSNBCABC, Broadway comedy, and Hollywood have decided to make of them. Dissent, the press has clearly decided, is hot copy. But if anything, the media tend to isolate the weirdest aberrations *and* consequently to attract to the movement many extroverted poseurs. But what does bohemia do when it finds itself massively infiltrated by well-intentioned sociologists (and we now all of a sudden have specialized "sociologists of adolescence"), sensationalizing journalists, curious tourists, and weekend fellow travelers? What doors does one close on them? The problem is a new and tough one: a kind of cynical smothering of dissent by saturation coverage, and it begins to look like a far more formidable weapon in the hands of the establishment than outright suppression.

Again, in his excellent article on the Italian students quoted above, Nicola Chiaromonte tells us that dissenters

must detach themselves, must become resolute "heretics." They must detach themselves quietly, without shouting or riots, indeed in silence and secrecy; not alone but in groups, in real "societies" that will create, as far as possible, a life that is independent and wise. . . . It would be . . . a non-rhetorical form of "total rejection."

But how is one to develop such strategies of dignified secrecy when the establishment has discovered exactly the weapon with which to defeat one's purposes: the omniscient mass media? The only way anybody or anything stays underground these days is by trying outlandishly hard—as when

Ed Saunders and a group of New York poets titled a private publication *Fuck You* to make sure it stayed off the newsstands. But it can be quite as distortive to spend all one's time evading the electronic eyes and ears of the world as to let oneself be inaccurately reported by them.

Yet to grant the fact that the media distort is not the same as saying that the young have evolved no life style of their own, or that they are unserious about it. We would be surrendering to admass an absolutely destructive potential if we were to take the tack that whatever it touches is automatically debased or perhaps has no reality at all. In London today at some of the better shops one can buy a Chinese Army-style jacket, advertised as "Mao Thoughts in Burberry Country: elegant navy flannel, revolutionary with brass buttons and Mao collar." The cost: £28 . . . a mere $68. Do Mao and the cultural revolution suddenly become mere figments by virtue of such admass larks?

Commercial vulgarization is one of the endemic pests of twentieth-century Western life, like the flies that swarm to sweets in the summer. But the flies don't create the sweets (though they may make them less palatable); nor do they make the summer happen. It will be my contention that there is, despite the fraudulence and folly that collects around its edges, a significant new culture a-borning among our youth, and that this culture deserves careful understanding, if for no other reason than the sheer size of the population it potentially involves.

But there *are* other reasons, namely, the intrinsic value of what the young are making happen. If, however, we want to achieve that understanding, we must insist on passing over the exotic tidbits and sensational case histories the media offer us. Nor should we resort to the superficial snooping that comes of cruising bohemia for a few exciting days in search of local color and the inside dope, often with the intention of writing it all up for the slick magazines. Rather, we should look for major trends that seem to outlast the current fashion. We should try to find the most articulate public statements of belief and value the young have made or have given ear to; the thoughtful formulations, rather than the off-hand gossip. Above all, we must be willing, in a spirit of critical helpfulness, to sort out what seems valuable and promising in this dissenting culture, as if indeed it mattered to us whether the alienated young succeeded in their project.

Granted this requires a deal of patience. For what we are confronted with is a progressive "adolescentization" of dissenting thought and culture, if not on the part of its creators, then on the part of much of its audience. And we should make no mistake about how far back into the early years of adolescence these tastes now reach. Let me offer one illuminating example. In December of 1967, I watched a group of thirteen-year-olds from a London settlement house perform an improvised Christmas play as part of a therapeutic theater program. The kids had concocted a show in which Santa Claus had been imprisoned by the immigration authorities for entering the country without proper permission. The knock at official society was especially stinging, coming as it did instinctively from some very ordinary youngsters who had scarcely been exposed to any advanced intellectual influences. And whom did the thirteen-year-olds decide to introduce as Santa's liberators? An exotic species of being known to them as "the hippies," who shiva-danced to the jailhouse and magically released Father Christmas, accompanied by strobelights and jangling sitars.

However lacking older radicals may find the hippies in authenticity or revolutionary potential, they have clearly succeeded in embodying radical disaffiliation—what Herbert Marcuse has called the Great Refusal—in a form that captures the need of the young for unrestricted joy. The hippy, real or as imagined, now seems to stand as one of the few images toward which the very young can grow without having to give up the childish sense of enchantment and playfulness, perhaps because the hippy keeps one foot in his childhood. Hippies who may be pushing thirty wear buttons that read "Frodo Lives" and decorate their pads with maps of Middle Earth (which happens to be the name of one of London's current rock clubs). Is it any wonder that the best and brightest youngsters at Berkeley High School (just to choose the school that happens to be in my neighborhood) are already coming to class barefoot, with flowers in their hair, and ringing with cowbells?

Such developments make clear that the generational revolt is not likely to pass over in a few years' time. The ethos of disaffiliation is still in the process of broadening down through the adolescent years, picking up numbers as time goes on. With the present situation we are perhaps at a stage comparable to the Chartist phase of trade unionism in Great Britain, when the ideals and spirit of a labor movement had been formulated but had not reached anything like class-wide dimensions. Similarly, it is still a small, if boisterous minority of the young who now define the generational conflict. But the conflict will not vanish when those who are now twenty reach thirty; it may only reach its peak when those who are now eleven and twelve reach their late twenties. (Say, about 1984.) We then may discover that what a mere handful of beatniks pioneered in Allen Ginsberg's youth will have become the life style of millions of college-age young. Is there any other ideal toward which the young can grow that looks half so appealing?

"Nothing," Goethe observed, "is more inadequate than a mature judgment when adopted by an immature mind." When radical intellectuals have to deal with a dissenting public that becomes this young, all kinds of problems accrue.

The adolescentization of dissent poses dilemmas as perplexing as the proletarianization of dissent that bedeviled left-wing theorists when it was the working class they had to ally with in their effort to reclaim our culture for the good, the true, and the beautiful. Then it was the horny-handed virtues of the beer hall and the trade union that had to serve as the medium of radical thought. Now it is the youthful exuberance of the rock club, the love-in, the teach-in.

The young, miserably educated as they are, bring with them almost nothing but healthy instincts. The project of building a sophisticated framework of thought atop those instincts is rather like trying to graft an oak tree upon a wildflower. How to sustain the oak tree? More important, how to avoid crushing the wildflower? And yet such is the project that confronts those of us who are concerned with radical social change. For the young have become one of the very few social levers dissent has to work with. This is that "significant soil" in which the Great Refusal has begun to take root. If we reject it in frustration for the youthful follies that also sprout there, where then do we turn?

Chapter II

AN INVASION OF CENTAURS

In the "today," in every "today," various generations coexist and the relations which are established between them, according to the different condition of their ages, represent the dynamic system of attractions and repulsions, of agreement and controversy which at any given moment makes up the reality of historic life.[1]

If we agree with Ortega that the fitful transition of the generations is a significant element in historical change, we must also recognize that the young may do little more than remodel the inherited culture in minor or marginal ways. They may settle for alterations that amount to a change of superficial fashion, undertaken out of mere pique or caprice. What is special about the generational transition we are in is the scale on which it is taking place and the depth of antagonism it reveals. Indeed, it would hardly seem an exaggeration to call what we see arising among the young a "counter culture." Meaning: a culture so radically disaffiliated from the mainstream assumptions of our society that it scarcely looks to many as a culture at all, but takes on the alarming appearance of a barbaric intrusion.

An image comes at once to mind: the invasion of centaurs that is recorded on the pediment of the Temple of Zeus at Olympia. Drunken and incensed, the centaurs burst in upon the civilized festivities that are in progress. But a stern Apollo, the guardian of the orthodox culture, steps forward to admonish the gate-crashers and drive them back. The image is

[1] José Ortega y Gasset, *Man and Crisis*, trans. Mildred Adams (London: Allen & Unwin, 1959), p. 45.

a potent one, for it recalls what must always be a fearful experience in the life of any civilization: the experience of radical cultural disjuncture, the clash of irreconcilable conceptions of life. And the encounter is not always won by Apollo.

Toynbee has identified such cultural disjunctures as the work of a disinherited "proletariat," using as his paradigm the role of the early Christians within the Roman Empire —a classic case of Apollo being subverted by the unruly centaurs. The Christian example is one that many of the hip young are quick to invoke, perhaps with more appropriateness than many of their critics may recognize. Hopelessly estranged by ethos and social class from the official culture, the primitive Christian community awkwardly fashioned of Judaism and the mystery cults a minority culture that could not but seem an absurdity to Greco-Roman orthodoxy. But the absurdity, far from being felt as a disgrace, became a banner of the community.

For it is written [St. Paul boasted] I will destroy the wisdom of the wise, and will bring to nothing the understanding of the prudent. . . . For the Jews require a sign, and the Greeks seek after wisdom. . . . But God hath chosen the foolish things of the world to confound the wise; and God hath chosen the weak things of the world to confound the things which are mighty. (I Cor. 1.19, 22, 27)

It is a familiar passage from what is now an oppressively respectable source. So familiar and so respectable that we easily lose sight of how aggressively perverse a declaration it is . . . how loaded with unabashed contempt for a long-established culture rich with achievement. And whose contempt was this? That of absolute nobodies, the very scum of the earth, whose own counter culture was, at this early stage, little more than a scattering of suggestive ideas, a few crude symbols, and a desperate longing. It was the longing that counted most, for not all the grandeur of Greco-Roman civilization could fill the desolation of spirit Christianity bred upon. Since we know now with an abundance of hindsight what the Christian *scandalum* eventually led to, the comparison with the still fledgling counter culture of our youth is bound to seem outlandish. But then, all revolutionary changes are unthinkable until they happen . . . and then they are understood to be inevitable. Who, in Paul's time, could have anticipated what would come of the brazen hostility of a handful of scruffy malcontents? And what would the nascent Christian movement have looked like under the merciless floodlights of any then-existing mass media? Would it even have survived the saturation coverage?

Perhaps the young of this generation haven't the stamina to launch the epochal transformation they seek; but there should be no mistaking the fact that they want nothing less. "Total rejection" is a phrase that comes readily to their lips, often before the mind provides even a blurred picture of the new culture that is to displace the old. If there is anything about the ethos of Black Power that proves particularly attractive even to young white disaffiliates who cannot gain access to the movement, it is the sense that Black Power somehow implies an entirely new way of life: a black culture, a black consciousness . . . a black soul which is totally incompatible with white society and aggressively proud of the fact. Black Power may build any number of barriers between white and Negro youth, but across the barriers a common language can still be heard. Here, for example, is Bobby Seale of the Oakland Black Panthers speaking to a meeting of the Center for Participative Education held at the University of California at Berkeley in September 1968. The crisis at hand stemmed from a decision of the UC regents to deny a Black Panther spokesman access to the campus. But for

Seale, as for the students, the issue had deeper cultural implications. Everything—the meaning of authority, of personal identity, of Judeo-Christian ethics, of sexual freedom—was somehow involved in this single act of administrative censorship.

Archie and Jughead never kissed Veronica and Betty. Superman never kissed Lois Lane. We are tired of relating to comic book conceptions. Adam should have defended the Garden of Eden against the omnipotent administrator. Life, liberty, and the pursuit of happiness don't mean nothing to me if I can't go home and feel safe with my wife in bed replenishing the earth.[2]

At first glance, it may not be apparent what sentiments of this kind (and they were the substance of the address) have to do with an issue of academic freedom. But Seale's audience had no trouble understanding. They readily recognized that authoritarianism in our society operates overtly or subtly at every level of life, from comic strip imagery to Christian theology, from the college classroom to the privacy of the bedroom—and they were prepared to discard the culture that relied on such sleazy coercion, root and branch.

Or to take another example of these apocalyptic yearnings that beset our young. When the Antiuniversity of London, the first English version of our free universities, was opened in early 1968, its prospectus was filled with courses devoted to "anti-cultures," "anti-environments," "anti-poetry," "anti-theatre," "anti-families," and "counter institutions." Seemingly nothing the adult society had to offer any longer proved acceptable. The superheated radicalism of the school was eventually to reach such a pitch that even the age-old student-teacher relationship came under fire as an intolerable

[2] From a recording of the address presented over KPFA (Berkeley) on September 24, 1968.

form of authoritarianism. So it too was scrapped, on the assumption that nobody any longer had anything to teach the young; they would make up their own education from scratch. Unfortunately—but was the misfortune more comic or more tragic?—the school failed to survive this act of radical restructuring.

Such white-hot discontent always runs the risk of evaporating into a wild, amorphous steam—so that it becomes difficult to tell the chiliastic illuminations from mere inanities. The typical fare offered at the Antiuniversity can be sampled in one of the "courses," called "From Comic Books to the Dance of Shiva: Spiritual Amnesia and the Physiology of Self-Estrangement." (Again one notes the bizarre but cunning association of the comic strip and high religion.)

Description of course: A free-wheeling succession of open-ended situations. Ongoing vibrations highly relevant. Exploration of Inner Space, de-conditioning of human robot, significance of psycho-chemicals, and the transformation of Western European Man. Source material: Artaud, Zimmer, Gurdjieff, W. Reich, K. Marx, Gnostic, Sufi, and Tantric texts, autobiographical accounts of madness and ecstatic states of consciousness—Pop art and twentieth century prose.

Heavy weather indeed. But altogether representative of the free-university style. Often enough, such madcap brainstorming under the auspices of instructors hardly out of their teens degenerates into a semiarticulate, indiscriminate celebration of everything in sight that is new, strange, and noisy; a fondling of ideas that resembles nothing so much as an infant's play with bright, unfamiliar objects. The appetite is healthily and daringly omnivorous, but it urgently requires mature minds to feed it. It will in large part be my purpose in the chapters that follow to examine a few of the more important figures that are now doing just that. But to make my own point of view quite clear from the outset, I believe that, despite their follies, these young centaurs deserve to win their encounter with the defending Apollos of our society. For the orthodox culture they confront is fatally and contagiously diseased. The prime symptom of that disease is the shadow of thermonuclear annihilation beneath which we cower. The counter culture takes its stand against the background of this absolute evil, an evil which is not defined by the sheer *fact* of the bomb, but by the total *ethos* of the bomb, in which our politics, our public morality, our economic life, our intellectual endeavor are now embedded with a wealth of ingenious rationalization. We are a civilization sunk in an unshakeable commitment to genocide, gambling madly with the universal extermination of our species. And how viciously we ravish our sense of humanity to pretend, even for a day, that such horror can be accepted as "normal," as "necessary"! Whenever we feel inclined to qualify, to modify, to offer a cautious "yes . . . *but*" to the protests of the young, let us return to this fact as the decisive measure of the technocracy's essential criminality: the extent to which it insists, in the name of progress, in the name of reason, that the unthinkable become thinkable and the intolerable become tolerable.

If the counter culture is, as I will contend here, that healthy instinct which refuses both at the personal and political level to practice such a cold-blooded rape of our human sensibilities, then it should be clear why the conflict between young and adult in our time reaches so peculiarly and painfully deep. In an historical emergency of absolutely unprecedented proportions, we are that strange, culture-bound animal whose biological drive for survival expresses itself *generationally*. It is the young, arriving with eyes that can see the obvious, who must remake the lethal culture of their elders, and who must remake it in desperate haste.

*   *   *   *

To take the position I assume here is undeniably risky. For once a cultural disjuncture opens out in society, nothing can be guaranteed. What happens among the minority that finds itself isolated by the rift is as apt to be ugly or pathetic as it is to be noble. The primitive Christian absurdity can be credited at least with the capacity to produce mighty works of intellect and mystic insight, as well as an ideal of saintly service. On the other hand, the alienated stock clerks and wallpaper hangers of post-World War I Germany sullenly withdrew to their beer halls to talk imbecile anthropology and prepare the horrors of Buchenwald. So, too, contemporary America's isolated minorities include the Hell's Angels and the Minutemen, from whom nothing beautiful or tender can be expected.

And our alienated young: how shall we characterize the counter culture they are in the way of haphazardly assembling? Clearly one cannot answer the question by producing a manifesto unanimously endorsed by the malcontented younger generation: the counter culture is scarcely so disciplined a movement. It is something in the nature of a medieval crusade: a variegated procession constantly in flux, acquiring and losing members all along the route of march. Often enough it finds its own identity in a nebulous symbol or song that seems to proclaim little more than "we are special . . . we are different . . . we are outward-bound from the old corruptions of the world." Some join the troop only for a brief while, long enough to enter an obvious and immediate struggle: a campus rebellion, an act of war-resistance, a demonstration against racial injustice. Some may do no more than flourish a tiny banner against the inhumanities of the technocracy; perhaps they pin on a button declaring "I am a human being: do not mutilate, spindle, or tear." Others, having cut themselves off hopelessly from social acceptance, have no option but to follow the road until they reach the Holy City. No piecemeal reforms or minor adjustments of what they leave behind would make turning back possible for them.

But where is this Holy City that lies beyond the technocracy—and what will it be like? Along the way, there is much talk about that, some of it foolish, some of it wise. Many in the procession may only be certain of what it must *not* be like. A discerning few—and among them, the figures I will be discussing in the chapters that follow—have a shrewd sense of where the technocracy leaves off and the New Jerusalem begins: not at the level of class, party, or institution, but rather at the non-intellective level of the personality from which these political and social forms issue. They see, and many who follow them find the vision attractive, that building the good society is not primarily a social, but a psychic task. What makes the youthful disaffiliation of our time a cultural phenomenon, rather than merely a political movement, is the fact that it strikes beyond ideology to the level of consciousness, seeking to transform our deepest sense of the self, the other, the environment.

The psychiatrist R. D. Laing captures the spirit of the matter when he observes: "We do not need theories so much as the experience that is the source of the theory." Such a distinction between theory and experience, challenging as it does the validity of mere analytical clarity as a basis for knowledge or conviction, cannot help but carry an antiintellectual tone. The tone becomes even more pronounced when Laing goes on to define the goal of "true sanity" as being

in one way or another, the dissolution of the normal ego, that false self competently adjusted to our alienated social reality: the emergence of the "inner" archetypal mediators of divine power, and through this death a rebirth, and the eventual re-establishment of a new kind of ego-functioning, the ego now being the servant of the divine, no longer its betrayer.[3]

When psychiatry begins to speak this language, it moves well beyond the boundaries of conventional scientific respectability. But if the dissenting young give their attention to figures like Laing (he is one of the leading mentors of Britain's burgeoning counter culture), it is surely because they have seen too many men of indisputable intelligence and enlightened intention become the apologists of a dehumanized social order. What is it that has allowed so many of our men of science, our scholars, our most sophisticated political leaders, even our boldest would-be revolutionaries to make their peace with the technocracy—or indeed to enter its service so cheerfully? Not lack of intellect or ignorance of humane values. It is rather that technocratic assumptions about the nature of man, society, and nature have warped their experience at the source, and so have become the buried premises from which intellect and ethical judgment proceed.

In order, then, to root out those distortive assumptions, nothing less is required than the subversion of the scientific world view, with its entrenched commitment to an egocentric and cerebral mode of consciousness. In its place, there must be a new culture in which the non-intellective capacities of the personality—those capacities that take fire from

[3] R. D. Laing, *The Politics of Experience and The Bird of Paradise* (London: Penguin Books, 1967), p. 119.

visionary splendor and the experience of human communion
—become the arbiters of the good, the true, and the beautiful.
I think the cultural disjuncture that generational dissent is
opening out between itself and the technocracy is just this
great, as great in its implications (though obviously not as
yet in historical import) as the cleavage that once ran between Greco-Roman rationality and Christian mystery. To
be sure, Western society has, over the past two centuries,
incorporated a number of minorities whose antagonism toward
the scientific world view has been irreconcilable, and who
have held out against the easy assimilation to which the
major religious congregations have yielded in their growing
desire to seem progressive. Theosophists and fundamentalists,
spiritualists and flat-earthers, occultists and satanists . . . it
is nothing new that there should exist anti-rationalist elements in our midst. What *is* new is that a radical rejection
of science and technological values should appear so close to
the center of our society, rather than on the negligible mar-
gins. It is the middle-class young who are conducting this
politics of consciousness, and they are doing it boisterously,
persistently, and aggressively—to the extent that they are in-
vading the technocracy's citadels of academic learning and
bidding fair to take them over.

The task of characterizing the non-intellective powers of
the personality in which our young have become so deeply involved is far from easy. Until the advent of psychoanalysis,
the vocabulary of our society was woefully impoverished when
it came to discussion of the non-intellective aspects of life.
The mystics and Romantics who have worked most closely to
the dark side of the mind provide us with a repertory of
brilliant metaphors and images to explain their experience.
Similarly, the Hindu and Buddhist traditions contain a vocabulary of marvelous discrimination for speaking of the non-
intellective consciousness—as well as a number of techniques

for tapping its contents. But the scientific intelligence rejects metaphor and mystical terminology the way a vending machine tosses out counterfeit coins (with a single revealing exception: the metaphor of natural "law," without which the scientific revolution might never have gotten off the ground). It leaves us devoid of language as soon as we enter that province of experience in which artists and mystics claim to have found the highest values of existence. Even psychoanalysis has been of little help in the discussion of the nonintellective, mainly because its approach has been burdened with a mechanistic vocabulary and an objective stand-offishness: a prying examination from the "outside," rather than a warm experiencing from the "inside." In reviewing the intellectual history of the generation that saw the appearance of Freud, Sorel, Weber, and Durkheim—the first generation to undertake what it hoped would be respectably scientific research into man's irrational motivations—H. Stuart Hughes observes:

The social thinkers of the 1890's were concerned with the irrational only to exorcize it. By probing into it, they sought ways to tame it, to canalize it for constructive human purposes.[4]

As the spell of scientific or quasi-scientific thought has spread in our culture from the physical to the so-called behavioral sciences, and finally to scholarship in the arts and letters, the marked tendency has been to consign whatever is not fully and articulately available in the waking conscious-

[4] H. Stuart Hughes, *Consciousness and Society* (New York: Vintage Books, 1958), pp. 35–36. Only Bergson and Jung, among major thinkers of the period outside the arts, treated the non-rational side of human nature with an intuitive sympathy. But who, in the scientific community or the academy, any longer regards them as "major thinkers"?

ness for empirical or mathematical manipulation, to a purely negative catch-all category (in effect, the cultural garbage can) called the "unconscious" . . . or the "irrational" . . . or the "mystical" . . . or the "purely subjective." To behave on the basis of such blurred states of consciousness is at best to be some species of amusing eccentric, at worst to be plain mad. Conversely, behavior that is normal, valuable, productive, mentally healthy, socially respectable, intellectually defensible, sane, decent, and practical is supposed to have nothing to do with subjectivity. When we tell one another to "be reasonable," to "talk sense," to "get down to brass tacks," to "keep one's feet on the ground," to "stick to the facts," to "be realistic," we mean that one should avoid talking about one's "inner" feelings and look at the world rather in the way an engineer looks at a construction project or a physicist views the behavior of atomic particles. We feel that worthwhile things come of such a state of mind—knowledge, solutions to problems, successful projects, money, power—whereas only some manner of unproductive self-indulgence comes of wallowing in "mere feelings." The more sophisticated may admit the legitimacy of allowing artists to moon and daydream. But the world, as every practical man knows, can do without poems and paintings; it can scarcely do without dams and roads and bombs and sound policy. Art is for the leisure hours: the time left over from dealing with realities and necessities.[5]

[5] One might expect some softening of this compulsively utilitarian rationality to stem from the new and now lavishly subsidized field of sleep research, which tells us of the absolute necessity of non-intellective experience. For a fascinating survey of this work, see Gay G. Luce and J. Segal, *Sleep* (London: Heinemann, 1967). Whatever else the sleep researchers may prove, however, they have already revealed the pathos of a society that must have it demonstrated by way of encephalographs and computers that the relaxation of rational consciousness and the experience of dreaming are vital to healthy life. But they do so seemingly without any awareness of the part science, with its militant intellectuality, has played in obscuring

We will return in later chapters to a fuller consideration of the scientific world view and its deficiencies. What is said here is meant only to suggest the difficulty the counter culture faces in simply trying to designate its project. It has removed itself to a position so wide of our cultural mainstream that it can scarcely speak without seeming to fall into a foreign tongue. In a world which more and more thinks of society as the subordinate adjunct of a gigantic technological mechanism requiring constant and instantaneous co-ordination from the center, the young begin to speak of such impracticalities as "community," and "participative democracy." Thus they revert to a style of human relations that characterizes village and tribe, insisting that real politics can only take place in the deeply personal confrontations these now obsolete social forms allow. Where are they to find understanding for such a homely ideal in a world dominated by vast political abstractions decked out in glittering propagandistic symbols, slogans, and statistical measures: nation, party, corporation, urban area, grand alliance, common market, socioeconomic system . . . ? The lively consciousness of men and women *as they are* in their vital daily reality is missing from our culture, having been displaced by these grandiose figments. To assert that the essence of human sociability is, simply and beautifully, the communal opening-up of man to man, rather than the achievement of prodigious technical and economic feats—what is this but to assert an absurdity?

Further, what is it to assert the primacy of the non-intellective powers but to call into question all that our culture

this fact. It is this blind spot which will probably lead to their research, like all science worth its subsidies these days, being used for idiotic ends. For example, Herman Kahn and Anthony Wiener, in their book *The Year 2000* (New York: Macmillan, 1967) give us a prognosis of "programmed dreams." Another instance of the technocratic principle: never let happen naturally and enjoyably what can be counterfeited by the technicians.

values as "reason" and "reality"? To deny that the true self is this small, hard atom of intense objectivity we pilot about each day as we build bridges and careers is surely to play fast and loose with psychopathology. It is to attack men at the very core of their security by denying the validity of everything they mean when they utter the most precious word in their vocabulary: the word "I." And yet this is what the counter culture undertakes when, by way of its mystical tendencies or the drug experience, it assaults the reality of the ego as an isolable, purely cerebral unit of identity. In doing so, it once again transcends the consciousness of the dominant culture and runs the risk of appearing to be a brazen exercise in perverse nonsense.

Yet what else but such a brave (and hopefully humane) perversity can pose a radical challenge to the technocracy? If the melancholy history of revolution over the past half-century teaches us anything, it is the futility of a politics which concentrates itself single-mindedly on the overthrowing of governments, or ruling classes, or economic systems. This brand of politics finishes with merely redesigning the turrets and towers of the technocratic citadel. It is the foundations of the edifice that must be sought. And those foundations lie among the ruins of the visionary imagination and the sense of human community. Indeed, this is what Shelley recognized even in the earliest days of the Industrial Revolution, when he proclaimed that in the defense of poetry we must invoke "light and fire from those eternal regions where the owl-winged faculty of calculation dare not ever soar."[6]

* * * *

[6] Shelley's magnificent essay "The Defence of Poetry" could still stand muster as a counter cultural manifesto. If only our technicians, our scientists, our experts of all description could be brought face to face with such statements! Surely that would do the trick.

When one first casts an eye over the varieties of youthful dissent, it may seem that there is considerably less coherence to this counter culture than I have suggested. To one side, there is the mind-blown bohemianism of the beats and hippies; to the other, the hard-headed political activism of the student New Left. Are these not in reality two separate and antithetical developments: the one (tracing back to Ginsberg, Kerouac, & Co.) seeking to "cop out" of American society, the other (tracing back to C. Wright Mills and remnants of the old socialist left) seeking to penetrate and revolutionize our political life?

The tension one senses between these two movements is real enough. But I think there exists, at a deeper level, a theme that unites these variations and which accounts for the fact that hippy and student activist continue to recognize each other as allies. Certainly there is the common enemy against whom they combine forces; but there is also a positive similarity of sensibility.

The underlying unity of these differing styles of dissent is revealed by the extraordinary personalism that has characterized New Left activism since its beginnings. New Left groups like SDS have always taken strong exception to the fashionable thesis that we have reached the "end of ideology" in the Great Society.[7] But there is a sense in which ideology *is* a thing of the past among politically involved dissenters. By and large, most New Left groups have refused to allow doctrinal logic to obscure or displace an irreducible element

[7] This thesis is, of course, untrue. Ideology is not absent in the technocracy; it is simply invisible, having blended into the supposedly indisputable truth of the scientific world view. Thus the technocrats deal in "rationality," "efficiency," and "progress," speak the purportedly value-neuter language of statistics, and convince themselves that they have no ideological orientation. The most effective ideologies are always those that are congruent with the limits of consciousness, for then they work subliminally.

of human tenderness in their politicking. What has distinguished SDS, at least in its early years, from old-line radical youth groups (as still represented, say, by the Progressive Labor Movement) is the unwillingness of the former to reify doctrine to the extent of granting it more importance than the flesh and blood. For most of the New Left, there has ultimately been no more worth or cogency in any ideology than a person lends it by virtue of his own action: personal commitments, not abstract ideas, are the stuff of politics. Such is the burden of the observation Staughton Lynd offered to the 1968 New University Conference when he lamented the fact that even radically inclined academics too often fail to "provide models of off-campus radical vocation." They teach Marxism or socialism; but they do not "pay their dues."

The intellectual's first responsibility is, as Noam Chomsky says, "to insist upon the truth. . . ." But what truth we discover will be affected by the lives we lead. . . . to hope that we can understandingly interpret matters of which we have no first-hand knowledge, things utterly unproved upon the pulses . . . is intellectual hubris. . . . I think the times no longer permit this indulgence, and ask us, at the very least, to venture into the arena where political parties and workingmen, and young people do their things, seeking to clarify that experience which becomes ours as well, speaking truth to power from the vantage-point of that process of struggle.[8]

The remarks return us to R. D. Laing's distinction between "theory" and "experience." For the radical intellectual as much as for anyone else, Lynd contends, truth must have a biographical, not merely an ideological, context.

It is this personalist style that has led the New Left to identify alienation as the central political problem of the

[8] Lynd's address appears in *The New University Conference Newsletter*, Chicago, May 24, 1968, pp. 5–6.

day. Not alienation, however, in the sheerly institutional sense, in which capitalism (or for that matter any advanced industrial economy) tends to alienate the worker from the means and fruits of production; but rather, alienation as the deadening of man's sensitivity to man, a deadening that can creep into even those revolutionary efforts that seek with every humanitarian intention to eliminate the external symptoms of alienation. Wherever non-human elements—whether revolutionary doctrine or material goods—assume greater importance than human life and well-being, we have the alienation of man from man, and the way is open to the self-righteous use of others as mere objects. In this respect revolutionary terrorism is only the mirror image of capitalist exploitation. As the French students put it in one of their incisive May 1968 slogans: *"Une révolution qui demande que l'on se sacrifice pour elle est une révolution à la papa."* ("A revolution that expects you to sacrifice yourself for it is one of daddy's revolutions.")

The meaning of New Left personalism is cogently expressed by the SDS Port Huron Statement of 1962:

We are aware that to avoid platitudes we must analyze the concrete conditions of social order. But to direct such an analysis we must use the guideposts of basic principles. Our own social values involve conceptions of human beings, human relationships, and social systems.

We regard *men* as infinitely precious and possessed of unfulfilled capacities for reason, freedom, and love. . . . We oppose the depersonalization that reduces human beings to the status of things. If anything, the brutalities of the twentieth century teach that means and ends are intimately related, that vague appeals to 'posterity' cannot justify the mutilations of the present. . . .

Loneliness, estrangement, isolation describe the vast distance between man and man today. These dominant tendencies cannot be overcome by better personnel management, nor by improved gadgets, but only when a love of man overcomes the idolatrous worship of things by man.[9]

The issue the students are addressing themselves to here, with their sentimental regard for "love," "loneliness," "depersonalization," makes for a vivid contrast to the more doctrinaire style of many of their radical predecessors. A generation ago at the time of the Spanish Civil War, Harry Pollitt, the leader of the British Communist Party, could with a clear conscience tell the poet Stephen Spender that he ought to go to Spain and get himself killed: the party needed more martyred artists to bolster its public image. That is ideological politics—the total subordination of the person to party and doctrine. Nor have such perversions been confined to the Stalinist Left. It was an adamant anti-Stalinist, Sidney Hook, who in his famous exchange of letters with Bertrand Russell during the early fifties, logic-chopped his way to the conclusion that thwarting the ambitions of the Harry Pollitts of the world would justify wiping out the entire human species.[10] Such anti-Stalinist militancy required two billion martyrs, willy-nilly: surely a political position that wins the world's record for sheer bloody-minded fanaticism. Had the H-bomb existed in the sixteenth century, we might well have expected to hear Calvin and Loyola carrying on with the same hair-raising bravado . . . and meaning it . . . and then perhaps none of us should be here today.

Now this is precisely the sort of corrupted human relations that has been largely absent from New Left politics. Instead, there has been a precociously wise fear of wielding power

[9] From the statement as it appears in Mitchell Cohen and Dennis Hale, eds., The New Student Left (Boston: Beacon Press, revised ed. 1967), pp. 12–13.

[10] The Russell-Hook exchange appears in Charles McClelland, ed., Nuclear Weapons, Missiles, and Future War (San Francisco: Chandler, 1960), pp. 140–57.

over others and of unleashing violence in behalf of any ideal,
no matter how rhetorically appealing. In the New Left, you
pay your *own* dues; nobody pays them for you; and you, in
turn, don't enforce payment on anybody else. As Kenneth
Keniston of the Yale Medical School observes in a recent
study: ". . . in manner and style, these young radicals are
extremely 'personalistic,' focused on face-to-face, direct and
open relationships with other people; hostile to formally
structured roles and traditional bureaucratic patterns of
power and authority"—a characteristic Keniston traces to the
child-rearing habits of the contemporary middle-class family.
The trait is so well developed that Keniston wonders if "it is
possible to retain an open, personalistic, unmanipulative
and extremely trusting style, and yet mount an effective program on a national scale."[11] The worry is real enough; organizational slackness is bound to be the price one pays for pursuing the ideal of participative democracy. But then it is
perhaps a measure of our corruption as a society that we
should believe democracy can ever be anything other than
"participative."

As I write this, however, I am bleakly aware that an
ideological drift toward righteous violence is on the increase
among the young, primarily under the influence of the
extremist Black Powerites and a romanticized conception of
guerrilla warfare. This is especially true of the European
young, who rapidly fall back upon stereotyped ideas about
revolution; but "confrontation politics" and cheers for the
fiction of the "people's war" are becoming more prominent
in the United States, too, as frustration with the brutality
and sleazy deception of the establishment grows. The tragic
search may be on again among radical dissenters for ways to

[11] See Kenneth Keniston, *Young Radicals* (New York: Harcourt,
Brace & World, 1968). The study is based on the National Steering
Committee of the 1967 Vietnam Summer.

"make murder legitimate," as Camus phrased it—and with this tendency, the New Left runs the risk of losing its original soulfulness. For the beauty of the New Left has always lain in its eagerness to give political dignity to the tenderer emotions, in its readiness to talk openly of love, and non-violence, and pity. It is, therefore, depressing in the extreme when, in behalf of a self-congratulatory militancy, this humane spirit threatens to give way to the age-old politics of hatred, vindictiveness, and windy indignation. At this point, things do not simply become ugly; they become stupid. Suddenly the measure of conviction is the efficiency with which one can get into a fistfight with the nearest cop at hand

It would be my own estimate that those who give way to the vice of doctrinaire violence and its manipulative ways are still a strict minority among the dissenting young—though an obstreperous minority which, for obvious reasons, attracts much attention from the press. The very inexclusiveness of the New Left style—the willingness to let every man take his own stand even when this produces a hopeless muddle—makes it impossible to turn away those who come to the demonstrations with icons of "Che" and Chairman Mao, and with all the attendant bloodcurdling slogans. Nevertheless, the prevailing spirit of New Left politics remains that reflected in the SDS motto "One man, one soul." The meaning of the phrase is clear enough: at whatever cost to the cause or the doctrine, one must care for the uniqueness and the dignity of each individual and yield to what his conscience demands in the existential moment.

Colin MacInnes, discussing the difference between the youthful radicals of the thirties and the sixties, observes that the contemporary young "hold themselves more personally responsible than the young used to. Not in the sense of their 'duties' to the state or even society, but to themselves. I think they examine themselves more closely and their motives and their own behavior."[12] Anyone who has put in much time with New Left students knows what MacInnes is talking about. It is that quality of sober introspection which almost amounts to what the Catholic Church calls "scrupulosity." It can become nearly intolerable to sit through the soul-searching sessions of these young people, waiting in attendance upon their lint-picking analyses of motivation, their dogged pursuit of a directness and immediacy free of organizational-hierarchical distinctions. And yet it is, at worst, the exaggeration of a virtue to insist that neither theory nor rhetoric must submerge the living reality of our actions as they affect others and ourselves, to insist that the final appeal must be to the person, never to the doctrine.

But then the question arises: what *is* the person? What, most essentially, *is* this elusive, often erratic human *something* which underlies social systems and ideologies, and which now must serve as the ultimate point of moral reference? No sooner does one raise the question than the politics of the social system yields to what Timothy Leary has called "the politics of the nervous system." Class consciousness gives way as a generative principle to . . . *consciousness* consciousness. And it is at this juncture that New Left and beat-hip bohemianism join hands. For even in its most hostile caricatures, the bohemian fringe of our youth culture makes its distinctive character apparent. It is grounded in an intensive examination of the self, of the buried wealth of personal consciousness. The stereotypic beatnik or hippy, dropped-out and self-absorbed, sunk in a narcotic stupor or lost in ecstatic

---

[12] Colin MacInnes, "Old Youth and Young," *Encounter*, September 1967. For another discussion of the subject, in the course of which the same point emerges, see the symposium "Confrontation: The Old Left and the New," in *The American Scholar*, Autumn 1967, pp. 567–89.

contemplation . . . what lies behind these popular images but the reality of a sometimes zany, sometimes hopelessly inadequate search for the truth of the person?

Beat-hip bohemianism may be too withdrawn from social action to suit New Left radicalism; but the withdrawal is in a direction the activist can readily understand. The "trip" is inward, toward deeper levels of self-examination. The easy transition from the one wing to the other of the counter culture shows up in the pattern that has come to govern many of the free universities. These dissenting academies usually receive their send-off from campus New Leftists and initially emphasize heavy politics. But gradually the curricula tend to get hip both in content and teaching methods: psychedelics, light shows, multi-media, total theatre, people-heaping, McLuhan, exotic religion, touch and tenderness, ecstatic laboratories. . . .[13] The same transition can be traced in the career of Bob Dylan, who commands respect among all segments of the dissenting youth culture. Dylan's early songs were traditional folk-protest, laying forth obvious issues of social justice; anti-boss, anti-war, anti-exploitation. Then, quite suddenly, rather as if Dylan had come to the conclusion that the conventional Woody Guthrie ballad could not reach deep enough, the songs turn surrealistic and psychedelic. All at once Dylan is somewhere beneath the rationalizing cerebrum of social discourse, probing the nightmare deeps, trying to get at the tangled roots of conduct and opinion. At this point, the project which the beats of the early fifties had taken up—the task of remodeling themselves, their way of life, their perceptions and sensitivities—rapidly takes precedence over the public task of changing institutions or policies.

[13] See Ralph Keyes, "The Free Universities," *The Nation*, October 2, 1967.

One can discern, then, a continuum of thought and experience among the young which links together the New Left sociology of Mills, the Freudian Marxism of Herbert Marcuse, the Gestalt-therapy anarchism of Paul Goodman, the apocalyptic body mysticism of Norman Brown, the Zen-based psychotherapy of Alan Watts, and finally Timothy Leary's impenetrably occult narcissism, wherein the world and its woes may shrink at last to the size of a mote in one's private psychedelic void. As we move along the continuum, we find sociology giving way steadily to psychology, political collectivities yielding to the person, conscious and articulate behavior falling away before the forces of the non-intellective deep.

Unrelated as the extremes of this spectrum may seem at first, one would not be surprised to discover the men we name turning up at the same teach-in. The Congress on the Dialectics of Liberation held in London during summer 1967 was pretty much that kind of affair: an effort to work out the priorities of psychic and social liberation within a group of participants that included New Left revolutionaries and existential psychiatrists, with Allen Ginsberg on hand—not to speak, but to chant the Hare Krishna. As one would expect, the priorities never did get established. Significantly, it proved impossible for the congress to maintain more than a stormy rapport with Black Power spokesmen like Stokely Carmichael, for whom, tragically if understandably, real social power, despite all that history teaches us to the contrary, once more looks like something that flows from the muzzle of a gun. And yet, the common cause was undeniably there: the same insistence on revolutionary change that must at last embrace psyche and society. Even for the Black Powerites, the root justification of the cause derives from existentialist theorists like Frantz Fanon, for whom the prime value of the act of rebellion lies in its psychic liberation of the oppressed.[14]

So it is that when New Left groups organize their demonstrations, the misty-minded hippies are certain to join in, though they may tune out on the heavy political speechifying in favor of launching a yellow submarine or exorcizing the Pentagon. In Berkeley after the 1966 troubles, the New Left and local hippies had no difficulty in cosponsoring a "Human Be-In" to celebrate the students' quasi-victory over the administration. Under hip influence, the celebration rapidly took on the character of a massive "love feast"; but no one seemed to find that inappropriate. Perhaps the most important feature of the event was the fact that, of the forty thousand in attendence, a vast number were teen-agers from local high schools and junior high schools—the so-called "teeny-boppers," who currently seem to provide the bulk of the crowd along Berkeley's Telegraph Avenue. For these youngsters, the next wave of the counter culture, the neat distinctions between dissenting activism and bohemianism are growing progressively less clear. No doubt, as the local city fathers fear, these youngsters learn all sorts of bad habits on the avenue—but they probably take their corruption in-

[14] Black Power frequently gets drawn into the counter cultural style in other respects. In Eldridge Cleaver's book *Soul on Ice* (New York: McGraw-Hill, 1968) there is an ongoing analysis of the hidden sexual foundations of racism. See the essay "The Great Mitosis." Unhappily, however, the analysis suggests that, like some of the New Leftists, Cleaver seems to conceive of the struggle for liberation as the province of manly men who must prove themselves by "laying their balls on the line." Too often this suggests that the female of the species must content herself with keeping the home fires burning for her battle-scarred champion or joining the struggle as a camp follower. In either case, the community is being saved *for* her, not *by* her as well. I think this means that invidious sexual stereotyping lies at a deeper level of consciousness than racial prejudice. For a comment on the problem, see Betty Roszak, "Sex and Caste," in *Liberation*, December 1966, pp. 28–31.

discriminately from SDS handouts and psychedelic newspapers without much awareness of the difference between dropping out and digging in for the political fight. It all boils down to disaffiliation for them—and the distinctions are of secondary importance.

We grasp the underlying unity of the counter cultural variety, then, if we see beat-hip bohemianism as an effort to work out the personality structure and total life style that follow from New Left social criticism. At their best, these young bohemians are the would-be utopian pioneers of the world that lies beyond intellectual rejection of the Great Society. They seek to invent a cultural base for New Left politics, to discover new types of community, new family patterns, new sexual mores, new kinds of livelihood, new esthetic forms, new personal identities on the far side of power politics, the bourgeois home, and the consumer society. When the New Left calls for peace and gives us heavy analysis of what's what in Vietnam, the hippy quickly translates the word into *shantih*, the peace that passes all understanding, and fills in the psychic dimensions of the ideal. If investigating the life of *shantih* has little to do with achieving peace in Vietnam, perhaps it is the best way of preventing the next several Vietnams from happening. Perhaps the experiments we find at the hip fringe of the counter culture are still raw and often abortive. But we must remember that the experimenters have only been with us for a dozen or so years now; and they are picking their way through customs and institutions that have had more than a few centuries to entrench themselves. To criticize the experiments is legitimate and necessary; to despair of what are no more than beginnings is surely premature.

* * * *

It is precisely because New Left politics is related to an entire culture of disaffiliation that the possibility of any enduring alliance with even the most outcast elements of the adult generation is severely diminished. As long as the young in their politics emphasize the further integration of the poor and disadvantaged into technocratic affluence, they can expect to enjoy ad hoc liaisons with workers and their unions, or with the exploited minorities. But such alliances are not apt to outlast successful integration. When the lid blows off the black ghettos of our cities, the ensuing rebellion may look like the prologue to revolution. The dissenting young then give their sympathy and support to the insurrection—insofar as Black Power will permit the participation of white allies.[15] But soon enough, whatever the black guerrillas may intend, the main activity of the day becomes wholesale looting—which is the poor man's way of cutting himself in on the consumer society. And at that point, the angry agitation that fills the ghetto begins to sound like a clamor at the gates of the technocracy—*demanding in*.

If Allen Ginsberg's *Howl* stands as a founding document of the counter culture, we must remember what the poet had to tell the world: "I have burned all my money in a wastebasket." Will it be a victory, then, or a defeat for the counter culture when the black man has at last fought his way clear of desperate expedients and wrings from the Great Society the white man's legal equivalent of looting: a steady job, a secure income, easy credit, free access to all the local emporiums, and his own home to pile the merchandise in? The issue is critical because it reveals the bind in which the

[15] Here, for example, is a flyer which was distributed in Harlem in 1967 by the "Committee of Concerned Honkies": "We'll talk about screwing up the Tactical Police Force (or National Guard or Army) during any black rebellion in the New York area. We'll also talk about jamming National Guard 'riot control' training sessions this autumn and other things."

counter culture finds itself when confronted by undeniably urgent questions of social justice. What, after all, does social justice mean to the outcast and dispossessed? Most obviously, it means gaining admission to everything from which middle-class selfishness excludes them. But how does one achieve such admission without simultaneously becoming an integral and supportive element of the technocracy? How do Black Power, black culture, black consciousness stop short of becoming steppingstones to black consumption, black conformity, black affluence: finally, to a middle-class America of another color? The dilemma requires the most painstaking tact and sensitivity—qualities that are apt to be in short supply among the deprived in the heat and turmoil of political struggle.

Consider, for example, the situation which the French students faced in the May 1968 General Strike. The great ideal of the moment was "workers' control" of French industry. Very well; but is workers' control immune to the dangers of technocratic integration? Unhappily not. For it is hardly difficult to imagine the technocracy reconstituting itself atop an echelon of shop stewards and industrial soviets—and perhaps using these new, more friction-free shop-floor arrangements to its own great advantage! Surely the touchstone of the matter would be: how ready are the workers to disband whole sectors of the industrial apparatus where this proves necessary to achieve ends other than efficient productivity and high consumption? How willing are they to set aside technocratic priorities in favor of a new simplicity of life, a decelerating social pace, a vital leisure? These are questions which enthusiasts for workers' control might do well to ponder. Suppose the French workers *had* taken over the economy, an objective which seems to have lost its general appeal in the wake of the new wage agreements the de Gaulle government has granted. Would the Renault workers have been willing to consider closing the industry down on the grounds that cars and traffic are now more the blight than the convenience of our lives? Would French aircraft workers have been willing to scrap the Concorde SST on the grounds that this marvel of aeronautical engineering will surely become a social monstrosity? Would French munitions workers have been willing to end production of the *force de frappe*, recognizing that the balance of terror is among the vilest offenses of the technocracy? I suspect that the answer to all these questions would be "no." The social composition of the technocracy would alter, but the change would amount to nothing more than broadening the base on which the technocratic imperative rests.

Once the relations of the counter cultural young and the wretched of the earth get beyond the problem of integration, a grave uneasiness is bound to set in. The long-range cultural values of the discontented young must surely seem bizarre to those whose attention is understandably riveted on sharing the glamorous good things of middle-class life.[16] How baffling it must seem to the long-suffering and long-deprived to discover the children of our new affluence dressing themselves

---

[16] Cf. Daniel and Gabriel Cohn-Bendit: "The differences between the revolutionary students and the workers spring directly from their distinct social positions. Thus few students have had real experience of grinding poverty—their struggle is about the hierarchical structure of society, about oppression in comfort. They do not so much have to contend with a lack of material goods as with unfulfilled desires and aspirations. The workers, on the other hand, suffer from direct economic oppression and misery—earning wages of less than 500 francs per month, in poorly ventilated, dirty and noisy factories, where the foreman, the chief engineer and the manager all throw their weight about and conspire to keep those under them in their place." *Obsolete Communism: The Left-Wing Alternative*, p. 107. Yet despite these radically different political horizons, Cohn-Bendit argues that there can be a common cause between the two groups, based on his tactic of "spontaneous resistance" in the streets.

in rags and tatters, turning their "pads" into something barely distinguishable from slum housing, and taking to the streets as panhandlers. Similarly, what can the Beatles' latest surrealist LP mean to an unemployed miner or a migrant farm laborer? What are the downs-and-outs of Nanterre to make of the latest production of Arrabal on the Left Bank? Surely they do not see these strange phenomena as a part of *their* culture, but as curious, somewhat crazy things the spoiled middle-class young amuse themselves with. Perhaps, like the Marxist guardians of social justice, they even see them as intolerable displays of "decadence"—meaning the neurotic discontent of those who cannot settle down gratefully to the responsibilities of life in an advanced industrial order.

But the bind in which the counter culture finds itself in dealing with disadvantaged social elements is doubled at another level with a painful irony. As has been mentioned, it is the cultural experimentation of the young that often runs the worst risk of commercial verminization—and so of having the force of its dissent dissipated. It is the cultural experiments that draw the giddy interest of just those middle-class swingers who are the bastion of the technocratic order. And *their* interest is all of the wrong kind. Visiting bohemia to peer at the "flower children," dropping by the rock clubs, laying out the $5.00 minimum it costs to play voyeur at *Le Cimetière des Voitures*, has become the contemporary version of "slumming" for our big spenders: a breezy flirtation with the off-beat that inevitably distorts the genuineness of the phenomenon.

There is no diminishing the tendency of counter cultural dissent to fall prey to the neutralization that can come of such false attention. Those who dissent have to be supremely resourceful to avoid getting exhibited in somebody's commercial showcase—rather like bizarre fauna brought back alive from the jungle wilds . . . by *Time*, by *Esquire*, by David

Susskind. On such treacherous terrain, the chances of mis-calculation are immense. Bob Dylan, who laments the night-marish corruptions of the age, nevertheless wears his material thin grinding out a million-dollar album a year for Columbia —which is more apt to find its way to the shelf beside a polished mahogany stereophonic radio-phono console in sub-urbia than to any bohemian garret. Vanessa Redgrave, a veteran of Committee of 100 sit-downs in Whitehall who will don *fidelista* fatigues to sing Cuban revolutionary ballads in Trafalgar Square, also lends her talents to the glossy *Play-boy* pornography of films like *Blow-Up*. Even Herbert Marcuse, much to his chagrin, has of late become hot feature material throughout Europe and America in the wake of the 1968 student rebellions in Germany and France. "I'm very much worried about this," Marcuse has commented on the situation. "At the same time it is a beautiful verification of my philosophy, which is that in this society everything can be co-opted, everything can be digested."[17]

From such obfuscation of genuine dissenting talent, it isn't far to go before the counter culture finds itself swamped with cynical or self-deceived opportunists who become, or conven-iently let themselves be turned into, spokesmen for youthful disaffiliation. Accordingly, we now have clothing designers, hairdressers, fashion magazine editors, and a veritable phalanx of pop stars who, without a thought in their heads their PR man did not put there, are suddenly expounding "the philosophy of today's rebellious youth" for the benefit

[17] Marcuse, "Varieties of Humanism," in *Center Magazine* (Cen-ter for the Study of Democratic Institutions, Santa Barbara), June 1968, p. 14. On the other hand, at another social level, Marcuse has acquired more urgent worries. A threat of assassination from the local Ku Klux Klan drove him from his San Diego home in July 1968. The incident reminds us that there are dark corners of the technocracy (like southern California) where the troglodytes still hold out.

of the Sunday supplements . . . the feature to be sandwiched between a report on luxury underwear and a full-color spread on the latest undiscovered skin-diving paradise at which to spend that summer of a lifetime. And then, for good reason, the counter culture begins to look like nothing so much as a world-wide publicity stunt. One can easily despair of the possibility that it will survive these twin perils: on the one hand, the weakness of its cultural rapport with the disadvantaged; on the other, its vulnerability to exploitation as an amusing side show of the swinging society.

* * * *

Picking its way through this socio-political obstacle course is an undeniably demanding task for the counter culture, one which may take the better part of another generation. To overcome the commercializing and trivializing tactics of the technocratic society will require outlasting the atmosphere of novelty that now surrounds our youth culture and which easily assigns it the character of a transient fad. In the process, there will have to be a maturation of what are often for the young no more than shrewd insights and bright instincts, so that these can become the thoughtful stuff of an adult life. If the counter culture should bog down in a colorful morass of unexamined symbols, gestures, fashions of dress, and slogans, then it will provide little that can be turned into a lifelong commitment—except, and then pathetically, for those who can reconcile themselves to becoming superannuated hangers-on of the campus, the love-in, the rock club. It will finish as a temporary style, continually sloughed off and left behind for the next wave of adolescents: a hopeful beginning that never becomes more than a beginning. As for the task of introducing the oppressed minorities into the counter culture: I suspect that this may have to wait until the black revolution has run its course in America. At which point the new black middle class will produce its own ungrateful young, who, as the heirs of everything their parents thought worth struggling for, will begin, like their white counterparts, to fight their way free of technocratic entrapment.

But beyond the problems raised by such social maneuvering, there lies an even more critical project: that of defining the ethical dignity of a cultural movement which takes radical issue with the scientific world view. The project is vitally important because there must be a reply to the challenge raised by the many uneasy intellectuals who fear that the counter culture arrives, not trailing clouds of glory, but bearing the mark of the beast. No sooner does one speak of liberating the non-intellective powers of the personality than, for many, a prospect of the starkest character arises: a vision of rampant, antinomian mania, which in the name of permissiveness threatens to plunge us into a dark and savage age. It is not without justification that concerned men should then hasten to mount the barricades in the defense of reason. Here, for example, is Philip Toynbee reminding us of "the old nihilistic yearning for madness, despair, and total denial" which was a mainstay of fascist ideology:

. . . it is important to remember that Himmler was the truest nihilist of them all. It is important to remember that the most effective guardians against a resurgence of fascism in Europe are hope, decency, and rationality. This should be brought home, if it can be, to all those young people who consider that they belong to the Left but who love to play with nihilistic toys in art and argument. The ultimate fascist cry is Millan Astray's "Viva, viva la Muerte!"[18]

[18] Toynbee reviewing some recent studies of fascism in *The Observer* (London), July 28, 1968. In a similar vein, the British playwright Arnold Wesker has referred to the hippies as "pretty little fascists" and the social critic Henry Anderson has renamed the Sex-

To a disconcerting extent, such criticism is outrageously unfair. "Make Love Not War" is still the banner most of the dissenting young are rallying to, and those who cannot see the difference between that sentiment and any motto the Hitler *Jugend* voiced are being almost perversely blind. So, too, one of the most remarkable aspects of the counter culture is its cultivation of a feminine softness among its males. It is the occasion of endless satire on the part of critics, but the style is clearly a deliberate effort on the part of the young to undercut the crude and compulsive he-manliness of American political life. While this generous and gentle eroticism is available to us, we would do well to respect it, instead of ridiculing it.

And yet . . . there are manifestations around the fringe of the counter culture that one cannot but regard as worrisomely unhealthy. Elements of pornographic grotesquery and blood-curdling sadomasochism emerge again and again in the art and theater of our youth culture and intrude themselves constantly into the underground press. Many of the underground newspapers seem to work on the assumption that talking about anything frankly means talking about it as crudely and as savagely as possible. The supposedly libertarian eroticism of this style betrays a total failure to realize that professional pornography does not challenge, but rather battens off the essential prurience of middle-class sexuality and has a vested

---

ual Freedom League the Sexual Fascism League. For a heavier presentation of such fears, see David Holbrook's essay "R. D. Laing and the Death Circuit" in *Encounter*, August 1968. Peter Viereck's *Metapolitics: The Roots of the Nazi Mind* (New York: A. A. Knopf, 1941), is a thorough attempt to spell out the connections between Nazism and Romanticism—a line of argument that is relevant to such criticisms, since the relationship of the counter culture to the Romantic tradition in our society is readily apparent. Finally, for an absolutely vicious denunciation of "the Nazi hoodlums of the new freedom," see G. Legman's intemperate little tract *The Fake Revolt* (New York: Breaking-Point Press, 1967).

interest in maintaining the notion that sex is a dirty thing. What prohibition was to the bootlegger, the puritanical ethos is to the pornographer: both are the entrepreneurs of an oppressive prudishness.[19] Even where such crudity is meant to satirize or reply in kind to the corruptions of the dominant culture, there is bound to come a point where sardonic imitation destroys the sensibilities and produces simple callousness. I find it little short of disheartening to come across items like the following: a rave review of an acid-rock group called The Doors (after Huxley, after Blake, apparently) taken from the underground Seattle newspaper *Helix* (July 1967):

The Doors. Their style is early cunnilingual with overtones of the Massacre of the Innocents. An electrified sex slaughter. A musical blood-bath. . . . The Doors are carnivores in a land of musical vegetarians. . . . their talons, fangs, and folded wings are seldom out of view, but if they leave us crotch-raw and exhausted, at least they leave us aware of our aliveness. And of our destiny. The Doors scream into the darkened auditorium what all of us in the underground are whispering more softly in our hearts: we want the world and we want it . . . NOW!

In the face of such mock-Dionysian frenzy, it is no wonder that a fretful cry for "rationality" should be raised. How *is* one to make certain that the exploration of the non-intellective powers will not degenerate into a maniacal nihilism? The matter needs sorting out, and I am uncertain

---

[19] *The Berkeley Barb* has become a particularly grim example of what happens when one ignores such seemingly obvious facts. The *Barb* now regularly carries about three pages of advertising for blue movies, along with a vast amount of "velvet underground" classified ads. Such obscenity merchandisers make about as much of a contribution to sexual freedom as the Strategic Air Command— whose motto is "peace is our profession"—makes to healthy international relations.

that many of the young have reflected sufficiently upon it.
Let me close this chapter, then, by offering some thoughts
that may help contribute a less forbidding, but I think no
less radical meaning to the central project of the counter
culture.

The problem at hand confronts us with a familiar, but
much misunderstood, dichotomy: the opposition of reason
and passion, intellect and feeling, the head and the heart.
. . . Again and again in moral discourse this troublesome
polarity intrudes itself upon us, pretending to be a real ethical
choice. But what is that choice? None of the terms of the
dichotomy is by any means unambiguously related to some
well-defined faculty of the personality. Rather, at the ethical
level of discussion, the choice comes down most often to one
between two styles of conduct. One pursues a rational style
of life, we say, if one's behavior is characterized by dispassionate restraint, unfailing deliberateness, and an articulate logicality. Conversely, one is irrational if one's conduct
forsakes dispassion in favor of an intense and overt emotion-
alism, deliberation in favor of impulsiveness, articulation and
logic in favor of rhapsodic declamation or some manner of
non-verbal expression. Once these extremes have been marked
out, the discussion usually settles down to an interminable
listing of examples and counter-examples meant to prove the
virtues and dangers of any tendency to one or the other pole
of the continuum.

Those who opt for rationality darkly warn us against the
terrors that have come of submerging the intellect beneath a
flood tide of feeling. They remind us of the lynch mobs and
pogroms, the unreasoning mass movements and witch-hunts
to which impassioned men have given themselves. They
remind us that Hitler was but echoing the words of D. H.
Lawrence when he commanded his followers: "Think with
your blood!" Against such barbaric upheavals, the cause of

reason invokes the example of great humanitarian personalities: Socrates, Montaigne, Voltaire, Galileo, John Stuart Mill . . . and all the many more who pled for the dignity of intellect against the savagery and superstition of their day.

But if we think again, we see at once that the same line of argument is open to those who opt for the life of feeling. Can they not match every hot-blooded brutality in human history with an example of cold-blooded criminality just as dire? If thirteenth-century Christendom had been dominated by the impulsive compassion of the simple-minded St. Francis, rather than by the frigid intellectuality of Innocent III, would there ever have been an Inquisition? By what manner of men was St. Joan, an illiterate visionary, martyred if not by heartless schemers whose intellectual capacities can scarcely be questioned? How many men of surpassing rationality can equal the record that the Quakers, guided by moral passion and the Inner Light, have compiled in resisting war, slavery, and social injustice?

When we turn to the case most frequently cited as evidence of the dangers of unrestrained passion—that of the Nazis—I think the same sort of argument can be used. Perhaps the Nazis did assume the mantle of a vulgarized Romanticism. But if we ask with what manner of men its cadres were staffed, we get a rather different picture of the regime. Without utterly dispassionate, utterly rational technicians and administrative automatons like Adolf Eichmann, it is impossible to imagine the Nazi state lasting a year. Those who blame Nazism on the corrupting influence of the Romantic movement surely mistake the propagandistic surface for the underlying political reality. The New Order was hardly the creature of moon-struck poets and Dionysian revelers. It was, instead, as thorough a technocracy as any that survives today: a carefully wrought bureaucratic-military apparatus based on relentless regimentation and precisely managed terrorism. If the movement dealt in the hot passions of the masses, its success lay in *organizing* those passions into a disciplined machinery of state with all the cunning that our market researchers employ in manipulating the irrationalities of the consuming public. Hitler may have postured like a Siegfried, but his henchmen were such children of the forest as knew how to make the trains run on time. Behind the Wagnerian facade, the Nazi death camp stands as a masterpiece of social engineering in which the cry of the heart was systematically drowned out by the demands of genocidal efficiency.[20]

And simply to bring the catalogue up to date: what are we to identify as the basic deficiency of all the technical experts who now administer the world-wide balance of terror? Is it intellect our scientists and strategists and operations analysts lack? These men who preside with an impersonal eye over a system of mass murder capable of greater destruction than all the lynch mobs and witch-hunters in history: is it their capacity to *reason* that is flawed? Surely Lewis Mumford goes to the heart of the matter when he insists that the situation confronts us with something that can only be called "mad rationality"; and he reminds us of Captain Ahab's chilling confession: "All my means are sane: my motives and object mad."[21]

We are correct in feeling that serious ethical discussion must get beyond ad hoc evaluations of specific actions—which is essentially the area of life we leave to the law. But we are mistaken, I think, in believing that the dichotomy

[20] For a moving example of how one simple, compassionate soul held out to the point of martyrdom against the practical accommodation with which his intellectual superiors greeted the Nazis, see Gordon Zahn's study of the Austrian peasant Franz Jägerstätter, *In Solitary Witness* (New York: Holt, Rinehart and Winston, 1965).

[21] Lewis Mumford, *The Transformations of Man* (New York: Collier Books, 1956), p. 122.

between rational and impulsive, deliberate and passionate styles of action is a more meaningful level of discourse. Indeed, I would contend that this dichotomy confronts us with inherently non-moral considerations. Neither rationality nor passionate impulse, as they characterize styles of behavior, guarantees anything about the ethical quality of action. Instead, these styles comprise a vocabulary of conduct which can be used to express many different things. To arbitrate between them at this level, therefore, would be as pointless as trying to decide whether prose or poetry is the proper province of noble sentiments. Nor do I think we advance the discussion by trying to work out some fifty-fifty compromise on the issue, on the assumption that there is some golden mean between reason and feeling that assures good conduct. We have too many examples of utterly rational and utterly impassioned human decency to reject either as a style of action. Neither our impulsive saints nor our humanitarian intellectuals can be denied their ethical beauty.

We enter a searching discussion of moral action only when we press beyond the surface style of conduct in which men express their ethical sensibilities and seek the hidden source from which their action flows. If, again, we think of conduct as a vocabulary, then we can see that our use of that vocabulary will depend wholly upon what we try to "say" through what we do. Our action gives voice to our total vision of life —of the self and its proper place in the nature of things— as we experience it most movingly. For many men this vision may be pathetically narrow, bounded on all sides by socially prescribed rules and sanctions; they may have only the dimmest awareness of a good or evil which is not the product of social inculcation and enforcement. In that case, a man behaves as he does out of fear or ingrained subordination and with little personal authority. Perhaps the conduct of most men is shaped in this way—and too often it is just such automatized dutifulness that we take to be rational and responsible. Yet, even so, there lurks behind our socially certified morality some primordial world view which dictates what reality is, and what, within that reality, is to be held sacred.

For most of us, this world view may elude the grasp of words; it may be something we never directly attend to. It may remain the purely subliminal sense of our condition that spontaneously forms our perceptions and our motivations. Even before our world view guides us to discriminate between good and evil, it disposes us to discriminate between real and unreal, true and false, meaningful and meaningless. Before we act in the world, we must conceive of a world; it must be *there* before us, a sensible pattern to which we adopt our conduct. If, like the Jainist holy man, we regard all life as divine, then it will seem perfectly sensible to inconvenience ourselves endlessly with avoiding every act that might injure even the most minute insect. If, on the other hand, we regard all non-human beings as lower and less sentient forms of existence, we will regard the Jainist as highly superstitious and his activities as morally meaningless. Indeed, we will not bother to think twice before slaughtering whole herds of animals for pleasure or need. The impulsiveness or deliberation with which men do these things will be beside the point. As long as any man's moral sensibility squares with our world view, we are inclined to accept his conduct as quite sane and reasonable. But all the elegant rationalizing in the world will not convince us that someone who rejects our vision of reality is anything but mad or superstitiously irrational—though, to be sure, we may be willing to practice a pluralistic tolerance toward him within certain prescribed legal limits.

We have no serviceable language in our culture to talk about the level of the personality at which this underlying vision of reality resides. But it seems indisputable that it exerts its influence at a point that lies deeper than our intellective consciousness. The world view we hold is nothing we learn in the same conscious way in which we learn an intellectual subject matter. It is, rather, something we absorb from the spirit of the times or are converted into, or seduced into by unaccountable experiences. It is, indeed, this guiding vision that determines what we finally regard as sanity itself. We can, therefore, see why two men like Bertrand Russell and Herman Kahn—neither of whom can be fairly accused of despising reason, logic, or intellectual precision—can emerge as such implacable antagonists on so many great issues. Russell himself, in grasping the primacy of vision over the superficial style of thought, speech, and conduct, has said, "I would rather be mad with the truth than sane with lies." "Mad," to be sure, from the viewpoint of others; for what brings a man close to the truth will become his own standard of sanity.

When I say that the counter culture delves into the non-intellective aspects of the personality, it is with respect to its interest at this level—at the level of vision—that I believe its project is significant. Undeniably, this project often gets obscured, especially among the more desperate young who quickly conclude that the antidote to our society's "mad rationality" lies in flinging oneself into an assortment of mad passions. Like too many of our severely self-disciplined solid citizens and "responsible" leaders, they allow their understanding to stop at the level of surface conduct, accepting as final the dichotomy between "spontaneous" and "deliberate" styles of behavior. They also believe

. . . that the unsought and inspired belongs to special individuals in peculiar emotional states; or again to people at parties under the influence of alcohol or hasheesh; rather than being a quality of all experience. And correspondingly, calculated behavior aims at goods that are not uniquely appropriated according to one's fancy, but are in turn only good for something else (so that pleasure itself is endured as a means to health and efficiency). "Being oneself" means acting imprudently, as if desire could not make sense; and "acting sensibly" means holding back and being bored.[22]

But while a good deal of our contemporary youth culture takes off in the direction of strenuous frenzy and simulated mindlessness, there also moves through the scene a very different and much more mature conception of what it means to investigate the non-intellective consciousness. This emerges primarily from the strong influence upon the young of Eastern religion, with its heritage of gentle, tranquil, and thoroughly civilized contemplativeness. Here we have a tradition that calls radically into question the validity of the scientific world view, the supremacy of cerebral cognition, the value of technological prowess; but does so in the most quiet and measured of tones, with humor, with tenderness, even with a deal of cunning argumentation. If there is anything off-putting to the scientific mind about this tradition, it does not result from any unwillingness on the part of the Eastern religions to indulge in analysis and debate. It results, rather, from their assertion of the intellectual value of paradox and from their conviction that analysis and debate must finally yield to the claims of ineffable experience. Oriental mysticism comprehends argumentation; but it also provides a generous place for silence, out of wise recognition of the fact that it is with silence that men confront the great moments of life. Unhappily, the Western intellect is inclined to treat silence as if it were a mere zero: a loss for words indicating the absence of meaning.

However sternly one may wish to reject the world view of

[22] From Paul Goodman's contribution to Frederick Perls, Ralph Hefferline, and Paul Goodman, *Gestalt Therapy* (New York: Delta, 1965), p. 242.

Lao-tzu, of the Buddha, of the Zen masters, one cannot fairly accuse such figures of lacking intellect, wit, or humane cultivation. Though their minds lay at the service of a vision that is incompatible with our conventional science, such men are the prospective participants of neither a lynch mob nor a group-grope party. Fortunately, their example has not been lost on our dissenting young; indeed, it has become one of the strongest strains of the counter culture.

We will return to this line of thought in later chapters. It will be sufficient to say at this point that the exploration of the non-intellective powers assumes its greatest importance, not when the project becomes a free-for-all of pixilated dynamism, but when it becomes a critique of the scientific world view upon which the technocracy builds its citadel and in the shadow of which too many of the brightest splendors of our experience lie hidden.

Chapter III

THE DIALECTICS OF LIBERATION:
HERBERT MARCUSE AND NORMAN BROWN

The emergence of Herbert Marcuse and Norman Brown as major social theorists among the disaffiliated young of Western Europe and America must be taken as one of the defining features of the counter culture. For it is in their work that the inevitable confrontation between Marx and Freud takes place. This is nothing less than an encounter between the two most influential, but far from obviously compatible social critics of the modern West, an encounter that leads directly to the hard task of assigning an order of priority to the psychological and sociological categories Marx and Freud have bequeathed us for the understanding of man and society. Neither psyche nor social class can be dispensed with; but one or the other of these concepts as they exist in their mature form must be given precedence in any systematic critique. Psychic reality and social reality: which is the prime mover of our lives? Which is the substance and which the shadow?

At question in our rank ordering of the two is the nature of human consciousness and the meaning of liberation. While both Marx and Freud held that man is the victim of a false consciousness from which he must be freed if he is to achieve fulfillment, their diagnoses were built on very different principles. For Marx, that which is hidden from reason is the exploitive reality of the social system. Culture—"ideology" in the pejorative sense of the word—intervenes between reason and reality to mask the operation of invidious class interest

—often enough by a calculated process of brain-washing. Ultimately, however, Marx believed that a "scientific socialism" could penetrate this deception and transform the social reality behind it. For Freud that which is hidden from reason is the content of the unconscious mind. Culture plays its part in the deception not as a mask concealing social reality, but rather as a screen on which the psyche projects itself in a grand repertory of "sublimations." Can human reason ever come to understand and accept for what it is the suppressed source of these cultural illusions? With respect to that possibility, Freud grew ever more pessimistic as his life wore on amid an increasingly self-destructive civilization.

There we have the issue. Is the psyche, as Marx would have it, a reflection of "the mode of production of material life"? Or is the social structure, as Freud argued, a reflection of our psychic contents? Put like this, the question may seem too blunt. Yet, before we finish, we shall see Marcuse and Brown divided just that starkly on the issue. To take one example: in his latest book, Brown, who contends that the truth of psychoanalysis lies precisely in its most offensive exaggerations, develops a psychoanalytic conception of kingship. He tells us:

King James in 1603 said: "'What God hath conjoined then, let no man separate.' I am the husband, and the whole island is my lawful wife." The phallic personality and the receptive audience are in coitus; they do it together, when it comes off. . . . A king is an erection of the body politic. . . . In Daniel, the ten horns are the ten kings; in Cambodia, a lingam adored in the temple in the center of the capital represented Devaraja, the God-King. His Royal Highness, the personification of the penis.[1]

[1] Norman Brown, *Love's Body* (New York: Random House, 1966), pp. 132–33.

To which Marcuse vigorously objects:

> In terms of the latent content, the kingdoms of the earth
> may be shadows; but unfortunately, they move real men
> and things, they kill, they persist and prevail in the sunlight
> as well as in the night. The king may be an erected penis,
> and his relation to the community may be intercourse; but
> unfortunately, it is also something very different and less
> pleasant and more real.[2]

What is the king, then? Social exploiter whose power derives from armed force and economic privilege? Or projected
father figure whose power derives from the overbearing
phallus he personifies? The convenient answer—correct but
superficial—is *both*. But which is the king *primarily*, in origin
and in significance? Does social privilege generate the erotic
symbolism? Does the erotic symbolism generate social privilege? Philosophically, the issue raises the very question of the
locus of reality, the direction in which metaphor points.
Politically, it poses the question of how our liberation is to
be achieved. How shall we rid ourselves of the king or his
dominating surrogates? By social or psychic revolution? Again,
the convenient answer is *both*. But with which do we start?
Which revolution is the "more real"?

The contribution both Marcuse and Brown make to the
counter culture in taking up this murky debate lies in their
attempt to develop a radical social critique out of psychoanalytical insights. In so doing they seek to undercut the
traditional ideologies, for which the interests of class, nation,
or race could be taken at face value—as they are consciously
perceived and articulated—and used as axiomatic material.
With both Marcuse and Brown we find ourselves tunneling
under the rhetorical surface of political life, on the assump-

[2] Herbert Marcuse, "Love Mystified: A Critique of Norman O.
Brown," *Commentary*, February 1967, p. 73.

tion that politics, like the rest of our culture, lies within the province of pathological behavior; that even principled rebellion runs the risk of operating upon the body politic with instruments contaminated by the very disease from which the patient is dying.

But Marcuse and Brown come to Freud along different routes and they discern in him markedly divergent indications of the way forward. In the controversy that finally divides them, it will be Marcuse who assumes the more cautious position, drawing back sharply from Brown's excesses. For Marcuse, the psychoanalytical insights of Freud must lead to the *transformation* of conventional left-wing ideology, not, as Brown's latest work threatens, to its obliteration. From the outset, Marcuse's purpose has been to assimilate Freud to the Hegelian-Marxist tradition within which he finds his own intellectual roots. Prior to World War II, Marcuse maintained a long association with the Institute of Social Research at Frankfort am Main, a major center of Neo-Marxist studies. Then, as now, his foremost attachment has been to Hegelian social theory; but he retains from this academic background a strongly felt obligation to speak to the concerns of his Marxist colleagues. Moreover, as a social philosopher who works in the company of social scientists and political activists, Marcuse remains vividly aware of the need to make his speculations applicable to the lively dilemmas of the world, to keep them in productive dialogue with his practical-minded associates. When all is said and done, Marcuse is a faithful devotee of the left, one who still sees in socialism the hope of the future, but who seeks to enrich the socialist vision by grafting upon it a Freudian dimension. It is for this reason that the radical students of Europe, with their traditional left-wing leanings, readily identify Marcuse as the ideological successor of Marx.

Brown, in contrast, comes to social criticism as the complete maverick. His exploration of "the psychoanalytical meaning of history" in *Life Against Death* is a late and eccentric development in his career. His early classical research —tidy, modest, conventional—reveals little of the Nietzschean elan one now associates with him.[3] Moreover, Brown begins his social thought with Freud, and he takes his Freud straight. He brings with him to psychoanalysis no pre-existing left-wing loyalties. Indeed, Brown makes only marginal reference in his writing to Marx, though it is obvious enough how drastically he calls Marxism into question. He is, besides, notorious for eschewing political engagement and its encumbering factionalisms. If Brown's thought is more daring, as well as more bizarre, than Marcuse's, it is because he works with the freedom of an academic who has bolted his scholarly specialty and arrives at his social critique with no strings attached. The result is all the turbulent originality of the amateur who pursues his speculative adventures unworried by the conventional wisdom of the professionals in the field or of ideologically entrenched colleagues. For the orthodox Freudian, Brown's liberties of interpretation are scandalously broad. For the radical activist, his politics turn out to be perversely a-political. Still, it will be my position here that, in the realm of social criticism, the counter culture begins where Marcuse pulls up short, and where Brown, with no apologies, goes off the deep end.

*   *   *   *

Before we examine the issues that divide Marcuse and Brown, let us survey the characteristics they possess in common. It is well worth doing, because both men can be credited with having made major and very similar contributions to

---

[3] See, for example, his *Hermes the Thief* (Madison, Wis.: University of Wisconsin Press, 1947).

contemporary social thought. The best way to draw out the novelty of their work may be to compare it with traditional Marxism.

The challenge Marcuse and Brown pose to Marxism is, interestingly enough, offered from ground they share with Marx —or perhaps we should say with the shadowy young "Ur-Marx" who aspired to philosophy under the heady influence of German idealism. The manuscript essays in which Marx roughed out and then abandoned his youthful speculations were not destined to find their way into print until some fifty years after his death. But their career since then has been spectacular. They have become, meager as they are, the seed-bed of what is now called "Marxist Humanism," the Marxism which we are to believe still retains its revolutionary relevance under the conditions of capitalist and collectivist-bureaucratic affluence.[4]

Marcuse, who readily identifies himself with the school, finds the value of these writings in the emphasis they lay upon those "tendencies that have been attenuated in the post-Marxian development of his critique of society, namely, the elements of communistic individualism, the repudiation of any fetishism concerning the socialization of the means of production or the growth of the productive forces, the subordination of all these factors to the idea of the free realization of the individual."[5] Undeniably these novice efforts of Marx possess considerable charm, despite their crudity of style and their forbidding Hegelian abstruseness. Not only do the essays reveal a warm, personalist concern for the individual, but at this stage of his life Marx did not blush to

[4] The writings have been published as *Economic and Philosophic Manuscripts of 1844* (Moscow: Foreign Languages Publishing House, 1959).

[5] Herbert Marcuse, *Reason and Revolution: Hegel and the Rise of Social Theory* (Oxford: Oxford University Press, 1941), pp. 294–95.

elaborate imaginatively on poetry and music, on play and love, on beauty and the life of the senses. As we shall see, there are points in these essays where he develops insights of great psychological promise. Still, there is something both pathetic and zany about the Neo-Marxist pedantry which now insists that these discarded, rudimentary exercises are the "true" Marx, and that—if only we will comb the leavings closely enough—we shall find in them (and the suggestion is almost that we shall find in them *alone* of all the literature of the period) all the essential wisdom of modern humanist thought.[6]

Marcuse, by way of defending the overall continuity of Marx's work, has protested against the effort to confine Marx's humanism to the early writings. "What Marxist Humanism really is," he argues, "appears in *Das Kapital* and in his later writings." But Marcuse goes on to define this "humanism" as "the building of a world without the domination or the exploitation of man by man."[7] True enough, the protest against exploitation appears in Marx from start to finish—along with other continuities. But it appears as well in all the socialist and anarchist theorists of the last 150 years. If there is a distinctive quality in the early manuscripts, it lies in their unusual psychological and poetic sensibility. And if we are going to regard the manuscripts as the "find" which Marxist Humanists suggest they are, then the decisive fact in our assessment of their place in the Marxian corpus must surely

[6] For an example of such egregious eulogizing (in this case by someone who should know better) see Erich Fromm's exegesis on Marx's old notebooks in *Marx's Concept of Man* (New York: Ungar, 1961). The burden of Fromm's essay is that Marx was "the flowering of Western humanity," one who "penetrated to the very essence of reality. . . ." but who has been very much misunderstood ever since.

[7] Herbert Marcuse, "Varieties of Humanism," *Center Magazine*, June 1968.

be that Marx himself cast these unpolished efforts into obscurity, never to return to their spirit of free speculation and aesthetic depth—except with an obliqueness that only the keenest Marxist scholar can detect. What ceased to have any significant personal influence on Marx could not help thereafter to have even less historical influence on the majority of his followers. Except for the role it now plays—and a valuable one it is—in watering the imagination of desiccated Marxists, the *Economic and Philosophic Manuscripts* is, historically speaking, an intellectual non-starter. A fact for which no one is more to blame than Marx himself.

In placing so high an evaluation upon the early manuscripts, the Marxist Humanists may be attributing to Marx qualities of mind and heart they ought properly to claim for themselves. In the case of Marcuse, this is certainly so. I will therefore assume in this essay that what is unmistakably and centrally present in Marcuse and only marginally present in Marx should be credited to Marcuse as an authentic advance upon traditional Marxism.

With both Marcuse and Brown, then, we return to the mainstream of the rich German Romantic tradition that Marx abandoned in favor of a so-called "scientific" socialism. It is as if, with the benefit of hindsight, they have been able to see that the stormy Romantic sensibility, obsessed from first to last with paradox and madness, ecstasy and spiritual striving, had far greater insights to yield than Marx suspected. In particular, the tradition was to issue forth in the work of Freud and of Nietzsche, the major psychologists of the Faustian soul. Hence we find in Marcuse and Brown a supreme evaluation placed on exactly those cultural elements which Marx, with his compulsive hard-headedness, banished to the status of "shadowy forms in the brain of men."[8] Myth, reli-

[8] As H. B. Acton observes, the only "mental production" Marx seems to have excused from the derogatory category of ideology is

gion, dreams, visions: such were the dark waters Freud fished to find his conception of human nature. But for all this occult matter Marx had little patience. Instead, he chose to spend dismal hours poring over the industrial statistics of the British Blue Books, where man has little occasion to appear in any role but *homo economicus, homo faber*. In contrast, Marcuse and Brown insist that we have more to learn of man from the fabulous images of Narcissus, Orpheus, Dionysius, Apollo, than from the hard data of getting and spending.

When the stuff of myth and fantasy becomes our proper study of man, however, the range of our investigation expands enormously. Industrial statistics are the language of the present; myth is the language of the ages. For Marx, the modern era was uniquely significant; it was the "last antagonistic form of the social process of production." For this reason, Marx's major historical thinking is squeezed into this apocalyptic interval and its immediate antecedents. When one reads the correspondence and the pamphlets of Marx and Engels, one is struck by the fierce present-mindedness of their concerns, the myopic fixation on the affairs of here and now, the fervent taking of sides in all the petty wars and power politicking of the time (usually in favor of the German Reich)—as if the conscious political deliberations and actions of today, tomorrow, next week really *could* make all the difference. Within such a restricted perspective, it was only too obvious who one's enemies were, and how the evils of the day were to be overcome.

But for Marcuse and Brown, following Freud, it is not so easy to mark out the villains and the heroes, nor to take seriously the surface politics of the time. For them, the primary unit of study becomes the whole of civilization.

natural science, for science after all is "empirically establishable." *What Marx Really Said* (New York: Schocken Books, 1967), pp. 77–80.

Industrialism, whether under capitalist or collective auspices, is assimilated to the general historical category of what Marcuse calls "the logic of domination," or Brown, "the politics of sin, cynicism and despair." And beyond civilization the Freudian thrust carries both men tenuously back into the evolutionary past in search of the origins of instinctual conflict. Like Marx, they are concerned with the dialectics of liberation. Like Marx, too, they seek to give the Hegelian concept of history a "material" basis in which its dialectical movement can be grounded. But it is not Marxian class conflict—or for Marcuse not class conflict alone—which answers their quest; it is, instead, the human body, seen as that perennial battlefield where the war of the instincts is waged.

Liberation must therefore become, at one and the same time, a more sweeping, yet more subtly discriminating project than most social rebels have realized. Those who believe that the liberation of man can be achieved by one sharp revolutionary jab, by the mere substitution of a well-intentioned elite for a corrupt one, are courting that "element of *self-defeat*" which Marcuse sees in all the revolutions of the past.

Clearly then, the key problem of "alienation" has assumed a very different meaning for Marcuse and Brown than anything one can find in the work of the mature Marx. This would no doubt be disputed by many Marxist Humanists (perhaps by Marcuse as well), for whom "alienation" has become the great ideologue's passport to contemporary relevance. One wonders, indeed, if Marx would retain any vitality at all among Western intellectuals had he not chanced to use this now modish word. One must say "chanced" to use it, because, as Daniel Bell has amply demonstrated,[9] the prevailing no-

---

[9] Daniel Bell, "In Search of Marxist Humanism: The Debate of Alienation," *Soviet Survey*, No. 32, April–June 1960. Erich Fromm takes issue with Bell's conclusions in *Marx's Concept of Man*, pp. 77–79, but I think not successfully.

tion of alienation in the Marxian corpus has only the most marginal connection with the way in which this idea functions in the thinking of Kierkegaard or Dostoyevsky or Kafka. It is rather as if the Neo-Marxists are attempting to usher Marx into the contemporary world on the coattails of existentialist artists and philosophers for whom the immediate issues of social justice, class conflict, and industrial exploitation were a subsidiary concern, if that.

It is interesting to note, however, how the more philosophical young Marx confronted the concept of alienation. One of the early essays relates the idea of "estranged" or "alienated" labor to the psychic life of man and to man's relations with nature. This is a much more impressive (because more generalized) conception of alienation than anything that appears later in Marx's work—but it leads him to a strange conclusion. After a deal of involuted analysis, Marx decides that "private property is . . . the *product*, the *result*, the *necessary consequence* of alienated labor, of the external relation of the worker to nature and to himself." (Italics added.) This forces Marx to ask a deep question: "How . . . does man come to alienate, to estrange, his labor? How is this estrangement rooted in the nature of human development?"

This is an absolutely astonishing line of thought to find in Marx, whether the old Marx or the young! For he is suggesting here that some primordial act of alienation has taken place in "human development" which is *not* to be traced to the economic process, but which, in fact, *generates* private property and all its attendant evils. What was this act of alienation? Unhappily, the manuscript, which was intended to solve this crucial problem, breaks off before we have the answer. Did Marx have any answer?

Perhaps he did . . . but it may not have been a very "Marxist" one. Earlier in the same essay, Marx speculates again on the origins of alienation. He asks, what is the "alien power" which intervenes to appropriate man's labor and so to frustrate his self-fulfillment? Can it be "nature"? Of course not, Marx answers.

What a contradiction it would be if, the more man subjugated nature by his labor and the more the miracles of the gods were rendered superfluous by the miracles of industry, the more man were to renounce the joy of production and the enjoyment of the produce in favor of these powers.

What a contradiction indeed! A *dialectical* contradiction, one might almost say. But Marx failed to unravel the paradox of this insight—for at last he was neither Nietzsche nor Freud.[10]

If "alienation" means that nightmare of existential weightlessness we associate with Kafka's white-collared Joseph K. or Tolstoy's gentryman Ivan Ilych, then the socioeconomic alienation Marx finds in the life of the proletariat is at most a derivative special case of the universal phenomenon. As we shall see, Marcuse and Brown disagree significantly in their diagnosis of the condition; but they are at one in insisting that alienation in this generalized sense is primarily psychic, not sociological. It is not a proprietary distinction that exists *between* men of different classes, but rather a disease that is rooted *inside* all men. The true students of alienation, therefore, are not the social scientists, but the psychiatrists. (We might recall that in Freud's day the latter were still commonly referred to as "alienists.") And what the psychiatrist knows is that alienation results from deep

[10] For these speculations on "estranged labor," see *Economic and Philosophical Manuscripts of 1844*, pp. 67–83. In other essays, however, Marx sticks to his guns stubbornly, insisting that the abolition of private property is *the* guaranteed way of abolishing alienation.

and secret acts of repression that will not yield to a mere reshuffling of our society's institutional structures.

It may even be the case that alienation, properly understood, has been more heavily concentrated in the upper levels of capitalist society than in its long-suffering lower depths. How otherwise is one to account on Freudian grounds for the monomaniacal acquisitiveness and ascetic self-discipline of the typical robber baron, except to see such grotesque behavior as a fierce perversion of the life instincts into anal-sadistic aggressiveness? Undoubtedly the novelists and play-wrights who have tried to convince us that the poor live fuller lives than the rich have been guilty of sentimentalizing. But there is perhaps this much truth in what they say: that if one sets about looking for sane and happy people, one is not likely to find them at the top of the social pyramid. For by whom is the life-depriving fiction of money more pathetically reified than by the successful capitalist?

Marx was not unaware of the fact that exploitation distorts the life of the capitalist quite as seriously as it does the life of the laborer, though in subtler ways. He was prepared at many points to see the money-grubbing capitalist as the pitiful victim of his own despotic economic system. There is, in fact, in one of the early essays an incisive treatment along these lines of the mystery of money. It is only a rough fragment built up around some passages from Goethe and Shakespeare, but it is nonetheless a precocious insight. In the essay, Marx comes close to realizing the sad truth that money functions in the imagination of the alienated profiteer, not as a rational measure of value, but as a corrupted magic, a wish-fulfilling fantasy-stuff. This, he concludes, is the secret of its uncanny influence over us. "The divine power of money," Marx observes, "lies in its character as men's estranged, alienating, and self-disposing species-nature. Money is the alienated ability of mankind." One can see in this notion the germ of Marx's later "fetishism of commodities," the cruel illusion from which both exploiter and exploited suffer under capitalism.[11] Yet when Marx sought in his later writing for an explanation of the thoroughly irrational acquisitiveness one sees in the capitalist, he had to fall back on stereotypic moralisms like "werewolf greed." What Marx lacked at this critical point in his thinking was the sense of the pathological which Marcuse and Brown derive from Freud—a perspective which leads them beyond an economic analysis of capitalism to a general critique of man's behavior under civilization as a whole. From this viewpoint it becomes abundantly clear that the revolution which will free us from alienation must be primarily therapeutic in character and not merely institutional.

We will have to look more closely at the work of Marcuse and Brown to see how each proposes to lift the burden of alienation from man's soul. Here let us underscore once more the contrast with Marx. For Marx, it was "not the consciousness of men that determines their social being, but, on the contrary, their social being that determines their consciousness"—a thesis which never quite managed to account for Karl Marx himself and the bourgeois intellectual defectors he expected to take leadership of the proletariat. Marcuse and Brown, on the other hand, emphasize the *primacy* of consciousness in social change. This is especially true of Brown, who treats revolution exclusively in terms of an apocalyptic illumination; but even Marcuse, who is more ambiguous on the matter, concludes that the making of a "non-repressive

[11] The essay on money appears in *Economic and Philosophic Manuscripts of 1844*, pp. 136–41. It is interesting to compare Marx's highly metaphysical analysis of money with the psychoanalytical treatment Brown presents in the "Filthy Lucre" section of *Life Against Death*, pp. 234–304.

civilization" will require a clear vision of libidinal liberation from the outset.

The consciousness of this possibility, and the radical transvaluation of values which it demands, must guide the direction of such a change from the very beginnings, and must be operative even in the construction of the technical and material base. (p. viii.)[12]

Moreover, the tone in which Marcuse and Brown speak of liberation is distinctly non-Marxian. For Marcuse, it is the achievement of a "libidinal rationality"; for Brown, it is the creation of an "erotic sense of reality," a "Dionysian ego." When they seek to elucidate these ideals, both must perforce become rhapsodic, introducing the imagery of myth and poetry. So they sound a note that has been scandalously lacking from the literature of social ideology and even more so from that of the social sciences. Most of our social scientists, one feels, regard the introduction of poetic vision into their work in much the same way a pious monk would regard bringing a whore into the monastery. But for the counter culture it is indisputable that the poets have known better than the ideologues, that visions mean more than research.

Orpheus and Narcissus [Marcuse observes] have not become the culture-heroes of the Western world: theirs is the image of joy and fulfillment; the voice which does not command but sings; the gesture which offers and receives; the deed which is peace and ends the labor of conquest; the liberation from time which unites man with god, man and nature. (p. 147.)

[12] Unless otherwise specified, all the Marcuse quotations in this chapter are from *Eros and Civilization* (New York: Vintage Books, 1962); all the Brown quotations are from *Life Against Death* (Middletown, Conn.: Wesleyan University Press, 1959).

Man the dreamer, the lover, the conjuror with divine aspiration: one must grant that Marx, in certain of his un-characteristic moods, may not have been beyond appreciating these aspects of humanity. His conjecture that a truly *human* history might only begin after the era of class conflict has subsided, betrays at least the faint and passing recognition that life in its fullness, life as it cries out from the depths of us to be lived, transcends "the realm of natural necessity." Engels, too, speaks of a "kingdom of freedom" that stands beyond the "kingdom of necessity." But what are its contours? How shall we know that happy kingdom when we see it? How shall we keep clear the difference between the mere means of getting there and the *end* which is to enjoy the *being* of freedom?

What we take seriously we give serious attention to—and Marx spared notoriously little attention for such utopian vistas. Marx the incensed moralist, the smoldering prophet of doom, the scholarly drudge: what time did he have in the heat and pressure of the crisis at hand to think of man as anything but *homo economicus*, exploited and joyless?

What then would Marx's reply be to the exuberant aspirations of Marcuse and Brown? Very likely: "Yes . . . but later." "Yes . . . afterwards. *After* the revolution. *After* we have eliminated the profiteering bastards. Then . . . perhaps . . . we shall talk of these things. We shall call together the commissars and the apparatchiks, and we shall all sit down and have a good long talk about Orpheus and Narcissus."

Which is what it means to take your eye off the ball.

For the utopian urge quickly atrophies without exercise. That is why we sense at points in the Marxist critique that our liberation must forever be subordinated to rationalizing the "anarchy of production"; that, indeed, it has been ban-ished to Never-Never Land. Engels, in his essay "On Authority," drew the somber conclusion:

If man by dint of his knowledge and inventive genius has subdued the forces of nature, the latter avenge themselves upon him by subjecting him, insofar as he employs them, to a veritable despotism, *independent of all social organization.* Wanting to abolish authority in large-scale industry is tantamount to wanting to abolish industry itself, to destroy the power loom in order to return to the spinning wheel.[13]

And far be it from any good Marxist to consider destroying the power loom or to conceive of "nature" as anything but a wily foe. In tone and in content, the essay makes clear that, at last, Marxism is the mirror image of bourgeois industrialism: an image reversed, and yet unmistakably identical. For both traditions, the technocratic imperative with its attendant conception of life stands unchallenged. Ironically, it is the greatest single victory bourgeois society has won over even its most irreconcilable opponents: that it has inculcated upon them its own shallow, reductionist image of man. Like classical economics, scientific socialism approached society as Newton approached the behavior of the heavenly bodies, seeking their immutable "laws of motion." Despite the fact that it was principally his moral fervor and invective rhetoric that was to give his work its enduring vitality, Marx aspired to the myth of a social-scientific objectivity in which society would be understood as "a process of natural history." What was not science was "speculative cobwebs . . . flowers of rhetoric . . . sickly sentiment." It is the tough-mindedness

[13] Lewis S. Feuer, ed., *Marx & Engels: Basic Writings on Politics and Philosophy* (New York: Anchor Books, 1959), p. 483. (Italics added.) In the essay, which was written as a slap at the anarchists, Engels observes stoically that "the automatic machinery of a big factory is *much more despotic* than the small capitalists who employ workers ever have been," and that the best one can hope for from revolution is that authority will lose its "political character and be transformed into the *simple administrative functions* of watching over the true interests of society." (Italics added.) It is an astonishing anticipation of the technocracy.

of nineteenth-century realpolitik that speaks too often through Marx, mixed with the grizzly callousness of social Darwinism and a scurrilous, positivistic atheism.

This, then, is ideology written in the key of the prevailing reality principle: ideology that collaborates in diminishing consciousness, that weighs down and seeks to reconcile us to an existence without dreams, without fantasies. To immerse oneself in the old ideologies—with the notable exception of that anarchist tradition which flows from such figures as Kropotkin, Tolstoy, Thoreau—is to find oneself stifling in the stone and steel environment of unquestionable technological necessity. It is a literature of seriousness and grim resolve, tightly bounded by practicality, class discipline, the statistics of injustice, and the lust for retribution. To speak of the ecstasies of life in such a somber environment is to risk folly. Here where all men trudge, none may dance. Dancing is . . . for later.

If the demise of the old ideologies begins anywhere, it begins with this delaying gesture. For to postpone until "later" consideration of the humanly essential in the name of "being realistic" is to practice the kind of deadly practicality which now stands our civilization in peril of annihilation. It is to deliver us into the hands of dehumanized commissars, managers, and operations analysts—all of whom are professional experts at postponing the essential. These are the practitioners of what C. Wright Mills called "crackpot realism." The artist who clings to his impossible vision at least preserves that much of heaven among us; the mad realist who turns from that vision for the sake of another "practical" measure only takes us one step further into the hell of our alienation.

It is understandable that the old ideologies should have been characterized by the diminished conception of realism that stems from anger and desperation. The horizon of the time encompassed neither affluence nor the insights of depth psychology. Marx, as Norman Brown observes, "is not free from the tacit assumption . . . that the concrete human needs and drives sustaining economic activity are just what they appear to be and are fully in consciousness." The essential insanity of technological "progress" and its concomitant disciplines—whether under capitalist or collective auspices—only stands revealed in the light of misused abundance . . . unless, of course, one has the rare moral vision Tolstoy displays in a tale like "How Much Land Does a Man Need?" But there was little of the Tolstoyan sensibility in Marx—the more's the pity for the course that radical ideology was to run in our time.

Now, however, the madness of this fake progress we pursue thrusts itself upon us irresistibly each time men turn away from the task of transforming this lovely earth into the garden of delights it might be, devoting themselves instead to the black arts of mutual torment. Happiness, as Freud bleakly and rightly observed, *still* has no cultural value. The "happiness" most of us settle for is whatever transient relief or exuberant diversion we can sandwich in between atrocities: "the pause that refreshes" before the next calamity.

. . . intensified progress seems to be bound up with intensified unfreedom [Marcuse observes, isolating the great, central paradox of our time]. Concentration camps, mass exterminations, world wars, and atom bombs are no 'relapse into barbarism,' but the unrepressed implementation of the achievements of modern science, technology, and domination. And the most effective subjugation and destruction of man by man takes place at the height of civilization, when the material and intellectual attainments of mankind seem to allow the creation of a truly free world. (p. 4.)

In the situation, it is easy enough for the older ideologies to continue supplying us with villains. Recrimination has always been one of the central functions of the ideologue—the more wrathful, the better. And in the court of social conflict the guilty have no appeal to criminal insanity. Is there any better definition of ideology than to identify it as that rhetoric of high principle we use when we yield in our indignation to a murderous mood? But as Barrington Moore, Jr., has observed:

there is a sense in the air, especially among the young, that Marxism and liberalism have in good measure ceased to provide explanations of the world. Indeed in their official forms these doctrines have become part of what requires explanation. Such ideas are no longer sufficient to tell us why a decent society is impossible: they have become reasons why this society remains out of the question.[14]

* * * *

So much for what unites Marcuse and Brown *contra* Marx. The similarities are many and marked. But beyond the psychoanalytical sensitivity they hold in common, a new tension already begins to appear. From the ground they share, the horizon falls steeply away, revealing an exotically controversial landscape colored by issues the like of which no political culture has yet encountered.

Let us raise two questions which go at once to the heart of the difference between Marcuse and Brown: (1) *Why* is man the uniquely repressed or alienated animal? (2) *How* is alienation to be abolished?

(1) Marcuse's examination of psychoanalysis leads him to the conclusion that the repressiveness of the Freudian Reality Principle is *historically*, not biologically, given. Reality Principle rejects Pleasure Principle because we live in "a world too

---

[14] Barrington Moore, Jr., "The Society Nobody Wants: A Look Beyond Marxism and Liberalism," in Kurt H. Wolff and Moore, eds., *The Critical Spirit: Essays in Honor of Herbert Marcuse* (Boston: Beacon Press, 1967), p. 418.

poor for the satisfaction of human needs without constant restraint, renunciation, delay." It is economic scarcity that has necessitated all those "painful arrangements and undertakings" we sum up under the heading of hard labor. And "labor time . . . is painful time, for alienated labor is absence of gratification, negation of the pleasure principle." At this point, Marcuse's formulation is identical with Freud's earliest conception of the Reality Principle—but with one important modification. Marcuse argues that it is not the "brute *fact* of scarcity" that leads to "instinctual inhibition and restraint." Rather, repression is a product of the unequal distribution of scarcity in civilized society. It sets in when ruling classes intervene to impose their selfish will on subject populations, to deprive and exploit and tread down those who are weaker. So begins the "logic of domination."

Marcuse here invents two new terms to supplement the Freudian analysis of "civilization and its discontents." The first of these is the "performance principle"—by which he means the particular socio-historical form the Reality Principle has assumed in any particular age (feudalism, capitalist industrialism, etc.). The social forms have been many, but throughout civilized history they have *all* been based on domination.

Secondly, Marcuse gives us the term "surplus repression," which he distinguishes from "basic repression." Basic repression he takes to be necessary under *any* form of the Reality Principle, simply because "the rational exercise of authority" must impose limits on our capacity for immediate gratification. But this restraint, Marcuse feels, is normal, natural, and acceptable to the healthy human being. Surplus repression, on the other hand, is that *additional* measure of deprivation which the invidious logic of domination demands. Surplus repression is what "a particular group or individual" imposes on others "in order to sustain and enhance itself in a privileged position. Such domination does not exclude technical, material, and intellectual progress, but only as an unavoidable by-product while preserving irrational scarcity, want, and constraint." Freud's error, Marcuse argues, lay in believing that scarcity and the Reality Principle were synonymous, that domination was inevitable under civilized conditions of life, and that labor had, therefore, to be alienated and unfulfilling. In short, he mistook a sociological style for an unbudgeable biological fact. The longer we do that, Marcuse contends, the more we help to rationalize the logic of domination for the repressive elites of the world.

There are questions that come immediately to mind about this line of thought. A truly radical social critique would have to be considerably clearer about how the logic of domination got started. If we look back behind the horizon of civilization, we find a condition of life among our neolithic and paleolithic ancestors which, while materially impoverished in comparison to the absurd affluence of middle-class America, was nevertheless plentiful enough to support the vital needs of tribes and villages, and to allow a good deal of time for communal culture. It is not at all clear—as Marcuse would have it—that these simple folk spent their lives drudging away under the whiplash of near-starvation. In fact, we have reason to believe that many of them (especially during the neolithic period) lived a decently comfortable life in a wise symbiotic relationship with their environment. Most important, the evidence is that they lived mainly in egalitarian communities where domination, as Marcuse uses the term, did not take its toll.[15] At this stage of society, there-

[15] On the egalitarian ethos of primitive and peasant communities, see Robert Redfield, *The Primitive World and Its Transformations* (Ithaca, N.Y.: Cornell University Press, 1953), and *The Little Community and Peasant Society and Culture* (Chicago: The University of Chicago Press, 1960). See also G. Clark and S. Piggott, *Primitive Societies* (New York: A. A. Knopf, 1965), pp. 132–33. Any

fore, repression could not have existed in any form that satisfies Marcuse's definition. Repressive, class-based regimentation—the social form we call "civilization"—only *follows* upon the destruction of primitive tribal and village democracy. This transition to civilized life happened—but *why* did it happen?

Marcuse rather muddles this critical question by resorting to Freud's fanciful theory of the primal horde. Marcuse himself admits that there is little anthropological value in Freud's speculation on this score; he therefore treats the hypothesis as symbolic. But symbolic of what? Of the primordial act of domination—whatever that may have been—which created man's guilt-stricken conscience and generated civilization. This comes down to saying that *somehow* domination began. But clearly an important connective link in the argument is missing. We still do not know why the human race made the transition to repressive social forms and abandoned non-repressive ones. Elsewhere, in passing (p. 33), Marcuse suggests that the transition was brought about "first by mere violence . . ." Very well; but where did this violence come from? Why, under egalitarian conditions that Marcuse must call non-repressive, does man rise up aggressively against man? The supposition must be accounted for from Freudian first principles. And this Marcuse fails to do.

But Brown does. In doing so, however, he takes us well beyond Marcuse's more restricted psycho-sociology of scarcity-based domination. Brown, indeed, removes the argument to the level of human ontology. What is it that represses man and leads to the progressive desexualization of the body? In

---

ethnographic account of, for example, the American Plains Indians or the fishers and hunters of the Pacific Northwest makes clear that primitive groups can rise well above being wretched, toil-ridden savages. In fact, their "Reality Principle" looks a great deal less oppressive than that through which several proletarian generations lived during our Industrial Revolution.

Brown's reading of Freud, it is the peculiarly human awareness and rejection of death—a condition of being which traces
back to the remote reaches of our animal evolution. Repression is not something that begins, therefore, with the advent
of civilized domination. It is coeval with the emergence of
human nature itself.

Thus the germ of repression is man's anxiety in the face
of his own mortality, and the course the disease runs is called
"history"—the struggle to fill time with death-defying works.
The energy of our history making is derived from the tension
between the life and death instincts as they carry on their
neurotic project of rejecting one another. When this energy
is used in a socially acceptable way, we have "sublimation"—
that desexualization of conduct on which Freud pinned so
much of his hope for the survival of civilization. But underlying all forms of sublimation, as well as the recognized
neuroses, there is the same antagonism of the instincts, the
mutual thrusting away which finally segregates the death instinct and drives it into its independent career as the dark
terror brooding over Faustian man in his harried pursuit of
immortal achievement.

Brown, however, undertakes a revision of Freud at this
point. He insists that the strife of Eros and Thanatos is not
a frozen, dualistic stand-off; instead, it is *dialectical* in nature. It is dynamic and capable of change. It derives from
a primordial balance, to which it may return again: a prospect
which is enshrined in the great mythical motifs of redemp-
tion and resurrection, of the New Jerusalem, of Nirvana.

We thus arrive at the idea [Brown concludes] that life and
death are in some sort of unity at the organic level, that at
the human level they are separated into conflicting oppo-
sites, and that at the human level the extroversion of the
death instinct is the mode of resolving a conflict that does
not exist at the organic level. . . . If death is a part of life,

there is a peculiar morbidity in the human attitude toward death. . . . Animals let death be a part of life, and use the death instinct to die; man aggressively builds immortal cultures and makes history in order to fight death. (pp. 100–1.)

It would be little better than pedantic to ask if this is a "correct" reading of Freud. Nothing in Freud's later metapsychology has the character of consistent, let alone demonstrable, theory; it is adventurous, often nebulous speculation whose main value lies in its suggestiveness, and in its effort to bring psychoanalysis into the philosophical mainstream. (The fact is, both Marcuse and Brown weaken toward pedantry in treating their problems like geometric puzzles in which Freud's work functions as the axiomatic material. Marcuse, for example, speaks in *Eros and Civilization* of "theoretically validating" ideas—which seems to mean construing one's idea in such a way that Freud might have meant something like it.) One does feel, however, that Brown, in developing a deeper and more dramatic conception of the death instinct than one finds in Marcuse, at least does greater justice to the radical bent of Freud's later investigations.

But if repression *is* buried at this remote depth in our being, then, for Brown, it will not yield to anything so superficial as a readjustment of Marcuse's performance principle. Indeed, it is at this point that one begins to feel the two men are diagnosing very different diseases.

(2) *How* is alienation to be abolished? Marcuse's hope for a non-repressive civilization derives from the growing affluence of industrial society. He argues·

The historical factor contained in Freud's theory of instincts has come to fruition in history when the basis of [scarcity]—which, for Freud, provided the rationale for the repressive reality principle—is undermined by the progress of civilization. (p. 137)

As "the excuse of scarcity" wears thin, as work discipline with the coming of cybernation relaxes, the performance principle and the dominating regimes it supports are called radically and obviously into question. Like Marx in *Capital*, Marcuse takes "the shortening of the working day" to be the "fundamental premise" on which the "true reality of freedom" is founded.[16]

"The discrepancy between potential liberation and actual repression has come to maturity," Marcuse tells us. So we may now conceive of life under a new and gentler Reality Principle which does not exact surplus repression. Work can become play, and the harshly disciplined body, a "thing to be enjoyed." We grasp this possibility as soon as we set aside the "rationality of domination" in favor of a "libidinal rationality" which takes the possibility of freedom and joy as axioms.

This amounts to turning the Marxist theory of revolution (at least as we have it in Marx's most influential writings) upside down. For instead of assuming that the emancipating revolution breaks forth in the blackest depths of "immiserization," Marcuse argues that it comes at the *height of affluence*. As we have seen, he also differs from Marx by upholding, in preparation for the revolution, the primacy of the *idea*. We must *begin* with "consciousness of the possibility" that a non-repressive civilization can and should be created: "the idea of a gradual abolition of repression" is "the *a priori* of social change." At the same time, Marcuse insists that concrete social change must take place before the *idea* can, in turn, become a widespread reality.[17]

Needless to say, by "social change" Marcuse means the

[16] Karl Marx, *Capital* (Chicago: Charles King & Co., 1906), III, 945–46.
[17] Marcuse takes the trouble to spell out this rather complicated interrelationship in his 1962 preface to the Vintage edition of *Eros and Civilization*. It is an involuted explanation which begins to suggest that Marcuse wants to hedge some of his Freudian commitments.

cashing in of all those regimes, capitalist and collectivist, which continue to enforce the now antiquated performance principle upon their subjects. This will be no simple matter, however. For "the rationality of domination has progressed to the point where it threatens to invalidate its foundation; therefore it must be reaffirmed more effectively than ever before."

At this point we would have to turn to Marcuse's *One-Dimensional Man* and his *Soviet Marxism* to trace his full analysis of what he calls "the pleasant forms of social control and cohesion" by which the technocracy carries out this re-affirmation. It is these studies which have gained him his largest following among the radical young—and deservedly so. In these works Marcuse emerges as one of the shrewdest critics of the subtle technocratic regimentation which now bids fair to encompass the whole of our world-wide industrial order. The critique is anticipated, however, in *Eros and Civilization*, where Marcuse offers us the idea of "repressive desublimation" as his explanation of the technocracy's ingenious assimilation of the "erotic danger zone." Repressive de-sublimation is the "release of sexuality in modes and forms which reduce and weaken erotic energy." (The observations offered in a previous chapter regarding *Playboy* permissiveness will do as examples of the technique.) Just as Marx, in his analysis of capitalism during the period of primitive accumulation, found the secret of gross physical exploitation in the notion of "surplus value," so Marcuse, in his study of technocracy under the regime of affluence, finds the secret of psychic exploitation in repressive desublimation. It is an excellent example of psychological categories replacing sociological-economic categories in social theory—and in this case Marcuse's analysis leads to a much solider idea than Marx's rather foggy use of the labor theory of value. It also leads to a distinctly non-Marxist conclusion, namely that technology

exerts an influence upon society *in its own right* and independent of the social form under which it is organized.

For Marx, technology was always a neutral factor: a fluid
that filled the social vessel and assumed its shape. Technology
could be either exploitive or humanitarian, depending wholly
upon the class interest it served. But Marcuse, surveying the
practice of both the Western and Soviet technocracies, concludes somberly that "the two antagonistic social systems
. . . join in the general trend of technical progress." In both
cases, we have "the total mobilization of the individuals for
the requirements of competitive total industrialization."[18]
The infernal machine has its way with all ideologies.

Now, Marcuse is undoubtedly right in identifying dena-
tured permissiveness as one of the key strategies of contemporary social control—and it is a pressure to which the
dissenting young have become especially sensitive. What is
not clear is *why* these dismal forms of domination should
continue when the potentiality of liberating affluence is so
undeniably apparent. If domination was born *solely* of
scarcity, then it should vanish with the advent of affluence
—for in our time special privilege is obviously not the pre-
requisite of subsistence . . . or even of a standard of life
considerably above subsistence. But domination *does* continue. And it does not seem that Marcuse offers any better
explanation of the fact than to suggest that "mental development lags behind the real development, or . . . retards the
real development, denies its potentialities in the name of
the past." (p. 31.) So we have a kind of psycho-social inertia
in operation which keeps us living in a discipline appropriate to scarcity even while abundance is available.

But inertia is a rather feeble explanation for behavior,
especially within a Freudian framework, where everything

[18] Herbert Marcuse, *Soviet Marxism: A Critical Analysis* (London:
Routledge & Kegan Paul, 1958), p. 259.

must return to an instinctual basis. Moreover, it seems obvious that the elites of the world are fully conscious of the possibilities of affluence, since they have developed remarkably astute strategies for integrating comfort, ease, permissiveness, and even rebellion into the logic of domination. Such is the burden of Marcuse's one-dimensional man analysis. But *why* do the elites persist in struggling against readily accessible liberation? Is it an irrational bad habit that they do so? Then this should be accounted for as Freud would have accounted for a neurotic symptom: by reference to some underlying instinctual conflict. But Marcuse would seem to have nothing left, out of which to construct such a conflict, since he begins by relating repression to a real economic factor (scarcity) that has now lost its force. What is it, then, that props up domination? Unless there is an answer based on Freudian first principles, we will have to retreat to the pre-Freudian domain of black and white moralizing and say that the technocrats are simply "bad guys."

Before we turn to Brown's treatment of these problems, we must underscore two central aspects of Marcuse's conception of non-repressiveness. First of all, Marcuse does not hold out the prospect of total liberation. His object is to repeal *surplus* repression only. *Basic* repression remains in force because, as Marcuse reminds us, "human freedom is not only a private affair." His hope is that "the renunciations and delays demanded by the general will must not be opaque and inhuman; nor must their reason be authoritarian." He even makes the strange suggestion that a "natural self-restraint" may enhance "genuine gratification" by way of "delay, detour, and arrest." This, combined with the idea of basic repression, raises some worrisome hedges around Marcuse's version of liberation. He offers us, it would seem, freedom . . . within sensible limits. Does Freud, in Marcuse's reading, get us much beyond John Stuart Mill's notion of civil liberty?

Secondly, Marcuse holds out no real prospect of reintegrating the death instinct. His treatment of this problem is marked by great ambiguity—and finishes sounding like some very pedestrian homely philosophy. The "ultimate necessity" of death can never be overcome, but it can be "a necessity against which the unrepressed energy of mankind will protest, against which it will wage its greatest struggle." What is the object of this struggle against an invincible foe? To achieve the longest, happiest life possible for all; to make death as painless as we can; to comfort the dying with hope of a world in which their loved ones and values will be secure. To the end, death is for Marcuse the object of a heroic "Great Refusal—the refusal of Orpheus the liberator."

To protest, to refuse, to struggle against death. . . . What Marcuse's version of non-repressiveness promises us, then, is the capacity to continue this futile opposition with the prospect of marginal gains like greater longevity and consolations for the dying. By no means empty ideals—but very traditional ideals that scarcely need repetition from Marcuse.

We recall, however, the title of Brown's book: *Life Against Death*. Was it not precisely this opposition, which Marcuse champions to the last, that served as Brown's diagnosis of repression? In Brown's view, as long as we continue to pit life against death we perpetuate the ontological dilemma of man. No wonder, then, that Marcuse has to qualify his ideal of liberation with a tricky distinction between "surplus" and "basic" repression. It is as if, try as he will, Marcuse cannot conceive of life as being anything other than a tragic discontent. Man's freedom *must* at last acquiesce to the inhibiting claims of his fellows and to the melancholy necessity of death. That is simply the best we can do. Marcuse's reference is to Orpheus the abandoned singer. Yet the tone is unmistakably that of stoical renunciation.[19]

But such is not the stuff of Brown's "Dionysian ego."

The death instinct is reconciled with the life instinct only in a life which is not repressed, which leaves no "unlived lines" in the human body, the death instinct then being affirmed in a body which is willing to die. And, because the body is satisfied, the death instinct no longer drives it to change itself and make history, and therefore as Christian theology divined, its activity is in eternity. (p. 308.)

Where does Brown find his justification for such a prospective integration of the instincts? Not, to be sure, in the ever-pessimistic Freud; he discovers it, rather, in the tradition of such Dionysian seers as Blake, Nietzsche, Jakob Boehme, St. John of the Apocalypse.

It is only in *Love's Body* that the visionary dimension of Brown's thought unfolds its fiery wings. And then we find ourselves transported well beyond limits that even the most radical politics of the past have respected. If Marx taught us that to talk politics is to talk class interest, if Marcuse would teach us that to talk class interest is to talk psychoanalysis, then Brown would teach us that to talk psychoanalysis is to conjure with the diction of pentecostal tongues.

Freud is the measure of our unholy madness, as Nietzsche is the prophet of the holy madness, of Dionysus, the mad truth."[20]

[19] Freud, who was an arch stoic himself, did catch the glimmer of a brighter possibility. See his wise and lovely essay "The Theme of the Three Caskets." It appears in *The Standard Edition of the Complete Psychological Works*, ed. James Strachey, London: Hogarth Press, 1958, Vol. XII, pp. 289–302.

[20] "Apocalypse: The Place of Mystery in the Life of the Mind" in *Harper's*, May 1961, p. 47. This Phi Beta Kappa oration is an important introduction to *Love's Body*.

This is not the place to make a full critique of *Love's Body*.[21] It is, I feel, a silly-brilliant effort, similar in that respect to Joyce's *Finnegans Wake*. Like Joyce, Brown has tried to discover a language beyond language, unrestricted by such conventional disciplines as logicality, continuity, or even normal sentence structure. The result is a witch's caldron of puns, rhymes, etymological prestidigitation, and oracular outpouring. It is a style that speaks by allusion and indirection, suggestion and paradox, and which could mean, at too many points, everything or nothing. It might be called the literary analogue of peripheral vision. Here is no effort to prove or persuade, but to try out, to play with, to invoke portentous illuminations. Unhappily, the experiment, like *Finnegans Wake*, weakens toward pedantry, finally becoming a scholar's chapbook which reveals Brown to be a very professorial prophet indeed: a Dionysus with footnotes.

Nonetheless, the book serves to show us where Brown's search for the psychoanalytical meaning of history has at last led him. In *Life Against Death*, Brown concludes that culture is a diseased reification of body metaphors born of repression at the deepest instinctual level. In *Love's Body*, he takes the next step: the effort to recover from this pathological culture the traces of our disintegrated psychic wholeness and to fashion of these remnants a reality principle based on the organic unity which predated the advent of repression. This project in psychic archaeology takes Brown well beyond Freud into the province of the visionary imagination, which now is no longer to be understood as a fiction of cunningly wrought symbols, but as the *really* real, the scandalously, subversively, dumbfoundingly real. As Keats would have it: "the *truth* of imagination." Hence the closing words of *Love's Body*:

[21] For some negative remarks on the book, see Theodore Roszak, "Professor Dionysus," in *New Politics*, Spring 1966, pp. 123–24.

The antinomy between mind and body, word and deed, speech and silence, overcome. Everything is only a metaphor; there is only poetry.

Following which we have a long quotation from a study of Tibetan mysticism.

By taking this occult turn, Brown commits a heresy that Marcuse cannot but set his face against, staking himself more firmly than ever in the reality that science and conventional perception describe. In response to Brown, Marcuse becomes the defender of *this* world, this *tangible* world we can lay hands on and which is nothing other than our reason takes it to be; *this* world, where men taste fleeting joys, more often sorrows, and die reluctantly; the secular *here*, the time-bound *now*. To follow the path Brown follows, Marcuse warns, "obliterates the decisive difference between the real and the artificial . . ."

The roots of repression are and remain real roots; consequently, their eradication remains a real and rational job. What is to be abolished is not the reality principle; not everything, but such particular things as business, politics, exploitation, poverty.

To forget this is to "mystify the possibilities of liberation," to flee from "the real fight, the political fight."[22]

But what a remarkable criticism this is for Marcuse to make! Here he wields the word "real" as if it were as solid a thing as a club, with which all subtleties, all ambiguities could be beaten into submission. Suddenly he becomes Dr. Johnson refuting Bishop Berkeley by way of giving the nearest

[22] Marcuse, "Love Mystified: A Critique of Norman O. Brown," pp. 71–74. This review of *Love's Body* and Brown's reply in the March issue (pp. 83–84) are absolutely basic to an understanding of the work of the two men.

stone a swift kick. It is as if Freud had never discovered the existence of a "psychic reality" within which the dreams, the lies, the fantasies of his patients became more meaningful, indeed more "real," than their verifiable memories. As Marcuse uses the term here, no official decision maker, no member of the local Kiwanis Club would take issue with him.

The implication of Marcuse's adamant secularism is clear enough. He is telling us that the politics of the world *is* precisely what everyman has always consciously taken it to be: the struggle against injustice, against oppression, against privilege . . . as old as the plea of the Eloquent Egyptian Peasant, as old as Thucydides' Melian Dialogue. What is the meaning, then, of the unconscious? In *Eros and Civilization*, Marcuse guides us through a "philosophical inquiry into Freud"; but when all is said and done, this venture seems to come down to little more than filling in the psychological totals in the same old political leger. So we learn that injustice is mental, as well as physical, cruelty. To be sure, Freud opened up the realm of dreams, of myth, of the deep life instincts. But this apparently is only the exotic psychoanalytical version of what Spartacus knew about reality long ago: that "the real fight" is "the political fight." As Spartacus saw the world, as Machiavelli saw it, so it *is*: power against power, the strong against the weak. Freud is no more than a footnote attached to the business-as-usual of politics. Which is: to choose sides, draw the line, and fight again . . . and again . . . for the obvious causes, in the obvious ways. "Surplus repression" would seem to become a mere psychoanalytical transcription for social injustice, and "libidinal reason," a shorthand term for social conscience with a mental health program.[23]

[23] Marcuse's criticism of Brown in the *Commentary* article comes very close to being the doctrinaire Marxist reading of Freud. Cf.

For Marcuse, then, liberation begins when we untie the knot of social domination. But for Brown, there is a knot within that knot: the knot of the scientific world view from which neither Marx nor Freud nor Marcuse could ever loose themselves. He replies to Marcuse with unabashed paradox:

In the dialectical view . . . demystification becomes the discovery of a new mystery. . . . The next generation needs to be told that the real fight is not the political fight, but to put an end to politics. From politics to poetry. . . . Poetry, art, imagination, the creator spirit is life itself; the real revolutionary power to change the world. . . .

* * * *

As long ago as the early forties, in *Reason and Revolution*, Marcuse introduced the ideal of "transcendence" into his social theory. But even then he was careful to insist that the transcendent truth he invoked as a standard by which to evaluate society "is not a realm apart from historical reality, nor a region of eternally valid ideas. To be sure, it transcends the given historical reality, but only in so far as it crosses from one historical stage to another."[24] He has emphasized the stubbornly and conventionally secular character of his thinking more recently in making clear his opposition to any religious conception of transcendence. Religious transcendence, he insists:

. . . is absolutely contrary to Marxism, which believes that the human condition can and should be improved through man's own powers. . . . The transcendence I was talking about [in *Reason and Revolution*] was an empirical historical transcendence to a different form of society, whereas

Paul Baran, "Marxism and Psychoanalysis," *Monthly Review*, October 1959, pp. 186–200.

[24] Marcuse, *Reason and Revolution*, p. 315.

the Christian transcendence is out of this world to another world.[25]

Yet it is the Christian image of "resurrection" that Brown finally asserts as his ideal of liberation—an image that rapidly carries him forward toward a "body mysticism" which manages to be *both* secular *and* transcendent. It is the direction in which more gifted minds than Brown's—Blake, Boehme, and, along non-Christian lines, Buber—have gone before him to discover a wisdom that can only speak the language of paradox and poetic metaphor.

In the presence of such paradox, Marcuse reverts to playing the tough-minded, nineteenth-century skeptic, demanding hard-edged dichotomies. He takes up the part for understandable reasons. He is a political man and he shies from any form of transcendence that threatens to flee the glaring oppressions and long-suffering of mankind, *and* which smacks of letting the bastards who exploit us off the hook. The commitment is honorable . . . and yet, in its own way, its politicization of human experience may be the herald of a totalitarianization far subtler than any Marcuse has so far discovered. Where Brown strives to accept visionary experience on its own terms, Marcuse insists on closing off all the great metaphors by minimalist interpretations. Marcuse, who believes so admirably in the Great Refusal, defends behind that belief a still greater and most depressing refusal. For him, the symbols of poetic vision can have only a horizontal, historical significance. They guide us toward the secular future, never toward that ever-present sacramental dimension of life designated by Blake as "the real and eternal world of which this Vegetable Universe is but a faint shadow." On the other hand, Brown's next politics, which is "no-politics," is nothing so much as the struggle to save space for a tran-

[25] Marcuse, "Varieties of Humanism."

scendence that transports us to that "real and eternal world."

"But there is no such world," the secular temperament insists. The Great Refusal which Marcuse sees in visionary art and religion amounts to the rejection of social domination in the name of a joy and freedom tragically thwarted by worldly injustice. That, and no more. Marcuse thus comes perilously close to Freud's most reductionist interpretation of art and religion, wherein creativity functions as a bandage of fantasy for the wounded Pleasure Principle. Yet not all the visions of our great souls have been of forbidden pleasures. How often have they been tale-tellings of terrors and powers and awesome presences, of inscrutable divinities, dark nights of the soul, and dreadful illuminations! On what sure grounds are we to tell those who claim to have known these "things unseen" that they have not known them . . . not *really?* Or that what they have known is no part of our liberation?

When we begin to probe the psychic underworld, we would do well to remember the distinction R. D. Laing makes between studying and experiencing what we find there:

The inner does not become outer, and the outer become inner, just by the discovery of the "inner" world. That is only the beginning. As a whole generation of men, we are so estranged from the inner world that there are many arguing that it does not exist; and that even if it does exist, it does not matter.[26]

Brown and Marcuse, you and I, most of us, perhaps all of us who must now begin to dig our way out from under the ancient and entrenched estrangement of our being: how dare *we* specify the limits of the real while we stand on this benighted side of liberation?

[26] Laing, *The Politics of Experience and the Bird of Paradise,* p. 46.

THE SKYLARK AND THE FROGS

*A Postscript to Herbert Marcuse's Philosophical Inquiry into Freud,
Freely Adapted from the Fable by Chuang-tzu*

There was once a society of frogs that lived at the bottom
of a deep, dark well, from which nothing whatsoever could
be seen of the world outside. They were ruled over by a great
Boss Frog, a fearful bully who claimed, on rather dubious
grounds, to own the well and all that creeped or crawled
therein. The Boss Frog never did a lick of work to feed or
keep himself, but lived off the labors of the several bottom
dog frogs with whom he shared the well. They, wretched
creatures! spent all the hours of their lightless days and a
good many more of their lightless nights drudging about in
the damp and slime to find the tiny grubs and mites on which
the Boss Frog fattened.

Now, occasionally an eccentric skylark would flutter down
into the well (for God only knows what reason) and would
sing to the frogs of all the marvelous things it had seen in
its journeyings in the great world outside: of the sun and the
moon and the stars, of the sky-climbing mountains and fruit-
ful valleys and the vast stormy seas, and of what it was like
to adventure the boundless space above them.

Whenever the skylark came visiting, the Boss Frog would
instruct the bottom-dog frogs to attend closely to all the bird
had to tell. "For he is telling you," the Boss Frog would explain, "of the happy land whither all good frogs go for their
reward when they finish this life of trials." Secretly, however, the Boss Frog (who was half deaf anyway and never
very sure of what the lark was saying) thought this strange
bird was quite mad.

Perhaps the bottom-dog frogs had once been deceived by
what the Boss Frog told them. But with time they had grown
cynical about such fairy tales as skylarks had to tell, and had
reached the conclusion also that the lark was more than a
little mad. Moreover, they had been convinced by certain
free-thinking frogs among them (though who can say where

these free-thinkers come from?) that this bird was being used by the Boss Frog to comfort and distract them with tales of pie in the sky which you get when you die. "And that's a lie!" the bottom-dog frogs bitterly croaked.

But there was among the bottom-dog frogs a philosopher frog who had invented a new and quite interesting idea about the skylark. "What the lark says is not *exactly* a lie," the philosopher frog suggested. "Nor is it madness. What the lark is really telling us about in its own queer way is the beautiful place we might make of this unhappy well of ours if only we set our minds to it. When the lark sings of sun and moon, it means the wonderful new forms of illumination we might introduce to dispel the darkness we live in. When it sings of the wide and windy skies, it means the healthful ventilation we should be enjoying instead of the dank and fetid airs we have grown accustomed to. When it sings of growing giddy with its dizzy swooping through the heavens, it means the delights of the liberated senses we should all know if we were not forced to waste our lives at such oppressive drudgery. Most important, when it sings of soaring wild and unfettered among the stars, it means the freedom we shall all have when the onus of the Boss Frog is removed from our backs forever. So you see: the bird is not to be scorned. Rather, it should be appreciated and praised for bestowing on us an inspiration that emancipates us from despair."

Thanks to the philosopher frog, the bottom-dog frogs came to have a new and affectionate view of the skylark. In fact, when the revolution finally came (for revolutions always do come), the bottom-dog frogs even inscribed the image of the skylark on their banners and marched to the barricades doing the best they could in their croaking way to imitate the bird's lyrical tunes. Following the Boss Frog's overthrow, the once dark, dank well was magnificently illuminated and ventilated and made a much more comfortable place to live. In addition, the frogs experienced a new and gratifying leisure with many attendant delights of the senses—even as the philosopher frog had foretold.

But *still* the eccentric skylark would come visiting with tales of the sun and the moon and the stars, of mountains and valleys and seas, and of grand winged adventures it had known.

"Perhaps," conjectured the philosopher frog, "this bird *is* mad, after all. Surely we have no further need of these cryptic songs. And in any case, it is very tiresome to have to listen to fantasies when the fantasies have lost their social relevance."

So one day the frogs contrived to capture the lark. And upon so doing, they stuffed it and put it in their newly built civic (admission-free) museum . . . in a place of honor.

Chapter IV

JOURNEY TO THE EAST . . . AND POINTS BEYOND: ALLEN GINSBERG AND ALAN WATTS

On October 21, 1967, the Pentagon found itself besieged by a motley army of anti-war demonstrators. For the most part, the fifty thousand protestors were made up of activist academics and students, men of letters (among them, Norman Mailer leading his "armies of the night"), New Left and pacificist ideologues, housewives, doctors . . . but also in attendance, we are informed (by *The East Village Other*), were contingents of "witches, warlocks, holymen, seers, prophets, mystics, saints, sorcerers, shamans, troubadours, minstrels, bards, roadmen, and madmen"—who were on hand to achieve the "mystic revolution." The picketing, the sit-down, the speeches, and marches: all that was protest politics as usual. But the central event of the day was a contribution of the "superhumans": an exorcism of the Pentagon by long-haired warlocks who "cast mighty words of white light against the demon-controlled structure," in hopes of levitating that grim ziggurat right off the ground.[1]

They did not succeed—in floating the Pentagon, that is. But they did manage to stamp their generation with a political style so authentically original that it borders on the bizarre. Is the youthful political activism of the sixties any different from that of the thirties? If the difference shows up anywhere, it reveals itself in the unprecedented penchant for the occult, for magic, and for exotic ritual which has become

[1] *The East Village Other*'s report appears in the issue of November 1–15, 1967, p. 3.

an integral part of the counter culture. Even those protestors who did not participate in the rite of exorcism took the event in stride—as if they understood that here was the style and vocabulary of the young: one had simply to tolerate its expression. And yet how strange to see the classic rhetoric of the radical tradition—Marx, Bakunin, Kropotkin, Lenin—yielding place to spells and incantations! Perhaps, after all, the age of ideology is passing, giving way to the age of mystagogy.

An eclectic taste for mystic, occult, and magical phenomena has been a marked characteristic of our postwar youth culture since the days of the beatniks. Allen Ginsberg, who has played a major part in fostering the style, professes the quest for God in many of his earliest poems, well before he and his colleagues had discovered Zen and the mystic traditions of the Orient. In his poetry of the late forties, there is a sensitivity for visionary experience ("Angelic raving," as he was to call it), which suggested even then that the social dissent of the younger generation would never quite fit the adamantly secular mold of the Old Left. Already at that point, Ginsberg speaks of seeing

> all the pictures we carry in our mind
> images of the Thirties,
> depression and class consciousness
> transfigured above politics
> filled with fire
> with the appearance of God.

These early poems[2] contrast strongly and significantly in style with Ginsberg's more widely read later work. They are often brief, tightly written affairs, done in a short, well-

[2] They are collected in the volume *Empty Mirror: Early Poems* (New York: Totem Press, 1961).

ordered line. We have nothing of the familiar rambling and ham-fisted Ginsberg line (based, as he puts it, on "Hebraic-Melvillian breath") until the 1949 poem *Paterson*. But the religiosity is already there, giving Ginsberg's poetry a very different sound from the social poetry of the thirties. From the outset, Ginsberg is a protest poet. But his protest does not run back to Marx; it reaches out, instead, to the ecstatic radicalism of Blake. The issue is never as simple as social justice; rather, the key words and images are those of time and eternity, madness and vision, heaven and the spirit. The cry is not for a revolution, but for an apocalypse: a descent of divine fire. And, already in the later forties, we have the first experiments with marijuana and chiliastic poems written under the sway of narcotics.

In some respects, these early poems, modest as they are, are superior to anything Ginsberg has written since—or so I find. Without compromising their lurching power, and without by any means becoming finely wrought, they possess a far greater sense of control and structure than the work that was later to give him his reputation. There is the willingness to be brief and to the point—and then to break off before the energy has been dissipated. By the early fifties, however, Ginsberg has abandoned these conventional literary virtues in favor of a spontaneous and unchecked flow of language. From this point on, everything he writes has the appearance of being served up raw, in the first draft, just as it must have come from mind and mouth. There is never the trace of a revised line; there is, rather, another line added on. Instead of revision, there is accumulation. As if to revise would be to rethink, and hence to doubt and double back on the initial vision. For Ginsberg, the creative act was to be a come-as-you-are party and his poems would arrive unshaven and unwashed, and maybe without pants on, just as they happened to be lying around the house. The intention is clear: lack of grooming marks the poems as "natural," therefore honest. They are the *real* thing, and not artifice.

There is a good deal of Charlie Parker's improvisation in Ginsberg's work, as well as the spirit of the action painters. Jackson Pollack worked at a canvas with a commitment never to erase, or re-do, or touch up, but to add, add, add . . . and let the whole finally work itself out into a unique pattern appropriate to *this* man at *this* moment of his life. The same sense of haste and total self-absorption clings to Ginsberg's poetry, the same eagerness to project the unvarnished imaginative impulse—though it seems all too clear that such improvisation is much less at home in literature than in music or painting. The intention of his poetry of the middle fifties was, says Ginsberg, "to just write . . . let my imagination go, open secrecy, and scribble magic lines from my real mind." Two of his best-known poems of these years were written without either forethought or revision: the long first part of *Howl* was typed off in one afternoon; *Sunflower Sutra* was completed in twenty minutes, "me at desk scribbling, Kerouac at cottage door waiting for me to finish." Of *Howl*, Ginsberg says, "I'd had a beatific illumination years before during which I'd heard Blake's ancient voice and saw the universe unfold in my brain," and this served as the inspiration for the later outburst.[3] In a similarly improvisatory manner, Jack Kerouac was to come to the point of typing off his novels nonstop onto enormous rolls of paper—six feet per day—with never a revision.

That this improvisatory style of writing produces a great deal that is worthless as art is, for our purposes here, less important than what this choice of method tells us about the generation that accepted Ginsberg's work as a valid form

[3] Ginsberg's statement on aesthetics appears in Donald M. Allen, ed., *The New American Poetry 1945–1960* (New York: Grove Press, 1960), pp. 414–18.

of creativity. What we have here is a search for art unmediated by intellect. Or rather, since it is the application of intellectual control that makes art of impulse, it is an effort to extract and indulge the impulse, regardless of the aesthetic quality of the product.

Far from being an avant-garde eccentricity, Ginsberg's conception of poetry as an oracular outpouring can claim an imposing genealogy that reaches back to the rhapsodic prophets of Israel (and beyond them perhaps to the shamanism of the Stone Age). Like Amos and Isaiah, Ginsberg aspires to be a *nabi*, a mutterer: one who speaks with tongues, one who permits his voice to act as the instrument of powers beyond his conscious direction. If his work falls short of the highest aesthetic standards of this great tradition, he can scarcely be denied the virtue of having complied with the demands of his calling in what is perhaps a far more important respect. Ginsberg has committed himself totally to the life of prophecy. He has allowed his entire existence to be transformed by the visionary powers with which he conjures and has offered it as an example to his generation. It is as if, initially, Ginsberg set out to write a poetry of angry distress: to cry out against the anguished state of the world as he and his closest colleagues had experienced it in the gutters and ghettos and mental institutions of our society. What came of that suffering was a howl of pain. But at the bottom of that howl Ginsberg discovered what it was that the bourgeois god Moloch was most intent upon burying alive: the curative powers of the visionary imagination.

In making that discovery, Ginsberg uncovered at the heart of the poem what every artist has found in the creative process, to one degree or another. But what distinguishes his career is the project that followed upon that discovery. Having once experienced the visionary powers, Ginsberg found himself driven to reach beyond literary expression to a total life style. More than a poet, he has become, for the disaffiliated young of America and much of Europe, the vaga-bond proselytizer whose poems are but a subsidiary way of publicizing the new consciousness he embodies and the tech-niques for its cultivation. At poetry readings and teach-ins, he need not even read his verses: he need only appear in order to make his compelling statement of what young dis-sent is all about. The hair, the beard, the costume, the mis-chievous grin, the total absence of formality, pretense, or defensive posturing . . . they are enough to make him an exemplification of the counter cultural life.

There is something more that has to be observed about the visionary impulse in Ginsberg's poetry. The ecstatic venture to which Ginsberg and most of the early beat writers have been drawn is unexceptionally one of immanence rather than tran-scendence. Theirs is a mysticism neither escapist nor ascetic. It has not led them, like the ethereal quest of T. S. Eliot a generation earlier, into a rose garden far removed from the corruptions of the flesh. Instead, it is a this-worldly mysti-cism they seek: an ecstasy of the body and of the earth that somehow embraces and transforms mortality. Their goal is a joy that includes even (or perhaps especially) the com-monplace obscenities of our existence. As Ginsberg put it in one of his early poems:

> This is the one and only
> firmament . . .
> I am living in Eternity.
> The ways of this world
> are the ways of Heaven.

Or, even more powerfully:

> For the world is a mountain
> of shit: if it's going to
> be moved at all, it's got
> to be taken by handfuls.

William Carlos Williams, commenting on the poems of the young Ginsberg, observed in them "a beat that is far removed from the beat of dancing feet, but rather finds in the shuffling of human beings in all the stages of their life, the trip to the bathroom, to the stairs of the subway, the steps of the office or factory routine, the mystical measure of their passions."[4] The observation holds true for much of the work of the beat writers and is one of their defining features as a group: an appetite for ecstasies that have been buried and forgotten beneath the nitty-gritty scatological and sexual rubbish of existence.

For Ginsberg, who tells us he did not find the Zen satori until 1954, this salvaging of enchantment from the very dross of daily life served to resolve the acute personal tension one of the early poems reflects:

> I feel as if I am at a dead
> end and so I am finished
> All spiritual facts I realize
> are true but I never escape
> the feeling of being closed in
> and the sordidness of self,
> the futility of all that I
> have seen and done and said.

The way out of this corner was to arrive at a vision of sordidness and futility that made of *them* "spiritual facts" in their own right. The world might then be redeemed by the willingness to take it for what it is and to find its enchanting promise within the seemingly despiritualized waste. At least, in Ginsberg's development, some such psychic strategy seems to have been involved in his break from the stark pathos of the early poems. It is certainly a striking feature of his personal growth that, as time goes on, he moves further and

[4] From Williams' preface to *Empty Mirror: Early Poems*.

further from the despondency of these early efforts, through the impassioned outburst of *Howl*, toward a poetry of gentleness and charitable acceptance. Ginsberg, who went through the hell of our mental institutions, finishes by telling us that he can find only tears of pity for the madness of a Lyndon Johnson and for all the wrong-headed men of power who sacrifice their lives for debased objectives; but the sorrow does not grind down Ginsberg's wise and impish sense of humor. As time goes on, he progressively reverses Wordsworth's dictum.

We poets in our youth begin in gladness;
But thereof come in the end despondency and madness.

Whatever the explanation for Ginsberg's liberating enlightenment, what we have in the kitchen-sink mysticism to which the early poetry leads is a remarkable anticipation of the Zen principle of the illuminated commonplace.

If we can believe the account Jack Kerouac gives us in *The Dharma Bums* (1956)—the book which was to provide the first handy compendium of all the Zen catch phrases that have since become more familiar to our youth than any Christian catechism—it was from the West Coast poet Gary Snyder that he and Ginsberg learned their Zen upon coming to San Francisco in the early fifties. Snyder had by that time already found his way to a Zen-based pattern of life dedicated to poverty, simplicity, and meditation. He was soon to undertake formal Zen studies in Japan and to become, of all the early beats, the most knowledgeable practitioner of the tradition—as well as the poet whose work seems to express the pregnant calm of Zen most gracefully. But along with Snyder there was Alan Watts, who had recently begun teaching at the School of Asian Studies in San Francisco after leaving his position as an Anglican counselor at Northwestern

University. By the time he had reached San Francisco, Watts, who was only thirty-five years old in 1950, had behind him at least seven books dealing with Zen and mystical religion, dating back to 1935. He had, in fact, been a child prodigy in his chosen field of study. At nineteen he had been appointed editor of *The Middle Way*, an English journal of Buddhist studies, and at twenty-three, coeditor of the English "Wisdom of the East" series. Along with D. T. Suzuki, Watts, through his televised lectures, books, and private classes, was to become America's foremost popularizer of Zen. Much of what young America knows about the religion traces back to one or the other of these two scholars and to the generation of writers and artists whom they have influenced.

Of the two, I think it is Watts whose influence has been the more widespread, for often at the expense of risking vulgarization, he has made the most determined effort to translate the insights of Zen and Taoism into the language of Western science and psychology. He has approached his task with an impish willingness to be catchy and cute, and to play at philosophy as if it were an enjoyable game. It is a style easily mistaken for flippancy, and it has exposed him to a deal of rather arrogant criticism: on the one hand from elitist Zen devotees who have found him too discursive for their mystic tastes (I recall one such telling me smugly, "Watts has never experienced satori"), and on the other hand from professional philosophers who have been inclined to ridicule him for his popularizing bent as being, in the words of one academic, "The Norman Vincent Peale of Zen." It is the typical and inevitable sort of resistance anyone encounters when he makes bold to find a greater audience for an idea than the academy or any restricted cult can provide —and it overlooks the fact that Watts' books and essays include such very solid intellectual achievements as *Psycho-*

therapy East And West. Too often such aristocratic stricture comes from those who have risen above popularization by the device of restricting themselves to a subject matter that preserves its purity only because it has no conceivable relevance to anything beyond the interests of a small circle of experts.

There is a sense, however, in which it would seem to be impossible to popularize Zen. Traditionally, the insights of the religion have been communicated directly from master to student as part of an extremely demanding discipline in which verbal formulations play almost no part. Zen is neither a proselytizing creed nor a theology, but, rather, a personal illumination that one may have to be tricked into experiencing while intellectually off guard. Thus the best way to teach Zen, so it would seem, is to talk about anything but Zen, allowing the enlightening spark to break through of its own unpredictable accord—which is rather the way the composer John Cage, one of Suzuki's students, uses his music. Similarly, I have watched one of Watts' colleagues in San Francisco try to bring students around to the key experience by way of what purported to be rehearsals of a drama, but a drama that was never intended to reach production. Much the same intention seems to underlie the sensory awareness classes of Charlotte Selver, with whom Watts often works.[5] Watts himself is best at employing these outflanking strategies as part of his private courses, rather than as part of his writing or public lecturing.

Now, if this sort of psychic jiujitsu is the essence of Zen, then it may very well be that, on the religion's own terms,

[5] An exposition of Charlotte Selver's work can be found in "Sensory Awareness and Total Functioning," *General Semantics Bulletin* Nos. 20 and 21, 1957, pp. 5–16. Miss Selver's system is a forerunner of all the many tactile and self-expressive therapies that have now become the stock in trade of hip spas like California's Eselen.

all the youthful confabulation with Zen over the past decade or so has been less than useless. "Those who know do not speak; those who speak do not know"—and I would have to leave it to the Zen adepts to decide whether anything that deserves to be called authentic has actually taken root in our culture. It is indisputable, however, that the San Francisco beats, and much of our younger generation since their time, *thought* they had found something in Zen they needed, and promptly proceeded to use what they understood of this exotic tradition as a justification for fulfilling the need. The situation may be rather similar to Schopenhauer's attempt to elaborate his limited knowledge of the Upanishads into a philosophy that was primarily an expression of his generation's Romantic *Weltschmerz*.

What was it that Zen offered or seemed to offer to the young? It is difficult to avoid feeling that the great advantage Zen possesses (if it can be called an advantage) is its unusual vulnerability to what I have called "adolescentization." That is to say: Zen, vulgarized, dovetails remarkably with a number of adolescent traits. Its commitment to a wise silence, which contrasts so strongly with the preachiness of Christianity, can easily ally with the moody inarticulateness of youth. Why do Zen masters throw their disciples into a mud puddle, asks Kerouac's Sal Paradise in *The Dharma Bums*. "That's because they want them to realize mud is better than words." A generation that had come to admire the tongue-tied incoherence of James Dean and which has been willing to believe that the medium is the message, would obviously welcome a tradition that regarded talking as beside the point. Similarly, Zen's commitment to paradox and randomness could be conveniently identified with the intellectual confusion of healthily restless, but still unformed minds. Perhaps above all, Zen's antinomianism could serve as a sanction for the adolescent need of freedom, especially for those who possessed a justified discomfort with the competitive exactions and conformities of the technocracy. There could very well be a subtle, subterranean connection between the discovery of Zen by some young American writers in San Francisco of the early 1950s and the placards that appeared on the walls of the beleaguered Sorbonne in May 1968 proclaiming, "It is forbidden to forbid." As Lewis Mumford suggests:

Since ritual order has now largely passed into mechanical order, the present revolt of the younger generation against the machine has made a practice of promoting disorder and randomness . . .[6]

The amorality of Zen, as one might imagine, was rapidly given special emphasis where sex is concerned. And in this respect, the latest European-American journey to the East is a new departure. The Vedantism of the twenties and thirties had always been severely contemplative in the most ascetic sense of the term. One always has the feeling in looking through its literature that its following was found among the very old or very withered, for whom the ideal swami was a kindly orientalized version of an Irish Jesuit priest in charge of a pleasant retreat. The novels of Hermann Hesse, which are now once more so popular among the young, convey this ethos of ethereal asexuality. But the mysteries of the Orient we now have on hand in the counter culture have broken entirely from this earlier Christianized interpretation. In fact, nothing is so striking about the new orientalism as its highly sexed flavor. If there was anything Kerouac and his colleagues found especially appealing in the Zen they

[6] Lewis Mumford, *The Myth of the Machine* (New York: Harcourt, Brace & World, 1967), pp. 62–63. But Mumford warns that this style of revolt can also turn into "a ritual, just as compulsive and as 'meaningless' as the routine it seeks to assault."

adopted, it was the wealth of hyperbolic eroticism the religion brought with it rather indiscriminately from the *Kamasutra* and the tantric tradition. Again, this looks very much like postwar middle-class permissiveness reaching out for a religious sanction, finding it, and making the most of it. As Alan Watts observed in a widely circulated critique of 1958, a great deal of "Beat Zen" was a "pretext for license . . . a simple rationalization." Kerouac's brand of modish Zen, Watts gently criticized, ". . . confuses 'anything goes' at the existential level with 'anything goes' at the artistic and social levels." And such a conception of Zen runs the risk of becoming the banner of

the cool, fake-intellectual hipster searching for kicks, name-dropping bits of Zen and jazz jargon to justify disaffiliation from society which is in fact just ordinary, callous exploitation of other people. . . . Such types are, however, the shadow of a substance, the low-level caricature which always attends spiritual and cultural movements, carrying them to extremes which their authors never intended. To this extent beat Zen is sowing confusion in idealizing as art and life what is better kept to oneself as therapy.[7]

Even if Zen, as most of Ginsberg's generation have come to know and publicize it, has been flawed by crude simplifications, it must also be recognized that what the young have vulgarized in this way is a body of thought which, as formulated by men like Suzuki and Watts, embraces a radical critique of the conventional scientific conception of man and nature. If the young seized on Zen with shallow understanding, they grasped it with a healthy instinct. And grasping it, they bought the books, and attended the lectures, and

[7] Alan Watts, "Beat Zen, Square Zen, and Zen," in *This Is It, and Other Essays on Zen and Spiritual Experience* (New York: Collier Books, 1967).

spread about the catch phrases, and in general helped to provide the ambiance within which a few good minds who understood more deeply could speak out in criticism of the dominant culture. Perhaps what the young took Zen to be has little relationship to that venerable and elusive tradition; but what they readily adopted *was* a gentle and gay rejection of the positivistic and the compulsively cerebral. It was the beginning of a youth culture that continues to be shot through with the spontaneous urge to counter the joyless, rapacious, and egomaniacal order of our technological society.

This is another way of saying that, after a certain point, it becomes little better than pedantic to ask how authentically Buddhist" a poem like Ginsberg's *Sunflower Sutra* (1955) is. Perhaps not very. But it *is* a poem of great tenderness, expressing an unashamed wonder for the commonplace splendors of the world. It asserts a sensibility that calls into question the anthropocentric arrogance with which our society has gone about mechanizing and brutalizing its environment in the name of progress. And it is a commentary on the state of what our society regards as its "religion" that the poet who still commands the greatest attention among our youth should have had to cast about for such an exotic tradition from which to take inspiration in expressing these beautifully humane sentiments.

The same holds true for Ginsberg's more current Hinduism. It is, at the very least, a fascinating Odyssey of the contemporary spirit that takes a young Jewish poet from Paterson, New Jersey, to the banks of the Ganges in order to make of him America's greatest Hindu guru. But is his Hinduism the real thing? I suggest the question is beside the point. What is far more important is his deeply felt necessity to turn away from the dominant culture in order to find the spirit for such remarkable poems as *The Wichita Vortex Sutra* and *Who Be Kind To*—both such compelling expressions of humanity and compassionate protest. Even more important is the social fact: Ginsberg the mantra-chanting Hindu does not finish as an isolated eccentric, but rather as one of the foremost spokesmen of our younger generation. Following Ginsberg, the young don cowbells, tuck flowers behind their ears, and listen entranced to the chants. And through these attentive listeners Ginsberg claims a greater audience among our dissenting youth than any Christian or Jewish clergyman could hope to reach or stir. (Perhaps the one exception to this might be the late A. J. Muste in the last years of his life. But then it was always Muste's practice to keep his ministerial identity as unobtrusive as possible.)

Indeed, we are a post-Christian era—despite the fact that minds far more gifted than Ginsberg's, like that of the late Thomas Merton, have mined the dominant religious tradition for great treasures. But we may have been decidedly wrong in what we long expected to follow the death of the Christian God; namely, a thoroughly secularized, thoroughly positivistic culture, dismal and spiritless in its obsession with technological prowess. That was the world Aldous Huxley foresaw in the 1930s, when he wrote *Brave New World*. But in the 1950s, as Huxley detected the rising spirit of a new generation, his utopian image brightened to the forecast he offers us in *Island*, where a non-violent culture elaborated out of Buddhism and psychedelic drugs prevails. It was as if he had suddenly seen the possibility emerge: what lay beyond the Christian era and the "wasteland" that was its immediate successor might be a new, eclectic religious revival. Which is precisely what confronts us now as one of the massive facts of the counter culture. The dissenting young have indeed got religion. Not the brand of religion Billy Graham or William Buckley would like to see the young crusading for—but religion nonetheless. What began with Zen has now rapidly, perhaps too rapidly, proliferated into a phantasmagoria of exotic religiosity.

Who would have predicted it? At least since the Enlightenment, the major thrust of radical thought has always been anti-religious, if not openly, defiantly atheistic—perhaps with the exception of the early Romantics. And even among the Romantics, the most pious tended to become the most politically reactionary; for the rest, the Romantic project was to abstract from religion its essential "feeling" and leave contemptuously behind its traditional formulations. Would-be Western revolutionaries have always been strongly rooted in a militantly skeptical secular tradition. The rejection of the corrupted religious establishment has carried over almost automatically into a root-and-branch rejection of all things spiritual. So "mysticism" was to become one of the dirtiest words in the Marxist vocabulary. Since Diderot, the priest has had only one thing the radical wanted: his guts, with which to strangle the last king. Shaw, writing in 1921 on the intellectuals of what he called the "infidel half-century" (he was dating from the time of Darwin), summarized the situation thus:

We were intellectually intoxicated with the idea that the world could make itself without design, purpose, skill, or intelligence: in short, without life. . . . We took a perverse pleasure in arguing, without the least suspicion that we were reducing ourselves to absurdity, that all the books in the British Museum library might have been written word for word as they stand on the shelves if no human being had ever been conscious, just as the trees stand in the forest doing wonderful things without consciousness.

The first effect was exhilarating: we had the runaway child's sense of freedom before it gets hungry and lonely and frightened. In this phase we did not desire our God back again. We printed the verses in which William Blake, the most religious of our great poets, called the anthropomorphic idol Nobodaddy, and gibed at him in terms which the printer had to leave us to guess from his blank spaces. We had heard the parson droning that God is not mocked; and it was great fun to mock Him to our hearts' content and not be a penny the worse. (From the preface to *Back to Methusaleh*.)

When he wrote these words, Shaw had himself long since abandoned the crusading skepticism of his generation's intelligentsia in favor of a species of Vitalism, convinced that it was destined to become the new religion. Instead, it became only another of the enclaves from which alienated artists, eccentric psychiatrists, and assorted cranks could do no more than snipe at the secularized mainstream culture. Only the debased mysticism of the fascists, as the ideology of an aggressive war machine, has seriously troubled the scientized intellectual consensus of the twentieth century. Even so, the *Schwärmerei* of fascism, as I have remarked, really served as the facade behind which one of the most formidable technocracies of the age was consolidated.

But now, if one scans any of the underground weeklies, one is apt to find their pages swarming with Christ and the prophets, Zen, Sufism, Hinduism, primitive shamanism, theosophy, the Left-Handed Tantra. . . . The Berkeley "wandering priest" Charlie (Brown) Artman, who was in the running for city councilman in 1966 until he was arrested for confessing (quite unabashedly) to possession of narcotics, strikes the right note of eclectic religiosity: a stash of LSD in his Indian-sign necklace, a chatelaine of Hindu temple bells, and the campaign slogan "May the baby Jesus open your mind and shut your mouth." Satanists and Neo-Gnostics, dervishes and self-proclaimed swamis . . . their number grows and the counter culture makes generous place for them. No anti-war demonstration would be complete without a hirsute, be-cowbelled contingent of holy men, bearing joss sticks and intoning the Hare Krishna. An underground weekly like *The Berkeley Barb* gives official Washington a good left-wing slamming on page one, but devotes the center spread to a crazy mandala for the local yogis. And in the back pages, the "Servants of Awareness . . . a unique group of aware people using 136 symbols in their meditation to communicate directly with *Cosmic Awareness* . . ." are sure to take out a four-column ad. The San Francisco *Oracle* gives us photos of stark-naked madonnas with flowers in their hair, suckling their babies . . . and the effect is not at all pornographic, nor intended to be so.

At the level of our youth, we begin to resemble nothing so much as the cultic hothouse of the Hellenistic period, where every manner of mystery and fakery, ritual and rite, intermingled with marvelous indiscrimination. For the time being, the situation makes it next to impossible for many of us who teach to carry on much in the way of education among the dissenting young, given the fact that our conventional curriculum, even at its best, is grounded in the dominant Western tradition. Their interests, when not involved with the politics of revolution, are apt to be fathoming phenomena too exotic or too subterranean for normal academic handling. If one asks the hip young to identify (a) Milton and (b) Pope, their answers are likely to be: (a) Milton who? and (b) which Pope? But they may do no mean job of rehearsing their kabbala or *I Ching* (which the very hip get married to these days) or, of course, the *Kamasutra*.

What the counter culture offers us, then, is a remarkable defection from the long-standing tradition of skeptical, secular intellectuality which has served as the prime vehicle for three hundred years of scientific and technical work in the West. Almost overnight (and astonishingly, with no great debate on the point) a significant portion of the younger generation has opted out of that tradition, rather as if to provide an emergency balance to the gross distortions of our technological society, often by occult aberrations just as gross. As often happens, one cultural exaggeration calls forth another, which can be its opposite, but equivalent. In the hands of a Herman Kahn, science, logic, and the precision of numbers have become their own caricatures as part of the black arts of mass murder. But Kahn and his like are massively subsidized out of the public treasury and summoned to the corridors of power. Even official Washington calls its Sino-Soviet advisors "demonologists"—and the designation is scarcely a wisecrack. So mumbo jumbo is indeed at the heart of human affairs when so-called scientific decision-making reveals itself as a species of voodoo. "A communion of bum magicians," as Ginsberg has called it. What, then, does "reason" count for?

Expertise—technical, scientific, managerial, military, educational, financial, medical—has become the prestigious mystogogy of the technocratic society. Its principal purpose in the hands of ruling elites is to mystify the popular mind by creating illusions of omnipotence and omniscience—in much the same way that the pharaohs and priesthood of ancient Egypt used their monopoly of the calendar to command the awed docility of ignorant subjects. Philosophy, the hard-headed Wittgenstein once said, is the effort to keep ourselves from being hexed by language. But largely under the influence of logicians and technicians, and with the supposed purpose of de-hexing our thinking, we have produced the scientized jargon which currently dominates official parlance and the social sciences. When knowledgeable men talk, they no longer talk of substances and accidents, of being and spirit, of virtue and vice, of sin and salvation, of deities and demons. Instead, we have a vocabulary filled with nebulous quantities of things that have every appearance of precise calibration, and decorated with vaguely mechanistic-mathematical terms like "parameters," "structures," "variables," "inputs and outputs," "correlations," "inventories," "maximizations," and "optimizations." The terminology derives from involuted statistical procedures and methodological mysteries to which only graduate education gives access. The more such language and numerology one packs into a document, the more "objective" the document becomes—which normally means the less morally abrasive to the sources that have subsidized the research or to any sources that might conceivably subsidize one's research at any time in the future. The vocabulary and the methodology mask the root ethical assumptions of policy or neatly transcribe them into a depersonalized rhetoric which provides a gloss of military or political necessity. To think and to talk in such terms becomes the sure sign of being a certified realist, a "hard research" man.

Thus to bomb more hell out of a tiny Asian country in one year than was bombed out of Europe in the whole Second World War becomes "escalation." Threatening to burn and blast to death several million civilians in an enemy country is called "deterrence." Turning a city into radioactive rubble is called "taking out" a city. A concentration camp (already a euphemism for a political prison) becomes a "strategic hamlet." A comparison of the slaughter on both sides in a war is called a "kill ratio." Totaling up the corpses is called a "body count." Running the blacks out of town is called "urban renewal." Discovering ingenious new ways to bilk the public is called "market research." Outflanking the discontent of employees is called "personnel management." Wherever possible, hideous realities are referred to by cryptic initials and formulalike phrases: ICBM, CBR, megadeaths, or "operation" this, "operation" that. On the other hand, one can be certain that where more colorful, emotive terms are used—"the war on poverty," "the war for the hearts and minds of men," "the race for space," "the New Frontier," "the Great Society"—the matters referred to exist only as propagandistic fictions or pure distraction.

Such is the technocratic word magic Ginsberg rails against in his *Wichita Vortex Sutra:*

The war is language,
        language abused
            for Advertisement,
        language used
    like magic for power on the planet
Black Magic language,
    formulas for reality—
            Communism is a 9 letter word
                used by inferior magicians
with the wrong alchemical formula for transforming earth
into gold
            funky warlocks operating on guesswork,
                handmedown mandrake terminology. . .

Governments have no doubt always resorted to such linguistic camouflage to obscure realities. Certainly the vice is not limited to our own officialdom. Marcuse has shrewdly shown how the Soviet Union's endlessly reiterated verbal formulae—"warmongering capitalist imperialism," "the people's democratic" this or that, always the same adjective hitched to the same noun—use the Marxist lexicon to produce the same ritualistic obfuscations.[8] But the special irony of our situation is the employment of what purports to be a clinically objective vocabulary of technologisms for the purpose of hexing intelligence all over again.

When science and reason of state become the handmaidens of political black magic, can we blame the young for diving headlong into an occult Jungian stew in search of "good vibrations" that might ward off the bad? Of course, they are

[8] Marcuse, *Soviet Marxism: A Critical Analysis,* p. 88.

soon glutted with what they find. They swallow it whole—
and the result can be an absurdly presumptuous confabulation. Whole religious traditions get played with like so many
baubles. A light-show group in Detroit names itself The
Bulging Eyeballs of Gautama and the Beatles become the
contemplative converts of a particularly simple-minded swami
who advertises his mystic wares in every London underground station—only to drop him after a matter of months
like a *passé* fashion.

No, the young do not by and large understand what these
traditions are all about. One does not uncarth the wisdom
of the ages by shuffling about a few exotic catch phrases—
nor does one learn anything about anybody's lore or religion
by donning a few talismans and dosing on LSD. The most
that comes of such superficial muddling is something like
Timothy Leary's brand of easy-do syncretism: "somehow" all
is one—but never mind precisely how. Fifty years ago, when
Swami Vivekananda first brought the teachings of Sri
Ramakrishna to America, he persuaded a clique of high-
society dilettantes to believe as much. The results were often
as ludicrous as they were ephemeral. Yet things are just beginning in our youth culture. In the turgid floodtide of discovery, sampling, and restive fascination, perhaps it would be
too much to expect disciplined order of the young in their
pursuit—and surely it would be folly to try to deduce one
from their happy chaos. They have happened upon treasure-
trove long buried and are busy letting the quaint trinkets
spill through their fingers.

For all its frequently mindless vulgarity, for all its tendency
to get lost amid the exotic clutter, there is a powerful and
important force at work in this wholesale willingness of the
young to scrap our culture's entrenched prejudice against
myth, religion, and ritual. The life of Reason (with a
capital R) has all too obviously failed to bring us the agenda

of civilized improvements the Voltaires and Condorcets once foresaw. Indeed, Reason, material Progress, the scientific world view have revealed themselves in numerous respects as simply a higher superstition, based on dubious but well-concealed assumptions about man and nature. Science, it has been said, thrives on sins of omission. True enough; and for three hundred years, those omissions have been piling up rather like the slag tips that surround Welsh mining towns: immense, precipitous mountains of frustrated human aspiration which threaten dangerously to come cascading down in an impassioned landslide. It is quite impossible any longer to ignore the fact that our conception of intellect has been narrowed disastrously by the prevailing assumption, especially in the academies, that the life of the spirit is: (1) a lunatic fringe best left to artists and marginal visionaries; (2) an historical boneyard for antiquarian scholarship; (3) a highly specialized adjunct of professional anthropology; (4) an antiquated vocabulary still used by the clergy, but intelligently soft-pedaled by its more enlightened members. Along none of these approaches can the living power of myth, ritual, and rite be expected to penetrate the intellectual establishment and have any existential (as opposed to merely academic) significance. If conventional scholarship does touch these areas of human experience, it is ordinarily with the intention of compiling knowledge, not with the hope of salvaging value.

When academics and intellectuals arrogantly truncate the life of the mind in this way, we finish with that "middle-class secular humanism" of which Michael Novak has aptly said,

It thinks of itself as humble in its agnosticism, and eschews the "mystic flights" of metaphysicians, theologians and dreamers; it is cautious and remote in dealing with heightened and passionate experiences that are the stuff of great literature and philosophy. It limits itself to this world and its concerns, concerns which fortunately turn out to be largely subject to precise formulations, and hence have a limited but comforting certainty.[9]

I think we can anticipate that in the coming generation, large numbers of students will begin to reject this reductive humanism, demanding a far deeper examination of that dark side of the human personality which has for so long been written off by our dominant culture as "mystical." It is because this youthful renaissance of mythical-religious interest holds such promise of enriching our culture that one despairs when, as so often happens, the young reduce it in their ignorance to an esoteric collection of peer-group symbols and slogans, vaguely daring and ultimately trivial. Then, instead of culture, we get collage: a miscellaneous heaping together, as if one had simply ransacked The Encyclopedia of Religion and Ethics and the *Celestia Arcana* for exotic tidbits. For example, one opens the underground *International Times* of London and finds a major article on Aleister Crowley. The exuberant treatment goes no further than the sensational surface—and how much further does such a figure allow one to go? It is the simple principle of inversion which too often dominates the underground press: the straight papers would have said "scandalous"; we say "marvelous." But understanding gets no further. One does not seek to discriminate, but only to manipulate: don't ask questions about the subject; just put it on a stick and wave it like a flag. It is at this point that the young, who are offering us, I feel, a great deal that is good to work with, need the help of mature minds, in order

[9] Michael Novak, "God in the Colleges: The Dehumanization of the University," in Cohen and Hale, *The New Student Left*, pp. 253–65.

that enduring distinctions can be drawn between the deep and the shallow, the superstitious and the wise.

For what they are groping their way toward through all their murky religiosity is an absolutely critical distinction. The truth of the matter is: no society, not even our severely secularized technocracy, can ever dispense with mystery and magical ritual. These are the very bonds of social life, the inarticulate assumptions and motivations that weave together the collective fabric of society and which require periodic collective affirmation. But there is one magic that seeks to open and vitalize the mind, another that seeks to diminish and delude. There are rituals which are imposed from on high for the sake of invidious manipulation; there are other rituals in which men participate democratically for the purpose of freeing the imagination and exploring self-expression. There are mysteries which, like the mysteries of state, are no better than dirty secrets; but there are also mysteries which are encountered by the community (if such exists) in a stance of radical equality, and which are meant to be shared in for the purpose of enriching life by experiences of awe and splendor.

A presidential convention or campaign filled with phonied-up hoopla is an obvious example of a debased ritual meant to cloak disreputable politicking with a democratic sanction. Similarly, modern war fever, manufactured out of skillfully wrought propaganda and playing upon hysterical frustrations, is a perverted blood ritual. It is a throwback to the rite of human or animal sacrifice, but now so highly regimented that it is lacking in the immediate and personal, if ugly, gratifications of its primeval original. It therefore requires not one, but millions of victims: anonymous populations that are known only as stereotypes in the mass media. The blood of the killed is never seen and touched, either in dread or strong satisfaction. Instead, a warrior, perhaps reluctantly conscripted, drops a bomb from on high or triggers a remote control—and somewhere far off an entire city dies in agony. The deed has been mechanistically precise, objectively planned by headquarters, and accomplished in cold blood. The society participates even in the life and death of war by passively reading the statistics of genocide in the newspaper. As Paul Goodman has commented, our wars get more murderous and less angry all the time—or perhaps one should say less *authentically* angry, for the anger is a managed and inculcated emotion that attaches itself to concocted images and abstract ideological issues—like those Big Brother provides for the citizens of 1984.

Compare these empty alienative rituals with such rites as our hippies improvise for themselves out of potted anthropology and sheer inspiration, and the distinction between good and bad magic should be clear enough. The tribalized young gather in gay costume on a high hill in the public park to salute the midsummer sun in its rising and setting. They dance, they sing, they make love as each feels moved, without order or plan. Perhaps the folklore of the affair is pathetically ersatz at this point—but is the intention so foolish after all? There is the chance to express passion, to shout and stamp, to caress and play communally. All have equal access to the event; no one is misled or manipulated. Neither kingdom, nor power, nor glory is desperately at stake. Maybe, in the course of things, some even discover in the commonplace sun and the ordinary advent of summer the inexpressible grandeur that is really there and which makes those who find it more authentically human.

It would be easy to dismiss such merry displays as so much marginal *joi de vivre*, having no political relevance. But I think this would be a mistake. Here, in such improvised rituals, there is something postulated as sacred—and it is something worthy of the designation: the magnificence of the season, the joy of being this human animal so vividly alive to the world. And to this something sacred which stands above all men, causes, regimes, and factions, all are allowed equal access. Could this not be the ultimate expression and safeguard of a participative democracy, without which the popular control of institutions might always be corrupted by partisan interest or deference to expertise? These embryonic rituals may very well be an approximation of the "no-politics" Norman Brown speaks of. For what might this "no-politics" be, if not a politics that doesn't *look* like politics at all, and which it is therefore impossible to resist by conventional psychic and social defenses?

Ginsberg has made his own contribution to this bizarre strategy. In 1966 he wrote a poem titled *How to Make a March/Spectacle*, an effort too long and particularly awful to merit quotation.[10] The poem has, however, either influenced or summarized the character of much of the demonstrating the young have been doing ever since. Its thesis is that demonstrations should lay aside their usually grave and pugnacious quality in favor of a festive dancing and chanting parade that would pass out balloons and flowers, candy and kisses, bread and wine to everyone along the line of march—including the cops and any Hell's Angels in the vicinity. The atmosphere should be one of gaiety and affection, governed by the intention to attract or seduce participation from the usually impassive bystanders—or at least to overcome their worst suspicions and hostilities.

An eccentric notion—and yet is there not a certain crafty wisdom to it? How many demonstrations have there been over the years: angry, vituperative, morally fervent displays which have been compounded of morbid breast-beatings and fierce denunciations . . . and which have won not a soul to

[10] The poem appears in *Liberation*, January 1966, pp. 42–43.

the cause who was not already converted? What *is* the purpose of such activity? On what conception of human psychology is it based? Where unconvinced people hear harsh slogans and see massed ranks of grim faces, their defenses are well rehearsed: they grimace and shout back and become, before the sensed threat, more entrenched in their opposition. How many people are ever won over by being harangued or morally bullied? And winning over is a dissenting minority's only alternative to acts of factional violence.

In contrast, Ginsberg invokes the Zen principle of catching the opponent off guard, of offering no resistant target at which he can strike back. The cause of the happy parade is clearly anti-war (and that simple sentiment is really as much as *any* peace demonstration ever gets across anyway)—but it is declared without self-congratulatory indignation or heavy, heady argument. Instead, the effort is to create a captivating mood of peaceableness, generosity, and tenderness that may melt the rigidities of opponents and sweep them along despite their conscious objections. Perhaps most important, the Ginsberg stratagem suggests that the demonstrators have some idea of what innocence and happiness are . . . which is supposed to be what good political principles aim for.

In a somewhat better poem than Ginsberg's, Julian Beck, director of the Living Theater, catches the spirit of the enterprise:

> It is 1968
> i am a magic realist
> i see the adorers of che
>
> i see the black man
> forced to accept
> violence
>
> i see the pacifists
> despair
> and accept violence

i see all all all
corrupted
by the vibrations

vibrations of violence of civilization
that are shattering
our only world

. . . .

we want
to zap them
with holiness

we want
to levitate them
with joy

we want
to open them
with love vessels

we want
to clothe the wretched
with linen and light

we want
to put music and truth
in our underwear

we want
to make the land and its cities glow
with creation

we will make it
irresistible
even to racists

. . . .

we want to change
the demonic character of our opponents
into productive glory[11]

[11] Julian Beck, *Paradise Now*, *International Times* (London), July
12–25, 1968. The Becks, Julian and Judith, have, during their years

Over the past few years, while the demonstrations of the New Left have increased in conventional militancy, politicking of this gentler spirit has also proliferated among the young. New York hippies have invaded the Stock Exchange to tear up and scatter dollar bills like so much confetti; San Francisco hippies have staged "strip-ins" in Golden Gate Park—in both cases with every appearance of thoroughly enjoying the exercise. Are these such inappropriate ways of taking issue with the economic and sexual hang-ups of our society? Would handing out leaflets on the subjects be a more effective challenge? The style easily carries over into a form of theater—such as that of the New York Bread and Puppet Theater or R. G. Davis' San Francisco Mime Troupe, both of which have toured the country giving street-corner and public park performances attacking the Vietnam war and racial injustice. In England, too, protests have taken on the form of street theater. In 1968, an anarchist group called the Cartoon Archetypal Slogan Theater (CAST) staged, as one of its many demonstrations, the "capture" of a Fleet Street monument by actors dressed like U.S. soldiers. The players claimed the monument for the American Government and then comically set about recruiting everybody on hand who supported the war in Vietnam for the American Army. They finished by delivering a giant-sized draft card bearing Prime Minister Wilson's name to No. 10 Downing Street.

"Revolutionary festivals," "revolutionary carnivals," "revolu-

---

of European exile from America (they were hounded from New York by the Internal Revenue Service in 1964) become the foremost impresarios of revolutionary theater. "Paradise Now" is also the title of one of their audience-participation drama rituals, intended to "envelope the audience in churchly communion" and to finish with "a call for a non-violent revolution right now." (I quote from their program notes for the production.) Perhaps inevitably, the more therapy and tribal ritual such efforts offer, the less dramatic art one can expect of them.

tionary playgrounds" . . . actors instead of speakers, flowers instead of pamphlets, enjoying instead of reviling—these are no substitute certainly for the hard work of community organizing (which is the New Left's best and most distinctive form of politics); but they are, I think, a significant revision of the art of demonstrating. Still, old-style radicalism frowns on such antics. For surely politics is not a thing to be enjoyed: it is a crusade, not a carnival; a penance, not a pleasure. No doubt many a "revolutionary festival" will degenerate into a mere mindless frolic—even as the militancy of "serious" demonstrations has been known to degenerate into fistfights . . . and then nobody convinces anybody of anything. But before we decide that the strategy of "no-politics" cannot possibly work, with its recourse to indirection, involvement by seduction, and subliminal persuasion, let us be honest about one thing. If violence and injustice could be eliminated from our society by heavy intellectual research and ideological analysis, by impassioned oratory and sober street rallies, by the organization of bigger unions or lobbies or third parties or intricate coalitions, by "the flat ephemeral pamphlet and the boring meeting," by barricades or bombs or bullets . . . then we should long since have been living in the New Jerusalem. Instead, we are living in the thermonuclear technocracy. Given the perfectly dismal (if undeniably heroic) record of traditional radicalism in America, why should the dissenting young assume that previous generations have much to tell them about practical politics?

Chapter V

THE COUNTERFEIT INFINITY:
THE USE AND ABUSE OF PSYCHEDELIC
EXPERIENCE

> a dusky light—a purple *flash*
> crystalline splendor—light blue—
>   *Green* lightnings.—
> in that eternal and delirious misery—
>   wrathfires—
>   inward desolations—
> an horror of great darkness
> great things—on the ocean
>   counterfeit infinity—
>
>   —COLERIDGE
>   (From *The Notebooks for 1796.*)

At the bohemian fringe of our disaffected youth culture, all roads lead to psychedelia.[1] The fascination with hallucinogenic drugs emerges persistently as the common denominator of the many protean forms the counter culture has assumed in the post-World War II period. Correctly understood (which it all too seldom is), psychedelic experience participates significantly in the young's most radical rejection of the parental society. Yet it is their frantic search for the phar-

---

[1] I will for the most part be using the word "psychedelics" in this chapter to cover all the many psychotropic agents, both professionally concocted and home-brewed, which are currently employed to induce visionary experience. Connoisseurs may find this global usage of the term unsatisfactory, preferring the more fastidious classification of hallucinogens one finds in an essay like Timothy Leary's "The Molecular Revolution" in *The Politics of Ecstasy* (New York: Putnam, 1968), pp. 332–61. However, I will brazen out this less discriminating terminology on the grounds that the thesis of this chapter applies to all the psychotropic agents without distinction.

macological panacea which tends to distract many of the young from all that is most valuable in their rebellion, and which threatens to destroy their most promising sensibilities.

If we accept the proposition that the counter culture is, essentially, an exploration of the politics of consciousness, then psychedelic experience falls into place as one, but only one, possible method of mounting that exploration. It becomes a limited chemical means to a greater psychic end, namely, the reformulation of the personality, upon which social ideology and culture generally are ultimately based.

This was the spirit in which, at the turn of the century, both William James and Havelock Ellis undertook their study of hallucinogenic agents. The prospectus of these early experimenters—James using nitrous oxide and Ellis, the newly discovered peyote (on which James was able to achieve only bad stomach cramps)—was highly exuberant with respect to the cultural possibilities that might flow from an investigation of hallucinatory experience. Ellis, reporting to the Smithsonian Institution in 1898 on his introduction to the "saturnalia for the specific senses," observed that:

If it should ever chance that the consumption of mescal becomes a habit, the favorite poet of the mescal drinker will certainly be Wordsworth. Not only the general attitude of Wordsworth, but many of his most memorable poems and phrases cannot—one is almost tempted to say—be appreciated in their full significance by one who has never been under the influence of mescal. On all these grounds it may be claimed that the artificial paradise of mescal, though less seductive, is safe and dignified beyond its peers.[2]

James was even more emphatic in hailing the philosophical importance of the non-intellective powers he had dis-

[2] Quoted in Robert S. DeRopp, *Drugs and the Mind* (London: Gollancz, 1958), pp. 55–56.

covered not only directly through his experiments with narcotics, but more academically by way of his ground-breaking survey *The Varieties of Religious Experience*. The enthusiasm on James' part is especially noteworthy since, as a founder of both pragmatism and behavioral psychology, he was much beholden to the standard forms of cerebration that belong to the scientific world view. Still, James was convinced that:

. . . our normal waking consciousness, rational consciousness as we call it, is but one special type of consciousness, whilst all about it, parted from it by the filmiest of screens, there lie potential forms of consciousness entirely different. . . . No account of the universe in its totality can be final which leaves these other forms of consciousness quite disregarded. . . . they forbid a premature closing of our accounts with reality.[3]

When, some fifty years later, Aldous Huxley and Alan Watts undertook psychedelic experiments that were destined to have far greater social influence than those of Ellis and James, the investigations were still characterized by the same controlled samplings and urbane observations.[4] Once again, the object was to gain a new, internal perspective on modes of consciousness and on religious traditions that the narrowly positivist science of the day had swept into an outsized pigeonhole labeled "mysticism"—meaning . . . "meaningless." The exercise Watts and Huxley had set themselves was therefore essentially one of synthesis and assimilation.

[3] William James, *The Varieties of Religious Experience* (New York: Modern Library, 1936), pp. 378–79.
[4] Huxley reports his experiences in *Doors of Perception* (New York: Harper, 1954); Watts, his in *The Joyous Cosmology: Adventures in the Chemistry of Consciousness*, foreword by Timothy Leary and Richard Alpert (New York: Pantheon, 1962). There is also an earlier essay by Watts, "The New Alchemy," which is reprinted in *This Is It*.

In much the same spirit in which Freud had set out to re-claim the dream as a form of evidence that could bear the weight of scientific speculation, Watts and Huxley wanted to recapture the value of neglected cultural traditions for which no disciplined method of study existed. The method they proposed was the systematic cultivation of states of ab-normal consciousness that approached these traditions by out-flanking the discursive, logic-chopping intellect.

The hypothesis Ellis and James, Watts and Huxley were testing has always seemed to me wholly sensible, even from the most rigorously scientific viewpoint. If the province of science is the disciplined examination of human experience, then surely abnormal (or transnormal) states of conscious-ness must also constitute a field of scientific study. As James had contended, the mystics, by relating their insights to direct personal experience, would seem to qualify as rigorous empiricists. Why then should their experience and the knowl-edge that appears to flow from it be screened out by science as somehow illegitimate? Is it perhaps the case that the mys-tics, in accepting the fullness of human experience, have been more truly scientific than the conventional scientist, who insists that only what makes itself apparent to an arbitrarily limited range of consciousness deserves attention? Such a prej-udice would seem all the more untenable once artificial chem-ical agents have been developed which provide discriminate access to these transnormal forms of consciousness. Why should they not be used as a kind of psychic depth charge with which to open up courses of perception that have be-come severely log-jammed due to the entrenched cerebral habits of our Western intelligence?

As an intellectual proposition, such experimentation may have been sound. But the experiments were destined to be-come more than a form of exotic psychological research. In-stead, they have been sucked into the undertow of a major social movement—and in this context, their influence has been far from wholesome.

With hindsight, it is clear enough what went wrong. Both Huxley and Watts drew the analogy between the drug experience and such exploratory devices as the microscope. Accordingly, the hallucinogens were to function as a lens through which the shadowy layers of consciousness could be studied. But a microscope in the hands of a child or the laboratory janitor becomes a toy that produces nothing but a kind of barbarous and superficial fascination. Perhaps the drug experience bears significant fruit when rooted in the soil of a mature and cultivated mind. But the experience has, all of a sudden, been laid hold of by a generation of youngsters who are pathetically a-cultural and who often bring nothing to the experience but a vacuous yearning. They have, in adolescent rebellion, thrown off the corrupted culture of their elders and, along with that soiled bath water, the very body of the Western heritage—at best, in favor of exotic traditions they only marginally understand; at worst, in favor of an introspective chaos in which the seventeen or eighteen years of their own unformed lives float like atoms in a void.

I think one must be prepared to take a very strong line on the matter and maintain that there are minds too small and too young for such psychic adventures—and that the failure to recognize this fact is the beginning of disaster. There is nothing whatever in common between a man of Huxley's experience and intellectual discipline sampling mescaline, and a fifteen-year-old tripper whiffing airplane glue until his brain turns to oatmeal. In the one case, we have a gifted mind moving sophisticatedly toward cultural synthesis; in the other, we have a giddy child out to "blow his mind" and bemused to see all the pretty balloons go up. But when all the balloons have gone up and gone pop, what is there left behind but the yearning to see more pretty balloons? And so one reaches again for the little magic tube . . . and again and again.

At the level of disaffiliated adolescence, the prospect held forth by psychedelic experience—that of consciousness expansion—is bound to prove abortive. The psychedelics, dropped into amorphous and alienated personalities, have precisely the reverse effect: they diminish consciousness by way of fixation. The whole of life comes to center despotically on one act, one mode of experience. Whether or not marijuana, LSD, and amphetamine are addictive remains a moot point—largely because of the ambiguity of the term "addiction." Are fingernails addictive? We all know people who bite them constantly and compulsively. Is chess addictive? There are players who will go without food or drink rather than abandon the board. Where does the dependency of compulsive fascination leave off and addiction begin?

What *is* obvious, however, is that the psychedelics are a heavyweight obsession which too many of the young cannot get over or around. For them, psychic chemistry is no longer a means for exploring the perennial wisdom; it has become an end in itself, a source of boundless lore, study, and esthetic elaboration. It is becoming the whole works. It is not that the young have all become hopheads; it is rather that, at the bohemian fringe, they are in the process of trying strenuously to inflate the psychedelics to the size of an entire culture. Ironically, the vice is typical of the worst sort of American commercialism. Start with a gimmick; end with a *Weltanschauung*. Madison Avenue's strategy of strategies: don't just sell them a new can opener; sell them a new way of life.

Here, then, is an example of how, at last, the dimensions of "expanded consciousness" measure up in the hippest versions of the underground press. (In this case, the October 1967 issue of the Southern California *Oracle*—but the point could be made with any number of other underground journals.) The art throughout is officially psychedelic: melting, soft-edged, bejeweled . . . not *good*, but official. The lead article is an interview with Timothy Leary, the subject exclusively under discussion being (what else?) LSD. The substance is slight and garbled, but the tone is pontifical and the piece strings together all the right slogans.

There follows a feature by a local "philosopher-ecologist" who has permitted the *Oracle* "to plug a tape recorder into his frontal lobe for a view of paradise as he perceives it." It begins: "When I turned on once in Yosemite with 250 micrograms of acid . . ." Thereafter, we have another interview, this time with a rock star (again, "a tape recorded probe of his lobes"), and it is all about "How I Get High." Next, there is the first of a new series on "Ecstatic Living," which is described as "insights gleaned from a 3-year creativity study conducted in Mexico under the sponsorship of Sandoz Company, makers of LSD-25"—which would seem to be in about the same category as research in international relations under the sponsorship of the CIA. The subtitle of the piece is: "Your Ecstatic Home—cheap ways of changing your home to reflect the changes in your consciousness."

Everyone should invest in a little electric motor of the kind that revolves things from the ceiling. Then you can take a large tin can and puncture it with holes and cause it to revolve around a light bulb . . . it shines little bits of starlight all over the room. In addition . . . we might also have a little revolving stage of the kind you see in jewelry store windows. . . . Cover this with any visionary object. For a list of visionary objects, you can read Huxley's classic *The Doors of Perception*.

There follows the science department: how *not* to catch hepatitis—a widespread disease among users of amphetamine. (It comes of contaminated needles.) The tone of this piece is hip-avuncular:

. . . doing your thing doesn't have to include dumping bad Karma on your soul-brothers. Don't touch food or drink or prepare it, without first thoroughly washing your hands, especially if you've just been to the john. . . . You can even afford to get up tight about it, especially if your home is of the tribal kind.

(My pre-tribal father used to phrase this piece of folk wisdom as: "You wash up before you sit down at this table!" But I seem to remember being about five years old at the time.)

Finally, we have recommended reading ("books to expand your consciousness"), a page of ads for psychedelic posters, and an Art Nouveau back page: boy and girl in sexual congress below a curvacious "LOVE."

If one turns to other underground weeklies, one is likely to find much the same narrow obsession with psychedelic problems and paraphernalia. The letters columns bubble with new brews, some of them positively bloodcurdling. Editorials exaggerate the narcotics laws and dodging the narcotics squad into the alpha and omega of politics. Meanwhile, the advertising betrays the fact that the journals have grown progressively more dependent on a local hip economy most of whose wares—clothing, light shows, rock music and its clubs, posters, electronic strobes, jewelry, buttons, bells, beads, black-light glasses, dope pipes, and assorted "head equipment"—are designed to be perceived through a narcotic haze, or at any rate go a long way toward glamorizing the psychedelics, deepening the fascination or the need.

There is a word we have to describe such fastidious immersion in a single small idea and all its most trivial ramifications, such precious efforts to make the marginal part stand for the whole of culture. The word is "decadent." And that, unhappily, is the direction in which a substantial segment of our youth culture is currently weakening.

If the psychedelic obsession were no more than a symptom of cultural impoverishment, things would be bad enough. But one must complete the grim picture by adding the sweaty, often vicious, and, in a few instances, even murderous relationships that inevitably grow up around any illegal trade. Money is still what it takes to survive in an urban environment, even if one is only eking out a subsistence. And narcotics, with their subsidiary merchandise, are what brings the money into communities like the East Village and the Haight-Ashbury. In a perceptive series on the Haight-Ashbury dope commerce written for the Washington *Post* (October 15–29, 1967), Nicholas Von Hoffman was forced to the unhappy conclusion that, whatever else they may take themselves to be, the hippies constitute, willy-nilly, "the biggest crime story since prohibition." The account he has to offer is far from pretty. Even if most of the flower children manage to steer clear of the more cynical and criminal aspects of the trade, their communities have nevertheless become a market more and more dominated by hard-nosed entrepreneurial interests that have about as much concern for expanding consciousness as Al Capone had for arranging Dionysian festivals.

To be sure, the authorities with their single-minded determination to treat the use of psychedelics as a police problem, and the mass media with their incorrigible penchant for simplifying and sensationalizing, are both to blame for turning the often innocent curiosity of the young into ugly and furtive channels. But the young bear a primary responsibility for letting themselves be trapped in the vicious ambience that the dominant society has created. One must insist that, on their own terms, they are old enough to know better than to let themselves be driven into the same bag

with drug merchandisers, who are only the criminal caricature of the American business ethos, and who will scarcely
be reformed by being given docile new populations to exploit.

*   *   *   *

It is no easy matter to establish responsibility for the psychedelic fascination of the young. The high-touting of narcotics has been going on since the days of the San Francisco
Renaissance, and by now the number of those who have
added to their lore and glamor is legion. Still, one figure—that
of Timothy Leary—stands out as that of promoter, apologist,
and high priest of psychedelia nonpareil. Surely if we look
for the figures who have done the most to push psychedelic experience along the way toward becoming a total and
autonomous culture, it is Leary who emerges as the Ultra of
the campaign. Indeed, he would probably be insulted if we
denied him the distinction.

It is remarkable, and more than a little suspicious, how
Leary came to exert his brief but significant influence on the
youth culture of the sixties. For while Leary had been a much-
publicized pioneer in the field of psychedelic research since
the early sixties,[5] it was not until his academic career had
been washed up (he was dismissed from Harvard in 1963)
and he had twice run a-foul of the narcotics laws, that he
blossomed forth—and then almost overnight—as a self-
proclaimed cultic swami. This rather makes it difficult to
avoid seeing more than a fortuitous connection between
Leary's legal entanglements (one of which saddled him with
the absurdly severe sentence of thirty years imprisonment
and a $30,000 fine) and his subsequent claims to visionary

[5] See, as an example of Leary's more academic style, the letter
he coauthored to the *Bulletin of the Atomic Scientists* for May
1962.

prophecy. Such an interpretation of Leary's career may be too cynical, but the fact remains that the first, splashy "psychedelic celebration" of his League for Spiritual Discovery was held in September 1966, within six months of the time his lawyer had appealed that one of Leary's narcotics convictions be reversed as a violation of religious freedom.[6]

But even if Leary's psychedelic cult began as a legal gambit, it need not be lightly dismissed. There exists in psychiatry a condition of mind called the Ganser syndrome—or the syndrome of approximate answers. The syndrome describes the behavior of people who seem to be faking insanity, but faking it so well that they eventually take on their insane role permanently. In a sense, they calculatedly drive themselves mad. In Leary's case, the "madness" has assumed the mantle of the divine, but it seems to involve the same process of systematically losing oneself in an eccentric identity. Whatever the explanation for the turn Leary's career has taken, the change has been of great significance for the development of our youth culture. For it is Leary who has managed to embed the younger generation's psychedelic fascination solidly in a religious context. The connection which far more gifted minds had discovered between psychedelic experience and visionary religion is finally being retailed by Leary to masses of teen-agers and college students.

[6] See the report on the league's founding and its first public service in the New York *Times*, September 20, 1966, p. 33, and September 21, 1966, p. 94. For the "biblical account" of the league's history, see Leary's *High Priest* (New York: World, 1968). This projected four-volume work is designed to provide "the Old Testament background of the new witness of those born after 1946." Clearly, Leary sees himself as the Moses of these scriptures, since this first volume deals almost exclusively with his own adventures and martyrdoms. The book is, incidentally, a striking example of the new religiosity. From the very first sentence—"In the beginning was the Turn-On"—we are in the midst of a religious eclecticism so heavily laid on that it is almost suffocating.

There is no way to tell whether Leary has or has not turned on more of the younger generation than novelist Ken Kesey, creator of the "acid test" during the early sixties. Both can claim a notorious success at the specialty act of organizing mass public "trips." But Kesey's sessions were mainly fun and games: LSD served up in a heady brew of amplified rock bands, strobe lights, and free-form dance. The intention was, at best, aesthetic and entertaining. Leary, on the other hand, preferred to come on during his LSD camp meetings with all the solemnity of the risen Christ, replete with white cotton pajamas, incense, and the stigmata of his legal persecutions—though the light and sound effects were still part of the act. (So were the high admission prices: up to $4.00 per seat.) Doubtless the psychedelic fascination would have spread among the young, though more slowly, without the proselytizing of Kesey and Leary. But Leary, appearing at just the ripe moment and gaining ready access to thousands of college students and adolescents, has been the figure primarily responsible for inculcating upon vast numbers of young and needy minds (many of which do not easily hold more than one idea at a time) the primer-simple notion that LSD has "something" to do with religion. And it is that notion—even if imperfectly grasped—which makes psychedelic experimentation much more than a naughty hijinx.

When the flaming youth of the twenties took heavily to bootleg liquor, they were in no position to reach for metaphysics to justify their bad habits. For our contemporary young, however, dope wears the charisma of an esoteric wisdom, and they defend its uses with a religious fervor. What Leary has taught them is that getting turned on is not a kind of childish mischief; it is the sacred rite of a new age. They know, if only vaguely, that somewhere behind the forbidden experience lie rich and exotic religious traditions, occult powers, salvation—which, of course, the adult society fails to understand, and indeed fears. "They're like the Romans," a young psychedelic promoter is quoted as saying. "They don't realize this is a religious movement. Until they make it [the use of psychedelics] legal and do it up front, we'll find our sacraments where we can. And no sooner is one made illegal, we'll come up with another."[7]

By way of a mystic religiosity, Leary has succeeded in convincing vast numbers of the young that his "neurological politics" must function as an integral, if not a central, factor in their dissenting culture. "The LSD kick is a spiritual ecstasy. The LSD trip is a religious pilgrimage." Psychedelic experience is *the* way "to groove to the music of God's great song."

But the promise of nirvana is not all. Leary has begun of late to assimilate the psychedelics to a bizarre form of psychic Darwinism which admits the tripper to a "new race" still in the process of evolution. LSD, he claims, is "the sacrament that will put you in touch with the ancient two million year old wisdom inside you"; it frees one "to go on to the next stage, which is the evolutionary timelessness, the ancient reincarnation thing that we always carry inside."[8] After this fashion, the "politics of ecstasy" become the wave of the future, moving in mysterious ways to achieve the social revolution. When Leary is criticized, as he often is, for preaching a form of a-political quietism, his critics overlook the fact that his pitch to the young actually makes ambitious political claims.

[7] *The Berkeley Barb*, June 30, 1967, p. 6.
[8] The quotations are from a 1967 British Broadcasting Company TV program called "The Mind Alchemists." The evolutionary doctrines are also scattered through Leary's recent book *The Politics of Ecstasy*. They also appear in an interview carried in the New York *Post Magazine*, September 14, 1967, p. 45.

The last few years [Leary tells us] I've been advising every-one to become an ecstatic saint. If you become an ecstatic saint, you then become a social force. . . . The key to the psychedelic movement, the key to what's going on with the young people today, is individual freedom. . . . Liberals and left-wing people, Marxists, are opposed to this individual pursuit. . . . They're attempting to wash out these seed-nific energies. We do go into action on the political or social chessboard to defend our individual internal freedom. . . . We're trying to tell the youngsters that the psychedelic move-ment is nothing new. . . . the hippies and the acid heads and the new flower tribes are performing a classic function. . . . The empire becomes affluent, urbanized, completely hung-up in material things, and then the new underground movements spring up. . . . They're all subversive. They all preach a message of turn-on, tune-in, drop-out.[9]

So, we are to believe, dosing on LSD and going under-ground is enough to transform society and re-route the course of history. Leary at his psychedelic arcadia in Millbrook, New York, is, despite all appearances to the contrary, in the van-guard of *the* revolution. "It will be an LSD country within fifteen years," Leary predicted in a 1967 BBC interview. "Our Supreme Court will be smoking marijuana within fifteen years. It's inevitable, because the students in our best universities are doing it now. There'll be less interest in warfare, in power politics. You know, politics today is a disease—it's a real ad-diction."

The "psychedelic revolution" then, comes down to the sim-ple syllogism: change the prevailing mode of consciousness and you change the world; the use of dope *ex opere operato* changes the prevailing mode of consciousness; therefore, uni-versalize the use of dope and you change the world.

[9] From an interview in the Southern California *Oracle*, October 1967. Leary now feels that the "dropout" stage for the young need not last longer than two years. See his *The Politics of Ecstasy*, p. 355.

When the promise of so much gets tied into the opportunity for unlimited free sexuality—which is a basic aspect of Leary's cult—is it any wonder the alienated young go for it headlong? "CAN the World Do Without LSD?" a feature in *The East Village Other* asks. "Here's where those who have and those who have not had LSD part company—at least as far as knowing what the subject under discussion is. . . . Can a person be human without LSD? Or, let us say, without THE PSYCHEDELIC experience? The answer, as far as the writer of this article can see, is a highly qualified, cautiously rendered, but emphatic, definitely NOT. BUT, . . ." (One breathes a sigh of relief for the qualifying "BUT." Perhaps, after all, there is some special dispensation through which Socrates, Shakespeare, Montaigne, Tolstoy, and the like may be granted their humanity.) "BUT, the psychedelic experience is not tied exclusively to LSD. There are at least five other effective psychedelic drugs." (No such luck.)

When the claims of psychedelia take on such proportions, one is surely justified in digging in one's heels and registering heated protest. But the trouble is: dope is not simply an excrescence that can be surgically removed from our youth culture by indignant rejection. Leary and his followers have succeeded in endowing it with such a mystique that it now seems the very essence of that politics of the nervous system in which the young are so deeply involved. And this is ironic in the extreme, because one could make an excellent case that the revolution which Leary purports to be leading is the most lugubrious of illusions.

Within a wider context, the quest of the young for psychedelic adventures begins to look like the symptom of a much larger social development, in which their rejected elders participate. The fact is: our society is well on its way toward becoming distressingly drug-dependent. The reliance on chemical agents to control the various functions of the organism is now a standard feature of what we regard as "health." During 1967, Americans consumed some 800,000 pounds of barbiturates—and then some ten billion amphetamine tablets to counteract the barbiturates. We are also given to understand that one out of four of our population uses tranquilizers regularly.[10] At a recent congress of the World Psychiatric Association held in London during November 1967, it was revealed that in Great Britain (with a population of about fifty million) a "staggering total" of over forty-three million prescriptions for psychotropic drugs was issued within a recent three-year period. And this total did *not* include the tranquilizers, anti-depressants, and sedatives used in general and mental hospitals or in private practice, but only those dispensed under the National Health Service.[11]

Speaking at the congress on the subject, Dr. William Sargent concluded that drugs were fast becoming the standard technique for dealing with anxiety and emotional disorder, largely replacing psychotherapy, psychoanalysis, or, needless to say, any attempt to alter the environmental factors that generate the suffering. The largest single group in this growingly drug-dependent population was identified, not as rebellious adolescents, but as older women who needed help falling asleep and settling their nerves.

Thus adjustments and functions that used to be left to the unaided human organism—sleeping, waking, relaxing, sexual potency, digestion, bowel movements—are being unloaded on an expanding repertory of chemical concoctions. Clearly, old-fashioned organic processes are not measuring up to the demands of contemporary civilization. This is, in plain point of fact, a damning indictment of contemporary civiliza-

[10] New York *Herald-Tribune* (International Edition), May 28, 1968.
[11] *The Guardian* (London), November 14, 1967.

tion, since whatever it is we are designing our environment for, it isn't the human being. But the most convenient way to meet such an unlivable state of affairs without thwarting technocratic values is, obviously, to patch up the organism with a congeries of pharmacological bandages. How many of us are there now who—for lack of time, for lack of tranquility—must look to a pill or an injection to bring off the most ordinary natural functions?

Within this framework, discussion of the psychedelics assumes a rather different significance. If our society is already committed to solving its psychic and organic problems with chemical agencies, then for how long can the line be drawn at the so-called "consciousness expanders"? Why *not* a pill or a needle to provide temporary emotional liberation and perceptual diversion? The public attitude on the issue already betrays a strange mixture of permissiveness and resistance. Amphetamine is familiar enough to the general public as the Benzedrine which many a harried student and fatigued executive uses without qualms to change his state of consciousness from drowsy to wakeful. LSD has met with no serious resistance in any quarter with respect to its professional use by therapists and researchers. If the public still withholds its tolerance for the unrestricted use of these drugs, its ambivalence must, to a considerable extent, be set down to an honest concern for the health hazard involved when the agents are used without some degree of knowledgeable discipline. The drugs are undeniably potent and the concern is legitimate. Even the underground press has begun to circulate the word that "speed (amphetamine) kills." As for marijuana, the objection against its use has become, as many impeccably straight individuals and groups have already admitted, increasingly inconsistent in a society which allows free use of alcohol.[12]

[12] See, for example, the remarks of Food and Drug Administra-

If the continuum of drugs on which our society is willing to let itself grow dependent has been interrupted at the psychedelics, I rather think it is, besides concern for the health hazard, because these substances have gotten associated in the public mind with the aggressive bohemianism of the young. Ironically, it may not be the young who have suffered public obloquy because of their association with the psychedelics; it may be the psychedelics that have suffered because of their association with troublesome youngsters. Unwilling to blame themselves for the alienation of their children, mother and father have decided to blame the drugs. So the psychedelics become the convenient scapegoat for the misbehavior of the young. And the more banners the young fly for dope, the more the adult society is hardened in its hostility to what is essentially an epiphenomenon of youthful rebellion. In the last analysis, the psychedelic line the disaffected young have chosen to fight on is a false one: there is nothing to be won or lost in the skirmish. It wasn't bootleg liquor that created the bohemianism of the "lost generation," and it isn't dope that has bred the beat-hip generation.

One begins to entertain suspicions about the supposedly revolutionary character of the psychedelic crusade when one realizes that publications as squarely conservative as *Life* and *Time*, whose lead our rebellious young would not follow three faltering steps in any other direction, were giving the psychedelics some very glamorous attention as far back as 1957. That was the year *Life* produced in its May 13 issue, a splashy and appetizing feature called "Seeking the Magic Mushroom." The authors were R. Gordon Wasson, a J. P. Morgan vice-president, and his wife. The piece recounted the visionary adventures they and a New York society photographer had had in 1955 among psilocybe cultists in darkest

tion commissioner Dr. James Goddard along these lines. New York *Times*, October 19, 1967, pp. 1, 51.

Mexico. The article, replete with detailed illustrations and descriptions of the mushrooms, made all the familiar connections with occult and oriental religions, and, bowing in the direction of William Blake's ecstatic verse, finished by assuring its readers "that the mushrooms make those visions available to a much larger number." Since then, the psychedelics have had a glowing press in *Time-Life, except* (significantly) where they have gotten mixed up with obstreperous bohemians.

Whatever its failings, the Luce press has pretty sound instincts regarding what the technocratic society can and can't assimilate. I suspect it shrewdly recognized that a nice private thrill pill would, if anything, come in handy as a means of maintaining some degree of emotional stability in the status quo. The young who take their psychedelic text from Huxley's *Doors of Perception* forget that in his *Brave New World* Huxley envisaged the unbearable being made bearable by a visionary chemical called "soma"—the purpose of which was to produce "sane men, obedient men, stable in their contentment."

Recently, when some young Englishmen, aided by a small number of radical psychiatrists, launched a group whose purpose it is to investigate the psychotropic drugs and "methods of altering consciousness in general," and to liberalize the narcotics laws in Great Britain, they appropriated the name SOMA for the organization: Society of Mental Awareness. I suspect they are tempting fate. For, on the face of it, it is difficult to see why the psychedelics cannot be assimilated to the requirements of the technocracy. Such an incorporation would seem to be an excellent example of Marcuse's "repressive desublimation." The historical record certainly suggests that it is precisely the role of narcotic agents to tame and stabilize. De Quincey, confessing his own sensational vice in the 1820s (and at the same time hinting wickedly at the prominence of opium eating among English aristocrats and artists of the day), was convinced that addiction flourished among the most long-suffering cotton-mill operatives. While the role of dope in dampening down social unrest in early industrial England has never been extensively researched, every historian of the period knows that it was common practice at the time for working mothers to start their children on the habit from the cradle by dosing the hungry babies heavily on laudanum ("mother's blessing" it was called).[13]

Later, at the turn of the century, during the stress of American industrialization, our country passed through a fit of narcotics addiction that probably has not since been surpassed, on a national scale at any rate. The main agent then was the morphine one could, until the passage of the Harrison Narcotics Act in 1914, enjoy in most of the pain-killers physicians then open-handedly prescribed. Even if one turns to the more bohemian narcotics connoisseurs of the mid-nineteenth century—like those who congregated around Théophile Gautier's *Club des Hachischins*—one is scarcely in the company of social revolutionaries. All the familiar visions are there in their reports—"the lilies of gold," "the myriad butterflies," "the fireworks display"—but as Baudelaire made clear, the "artificial paradise" was, at last, an escape "from the hopeless darkness of ordinary daily existence."[14] The language is

[13] Laudanum and morphine also claimed their victims at a more elite social level in England, numbering among their habitual users Coleridge, Dickens, Carlyle, Rossetti, Elizabeth Barrett Browning, and the poet laureate Tennyson. It is striking that Victorian society had little trouble in accepting serious addiction on the part of such luminaries, while contemporary Britain threatens its John Lennons and Mick Jaggers with severe punishment for toying with the comparatively more innocuous cannabis. Why? Is it not because these young pop stars represent an ethos of disaffiliation that is fiercely obnoxious to the adult society, and which makes the once-private vice a public outrage?

[14] Robert S. DeRopp, *Drugs and the Mind*, pp. 61–77.

loftier, but the sentiment is the same one would no doubt elicit from any of the miserable, bleary-eyed dockworkers of Hong Kong who consume their meager substance "chasing the dragon." And yet, if narcotics consumption is the measure, then it is Hong Kong, rather than San Francisco, that we would have to regard as the world's most "turned-on" city.

In the late fifties, an English writer underwent a series of LSD sessions which were later written up and published under the pseudonym "Jane Dunlap."[15] One forms the impression, from the gushy and saccharine style, that Miss Dunlap is the sort of writer whose creations ordinarily come blazing out of the pages of the *Ladies' Home Journal*. Still, Miss Dunlap in her experiments with LSD is, I fear, a great deal more typical of the ordinary user than either an Aldous Huxley or an Allen Ginsberg. If so, the chances seem pretty slim that the psychedelic society for which Timothy Leary and his disciples are crusading is going to qualify as a cultural renaissance.

Miss Dunlap had heard about LSD by way of the Wasson feature in *Life*—a magazine whose "many excellent articles" she has admired and collected since its very first issue. She volunteered herself forthwith for a run of psychedelic sessions at the local university and proceeded to dictate reports of her revelations, which sound for all the world like an autistic collage of Jules Verne, Flash Gordon, and Nick Kenny. Already in Miss Dunlap's experiments one has the off-putting sense that she is finding what she feels she is *supposed* to look for, and that the experience is falling into a kitschy mold. "I saw the tiny grasses bend in prayer, the flowers dance in the breeze, and the trees lift their arms to God." And so on, and on . . . while the music in the background is, inevitably, "Ave Maria." By the time we reach Jane Dunlap, the psy-

[15] Jane Dunlap, *Exploring Inner-Space: Personal Experiences under LSD-25* (London: Gollancz, 1961).

chedelic breakthrough is well on its way to becoming a band-wagon. The visionary adventure that was supposed to vault ordinary humanity to the heights of Blake and Wordsworth has been scaled down to the cultural level of Forest Lawn's plaster reproductions of Michelangelo's David. And what could the most oppressive powers-that-be take exception to in a chemical that guides the Miss Dunlaps of the world to the consoling conclusion that "to one who accepts the God-pull of reversed gravity and maintains a geological time sense, the future seems gloriously bright"?

Why should not the technocratic society accept into its arsenal of social controls methods of emotional release as sophisticated as the psychedelics? An occasional turn-on, a periodic orgy, a weekend freak-out . . . what threat do such private kicks pose to the established order—provided always that they do not become associated with disruptive forms of dissent? The brainstormers at RAND have already flirted with the notion of introducing tranquilizers and sedatives into the most hideously repressive of situations—life in the post-attack fallout shelter—as a means of draining off the pressure of desperation.[16] Why not the psychedelics as well?

Moreover, one must bear in mind that a deal of narcotics is already being widely used, though with much more discretion than by the bohemian young, by very respectable citizens. Purged of its social nonconformity, it is becoming an integral part of the swinging society—like wife swapping in suburbia or the topless cocktail waitress. I know that within my own circle of acquaintances the number of those who indulge in private little trips—just for the fun of it—grows constantly. But it all has nothing to do with radical social or cultural attitudes. The practice is simply another safety valve.

[16] Herman Kahn, "Some Specific Suggestions for Achieving Early Non-Military Defense Capabilities," RAND Corporation Research Memo, RM-2206-RC, 1959, p. 48.

If anything, it allows one to bear up under any grim business-as-usual with a bit less anxiety.

What if the psychedelic boosters had their way then, and American society could get legally turned on? No doubt the marijuana trade would immediately be taken over by the major cigarette companies—which would doubtless be an improvement over leaving it in the hands of the Mafia. (It would not be surprising to discover that all the little "Legalize Pot" buttons are being turned out by American Tobacco: the business would be worth a billion dollars.) And surely the major pharmaceutical houses would move in on LSD just as readily. And what then? Would the revolution have been achieved? Would we suddenly find ourselves blessed with a society of love, gentleness, innocence, freedom? If that were so, what should we have to say about ourselves regarding the integrity of our organism? Should we not have to admit that the behavioral technicians have been right from the start? That we are, indeed, the bundle of electrochemical circuitry they tell us we are—and not persons at all who have it in our nature to achieve enlightenment by native ingenuity and a deal of hard growing.

"Better Things For Better Living Through Chemistry." So reads one of the prominent hippy buttons, quoting E. I. Du Pont. But the slogan isn't being used satirically. The wearers mean it the way Du Pont means it. The gadget-happy American has always been a figure of fun because of his facile assumption that there exists a technological solution to every human problem. It only took the great psychedelic crusade to perfect the absurdity by proclaiming that personal salvation and the social revolution can be packed in a capsule.

Chapter VI

EXPLORING UTOPIA:
THE VISIONARY SOCIOLOGY OF
PAUL GOODMAN

A middle-aged man—a novelist and social critic—is watching several kids play a game of "down the river" in a busy city street. In particular, his eyes fall admiringly on a seventeen-year old boy who has organized the game and who is his homosexual partner. The boy is a college dropout, a gifted social misfit in a society that cannot make place for his irrepressible, if tactless, honesty. But he knows how to organize a ball game and can lose himself gracefully in the spontaneous fun of the little community of players that has crystallized around him. And for this quality especially, the man loves him. The game gathers pace, taking on the beauty of lively young bodies immersed in play. But then the shop owner whose wall has been appropriated for the game appears and, for no sensible reason, calls in a cop to disperse the kids. The man does not, and the boy cannot, stand up to the cop's authority. The kids scatter. The boy turns on the man accusingly for having failed to take on the cop, for having "betrayed natural society." Afraid that the boy will go sour-cynical, the man skillfully maneuvers their confrontation through tears, outrage, sardonic humor. And yet the man himself is stricken with a shame and powerlessness that must be vented. That night he is scheduled to broadcast a social commentary over New York's listener subscription radio station. The subject he chooses is the metropolitan traffic problem, and he enters an impassioned plea for outlawing private automobiles from the city and giving the streets back to the natural activities of play and leisure. He also produces a practical proposal to that end.

The scene is from Paul Goodman's 1967 novel, *Making Do*. Located in the middle of a work of fiction, the chapter is called "Banning the Cars from New York" and is a serious treatment of that issue. Surrounded by fictitious characters, the central figure, the middle-aged social critic, is pure autobiography. Thus the scene, like the book as a whole, is a peculiar mix of the actual and the imaginary, which, in the small space of a single incident, neatly distills much of what Paul Goodman is all about. Focusing on a spontaneous and joyous human activity, the civic issue builds up from the problems of children. The wide-ranging social analysis is rooted in the thwarted animal needs of young bodies at play. The philanthropic care for society emerges from a man's physical love for a boy. The man and the boy in their confrontation relate as Gestalt therapist to patient, channeling their anger and frustration into a rough and immediate give and take aimed at producing tears and then humor. The man's political *modus operandi* is precise intellectual discourse via an anarchist radio station. The initial object of his practical proposal is the reclamation of the city, of a particular city—New York—in order that it might become a human community once again. And behind the contemporary scene there looms the Socratic paradigm: the wise citizen loitering in the agora to play mentor to a youth he loves body and soul, and in whom the future of the polis resides.

So the incident ends with the bittersweet credo: "This I did with all my will and apparently indefatigably (but I will one day drop with weariness)—I invented a different practical world that made no sense and took the heart out of me. Instead of resigning, I reacted, in moments of despair, by thinking up something else, and behaving as if this more pleasing landscape might indeed come to be the case."

*   *   *   *

Where and how does one begin to understand a figure as complex as Paul Goodman? His writing embraces poetry and fiction, literary and social criticism, city planning, psychotherapy, political theory, education, and economics. In all these areas he is a figure to be reckoned with, if for no other reason than that, whatever his subject matter, Goodman writes a style that annoys its way into being taken seriously. There runs through his work a quality of aggressive, wised-up cunning that never fails to lay a shrewd polemical edge against some vulnerable nerve of our conventional wisdom. His prevailing tone of argumentation is a wry "you've got it all wrong from the ground up," accompanied by an even more vexatious willingness to begin our education then and there from scratch. But Goodman knows how to be fruitfully vexatious about every issue he turns to—rather in the same way Socrates knew how to use outrage to force an opponent back from stuffy cocksureness to first principles.

The young, whose champion Goodman has wearily but willingly become, know him for the most part by way of his essays and lectures in social criticism. But if we begin, as we do here, with Goodman the novelist, it is because Goodman understands himself primarily as a novelist (and poet). His social thought reaches out from his creative work and takes its distinctive style from it. Indeed, if there is one piece of Goodman's writing that seems guaranteed to endure, it is his mammoth social-philosophical novel *The Empire City*, which, like *Making Do*, takes as its theme the frustrated aspiration of youth in quest of education. The several episodes of *The Empire City* span some seventeen years of Goodman's career (from 1941 to 1958). A sprawling compendium which mingles novel and pamphlet, treatise and reportage, the book serves as his running commentary on the steep American ascent to Empire as seen from the vantage point of a tiny communitarian circle surviving by its wits and the public welfare in megapolitan New York. What better way could there be to delineate and dramatize the flesh-and-blood implications of our emergent *Weltpolitik* than to immerse oneself in the plight of such sensitive human material?

Not only does the situation allow Goodman to develop an existential sociology of American society; from the imaginary perspective of his group of natural-born anarchists, Goodman was able to discern as early as the mid-forties the regime of kid-glove technocratic manipulation that would characterize our postwar life. Here, for example, is the incisive prediction which appears in a section of *The Empire City*, published in 1947; it is delivered by the ghost of the supercapitalist, Eliphaz, the last of the self-made men.

Sociolatry is the period when the great society that has inherited itself from me will be organized for the good of all, and will coordinate unchanged its wonderful productive capacities to heighten continually the Standard of Living. You will buy many expensive things that you do not absolutely need. . . .

Next, the great society will turn to assure the psychological well-being of most of its members. This is called "the education for democracy in the conditions of mass industrialization." This is the Sociolatry.

It is the adjustment of the individual to a social role without releasing any new forces of nature. . . . Please, I am not speaking of a crude regimentation but of a conformity with universal tolerance and intelligent distinction as among the collegians at Yale. Each person will warrant individual attention, for there is a man fitted, with alterations, for every job. . . .[1]

The recurrent chorus throughout the prophecy runs: "And millions will fall down on the streets of the Asphyxiation." Sure enough: no sooner is the fortune of the society told than Goodman's heroine, the stalwart Laura, swoons to death of sheer desperation at the oppressive prospect. Not only do novelists make better political weather vanes than our social scientists, they calculate the human costs with more precision.

It is essentially from his literary background that Goodman brings the gift of vision to his criticism, the inexhaustible capacity to imagine new social possibilities. Where our conventional sociology settles, in an attitude of premature senility, for analyzing structures and rearranging functions, Goodman restores social innovation to a position of preeminence. It is hardly surprising that one who thinks as a novelist and poet should do so. The artist who sets about making a critique of social ills is bound to play the role of utopian: one who cannot, like the academic sociologist, allow the grim tyranny of established fact to monopolize the discussion of human potentialities.

If Goodman's *Communitas* (his first major social statement, written in collaboration with his architect brother, Percival, in 1947) is the best study of city planning to come out of postwar America, it is not only because the critique insists on treating the problems of the city as an integral part of the national economy, but mainly because the spirit of artistry hovers over the book from start to finish. There is wit, there is satirical bite, there is the power of vivid imagery. Only a novelist could have depicted the impending idiocy

[1] Paul Goodman, *The Empire City* (New York: Macmillan, paper, 1964), p. 277.

of our postwar affluence as Goodman did in his projected "City of Efficient Consumption": one colossal department store whose citizen-shoppers indulge at the end of each year in a Walpurgis Night of riotous destruction which clears away the inventories and ungluts the economy. The city emerges from the pages of *Communitas* not as a depersonalized amalgam of technicalities—real estate values, traffic and utilities control, zoning legalities, etc.—but rather as the arena of human drama: "a choreography of society in motion and in rest." Thus the city becomes a background against which people loom large and primary in their erratic, inventive search for organic and spiritual fulfillment. Which is the city as a novelist sees it: life foremost—as Balzac saw Paris, as Joyce saw Dublin, as Dickens saw London. At once we realize that, compared to human community as Goodman discusses it, what passes for "city planning" in our society is a species of low-level gadgeteering. Lacking the utopian vision Goodman brings to the subject, we have no "city" and no "planning" but only bureaucratic tinkering within the disintegrating status quo.

Inevitably, the utopian theorist, in the lethargy of postwar America, finds his audience among the disaffiliated young. For it is the young, in their desperate need to grow up sanely amid an insane environment, who hunger for lively alternatives. To be sure, the depth and complexity of Goodman's thought deserves an audience of greater maturity. But where is it to be found? In October 1967, Goodman was by some weird happenstance invited to address a conference of the National Security Industrial Association, the adult power structure of the warfare state, official bulwark of the middle-class American consensus in behalf of cold war, arms race, and rampant proliferation of technical prowess. Being responsible adults endowed lavishly with the power and treasure of the nation, the conferees *should* have taken Goodman's words to heart as serious matter for discussion, even though his proposal was that the association phase itself out of existence as rapidly as possible. Of course they *should* have. But of course they didn't, as Goodman well knew they wouldn't. He did not, therefore, speak primarily to them or for them. And when he reached his conclusion—" . . . we believe . . . that [your] way of life itself is unnecessary, ugly, and un-American . . . we cannot condone your present operations; they should be wiped off the slate"—he was inevitably greeted by shouts of "Who are *we?*" His answer: "*We* are I and those people outside." And who were the "people outside" for whom the country's leading social theorist had now assumed the role of spokesman? They were a contingent of college students whom Goodman had invited to picket the auditorium during his presentation.[2]

Again and again Goodman bemoans the fact, but at last his force as a public voice derives from his "crazy young allies." Whenever he speaks one feels for sure there is a contingent of the young somewhere nearby already inscribing his words on a banner.

But it is not Goodman's utopianism alone that has made him the foremost tribune of our youthful counter culture. "Mad Ireland," Auden said, speaking of Yeats, "hurt him into poetry." So mad America hurt the poet Goodman not simply into political analysis, but into political activism. Goodman's criticism, like that of C. Wright Mills, is shot through with the imperative need to "*do* something" about the mess at hand. His utopianism functions as the hypothesis of a true pragmatism, the beginning of a real project. This urgent effort to marry action to idea has not only won him the allegiance of young radicals, but has served as a highly important discipline upon the mindlessness toward which they

[2] Paul Goodman, "A Message to the Military-Industrial Complex," *Peace News* (London), December 15, 1967.

weaken. This youthful restiveness with talk and thought—
the desire to get on with the picketing and demonstrating
and sitting-in—is obviously a reaction against the academicism
of many social critics who, despite their own spleen, have
been content to settle for a good analysis and some verbal
sniping.

Goodman, in contrast, has been the example of an intellectual in whom *both* precise, even scholarly, thought *and*
radical action can reside. He has shown that the delicate balance can be held gracefully. In an essay of the early sixties
on "The Ineffectuality of Some Intelligent People," Goodman coined the phrase "a practical syllogism" to illustrate
the intellectual paralysis of the time. "I need an X," the
academic critic says. And his analysis leads him to the conclusion, "Here is an X." Then *take* it, Goodman urges, and
use it.[3] Is it a "general strike for peace" we need? During
such a strike in 1961, Goodman was on the street outside
Random House picketing his own publisher. Is it a new form
of university we need? Very well, then: Goodman ends his
critique of higher education in *The Community of Scholars*
with the call for a mass defection from the universities and
for the establishment of new dissenting academies—a "something" that can be done *now*. The defection has since taken
place, spilling over into the many free universities that are
springing up across the land, and Goodman was on hand
at one of the best of them, San Francisco State's "Experimental College," to offer a year of his time in residence.
Most recently, he has been among those who, like Dr. Spock,
have been willing to place their own fortunes and sacred
honor behind the student draft-resisters. The contribution
he has made by such activity is inestimably great. For if the
essential values of intellect are to be preserved among a

[3] The essay appears in Paul Goodman, *Drawing the Line* (New
York: Random House, 1962), pp. 97–111.

disaffiliated youth who tend heavily toward action and non-intellective modes of consciousness, the job will be done by those intellectuals who have demonstrated that thought is not sheerly "academic," but the concomitant of principled action.

* * * *

There is another major reason why Goodman has caught on among the young. As we have seen, the counter culture provides a limited market for the Old Left ideologies with their final appeal to the metaphysics of the class conflict and their primary commitment to institutional reorganization. The fascination of the young for exotic religion and narcotics is a symptom of their quest for some new foundation that can support a program of radical social change. Accordingly, sociology has been forced to yield progressively to psychology as the generative principle of revolution. And here again Goodman makes a distinctive and significant contribution.

In 1951, well before he had made much of a mark as a social critic, Goodman contributed his lengthy theoretical section to the textbook *Gestalt Therapy*.[4] It is probably among the least read of his writings; it is certainly one of his most demanding; but it is perhaps one of his most important. For the ground of Goodman's style of thought lies as much in his work as a Gestalt therapist as in his novels. It is Gestalt psychiatry which provides the skeletal structure of any "system" Goodman's thought possesses.

It would be difficult to do full justice to Gestalt here. Both in theory and practice, it remains one of the most controversial schools of post-Freudian psychotherapy—perhaps for no reason more than that it makes a determined effort to integrate the psychoanalytic tradition with a sensibility

[4] Perls, Hefferline, and Goodman, *Gestalt Therapy*.

that derives essentially from oriental mysticism. Mixing oil and water might be a less formidable project. I will try simply to draw out four major characteristics of Gestalt which one finds echoed throughout Goodman's writings and which seem to be preceisely the kind of first principles the counter culture is moving toward.

(1) There is, first of all, the mystical "wholism" which the therapy inherits from Gestalt theories of perception. For the Gestaltists, perceptions are not piecemeal impressions printed by the "objective" world on the passive wax of the senses, but rather patterned wholes which are created by a strange and beautiful collaboration between the perceiver and the perceived. Generalizing this rich insight to life as a whole, Gestalt therapists envision a purposive give and take between every organism and its environment which has the same inexplicable spontaneity and self-regulation as the process of perception. Just as visual figures are co-operatively drawn against a ground by the seer and the seen, so, within their field, organism and environment are understood to be in a constant natural dialogue, an ongoing series of "creative adjustments" which make man at home in his body, his community, his natural habitat.

It is not the case, therefore, that the body need be *made* to function, that human beings need be *made* sociable, that nature need be *made* to support life. For the Gestaltist, individual and social neurosis sets in only when the seamless garment of the "organism/environment field" is divided by a psychic factionalism that segregates from the ecological whole a unit of defensive consciousness that must be pitted against an "external" reality understood to be alien, intractable, and, finally, hostile.

The sign of this losing of faith in self-regulating processes is the construction of an alienated self which fearfully retreats from the "outside world" and progressively diminishes in size until, at last, it is envisioned as some manner of homunculus besieged within the skull, manipulating the body as if it were an unwieldy apparatus, feverishly devising strategies of defense and attack. At this point, instead of spontaneous adjustment—what Goodman calls the "free interplay of the faculties"—we have a compulsive deliberateness and an aggressive urge to regiment all that which was originally merged in the unitary field: "others," "nature," "the body," "the passions," the "irrational." Health, which is properly a matter of letting the chips of life fall where they may, a trustful yielding to the needs and urges of body, community, nature, now becomes a matter of piecemeal cerebral organization via pills, dieting, authoritarian doctoring, etc. —all of which seem to finish by producing a degree of iatrogenic disease greater than any illness that existed in the unitary state of the organism/environment field. At last, we are left wondering how life ever survived before there was a civilized brain to watch out for it. But we find no answer, because the primordial "wisdom of the body" has hopelessly eluded us. We have lost touch with the self-regulation of a symbiotic system and have given over to a compulsive need to control, under pressure of which the organism freezes up and seems to become inutterably stupid. The major therapeutic technique of Gestalt, therefore, is an ingenious form of directed physical activity which aims at locating and thawing frozen organic energy.

Gestalt, then, finds the secret of health in the sub-intellective processes which, if left to their own ingenuity, take care of themselves. The culmination of healthy functioning is the moment of "final contact," during which "the deliberateness, the sense of 'I', spontaneously vanishes into the concern, and then boundaries are unimportant, for one contacts not a boundary but the touched, the known, the enjoyed, the made."[5] And then we achieve a spontaneity of thought, action, creation which approaches "the spontaneous pelvic movement before orgasm, and the spasm, or the spontaneous swallowing of food that has been well liquefied and tasted."[6]

It is easy enough to see how Gestalt's bad politics of the nervous system can then be projected into the surrounding social system. If one loses faith in the natural processes of body and emotion, one quickly loses faith in human sociability. *Everything* must then be *made* to happen properly and supervised at every turning by "experts." The state becomes the domineering brain of the body politic, which is also taken to be recalcitrant and stupid. The resultant authoritarianism will scarcely yield to a readjustment of institutions or restructuring of social classes. That, most likely, leads only to a change of managerial personnel. The problem has a metaphysical origin, stemming from a misconception of nature and of man's role within it.

Now, I think this Gestaltist conception of reality is true, but it is also fundamentally mysterious—by which I mean it is extremely difficult to find words that capture the elusiveness of the ideas. For one thing, in speaking of the Gestaltist "field," one's language must become trans-personal. Since it is the total ecological pattern, not the self, which the Gestaltists postulate as basic, one cannot speak of personal agencies which *do* this, or *cause* that. Rather, one must imagine processes happening of their own accord, producing the numberless symbiotic patterns and balances we call "nature," and among them that pattern of mind, body, and society we call human consciousness. Thus one recognizes that Gestalt theory is, fundamentally, a species of Taoism disguised rather

[5] *Gestalt Therapy*, p. 447.
[6] Ibid., p. 417.

cumbersomely as Western psychiatry. What is this "organism/environment field," after all, but Lao-tzu's *Way?* Goodman himself turns to the mystic tradition more than once to present a Gestalt idea. How do people lessen the pain of suffering? "By finally 'standing out of the way,' to quote the great formula of Tao. They disengage from their preconceptions of how it 'ought' to turn out. And into the 'fertile void' thus formed, the solution comes flooding."[7] Surely much of the charm the young discover in Goodman's thinking derives from its subtle underlying connection with the oriental mysticism that has enjoyed so much youthful popularity in the postwar period.

(2) One of Goodman's most distinctive and refreshing traits as a social critic is his irksome habit of arguing issues *ad hominem*—a characteristic which draws strongly on his experience as a Gestalt therapist. Unless one is on the receiving end of this tactic, it is an exciting new approach to public discussion. Here, for example, is Goodman commenting on John Kennedy's telltale predilection for words like "discipline," "sacrifice," "challenge":

It is the . . . moral Catholicism of the little boy who disciplines himself from masturbating and checks off his victorious days on the calendar. Masturbating proves you are weak and makes you weak. In this context, "challenge" is the kind of strenuous excitement possible to persons who, having given up their internal spontaneity, rally to an external demand . . . The sense of duty does not seem to be [Kennedy] himself, but his submissive—and evasive—obedience to some grownups; one who is not convinced of his moral courage.[8]

This is the intellectual counterpart of hitting below the belt, and it is not at all polite. But, in fact, it summarizes

[7] *Gestalt Therapy*, pp. 358–59.
[8] From the essay "The Devolution of Democracy," *Drawing the Line*, p. 68.

Kennedy more accurately than any analysis of policy or program could. And, in any case, it is the sort of style one must expect a psychotherapist to bring to bear on public argument.

The significance of this "contextual method of argument," as the Gestaltists call it, is that it short-circuits a deal of intellectual banter that may be totally beside the point and at once personalizes the debate—though perhaps painfully. It is a mode of intellectuality which brings into play the non-intellective substructure of thought and action. Goodman explains the technique in this way:

. . . a merely "scientific" refutation by adducing contrary evidence is pointless, for [the opponent] does not *experience* that evidence with its proper weight . . . Then the only useful method of argument is to bring into the picture the total context of the problem, including the conditions of experiencing it, the social milieu and the personal "defenses" of the observer. That is, to subject the opinion and his holding of it to a gestalt-analysis. . . . We are sensible that this is a development of the argument *ad hominem*, only much more offensive, for we not only call our opponent a rascal and therefore in error, but we also charitably assist him to mend his ways![9]

This is the principle underlying what one might well mistake in much of Goodman's debate and writing for a callous kind of one upmanship—which is what the technique does indeed degenerate into when inexpert hands take it over. It is easy to see how appealing such a style would be to a generation that had grown dubious about the reliability of speech, and had already attuned itself to "hearing" the character hidden behind the inarticulate grunts and shrugs of a James Dean and Marlon Brando. It was also bound to strike home with the New Left students, given their wise sus-

[9] Perls, Hefferline, and Goodman, *Gestalt Therapy*, p. 243.

picion of the ideology mongering that has always characterized radical politics, and their soulful search for personal honesty.

Goodman's special awareness of the sub-verbal level of speech—the significance not only of *what* is said, but of *how* it is said—contributes to that unadorned, offhand speaking style which has proved so attractive to student audiences. Where the usual academic posture is stilted, remote, defensively masked in a narrow expertise, Goodman comes on as a whole and vulnerable man. As if to say, "the truth is as much a matter of what I *am* as of what I *know*. So I will show you what I am"—thus opening himself to be addressed *ad hominem*. Such honesty usually puts to shame Goodman's professorial and official interlocutors by calling into question at once the protective formalities and role playing of public debate.

On the other hand, an inevitable and off-putting adjunct of this psychologizing approach is the irresistible need to lay bare the secrets of one's *own* heart in the name of candor. On Goodman's part, such psychic disarmament has led to a great deal of confessional outpouring (his journal *Five Years* is a particularly heartrending example)—as it has on the part of most of the beat-hip writers. Being a public figure in the counter culture means having very little that is private. Which can lead to a winsome kind of innocence, no doubt. But it can be such an embarrassment to find oneself sucked into other people's soul-searching: do they want you to respond with praise? shock? pity? love? or disgraceful confessions of your own? Or are you simply functioning as a sounding-board? Certainly this shameless letting down of the hair accounts for the vulnerability of beat-hip bohemianism to sensationalizing publicity. But then it may be that the most strategic bastion of traditional values the counter culture is attacking is precisely the bourgeois Christian pride in a well-developed guilty conscience.

(3) An especially significant feature of Gestalt is the dignity it confers on the predatory aspects of human nature. While traditional psychiatry confronts aggressiveness with suspicion or resistance, usually interpreting it as a prime pathological symptom, Gestalt readily embraces it in its natural manifestations and seeks to give it freedom. In Gestalt therapy, the practice is not to talk the patient around and out of the destructive violence he feels within himself, but rather to let him experience it deeply by way of vivid display, so that he might come to accept its necessary presence. The object is not to de-fuse the submerged charge of aggression, but to detonate it. The patient may be induced to deliver an infuriated scream or a good animal growl, or to undertake a kicking and punching session. In this way, the aggressiveness—bred of frustration, resentment, justified anger, hatred—that has been stored away in this or that dark corner of the organism has the chance to enjoy release.

Our society frowns on such displays of strong feeling, contending that they are bad manners or childish outbursts. Goodman shrewdly retorts that we are wrong to believe that children who howl or explode with disappointment have "no way to handle their anger." Kids get the potent emotion out of their system and bounce back quickly. It is we sternly self-controlled adults who have no successful way of handling our violent feelings. We stoically lock them away inside us, forming ulcers around them . . . or a variety of other diseases (including myopia and toothache) which Gestalt interprets as psychogenic. When we behave in such gentlemanly fashion, we overlook the fact that the human being carries forward from his prehistoric past a long career of predation and risk taking during which speed, strength, and aggressive cunning were as much a part of normal behavior as the tenderer emotions. Where is the juice and passion of this heritage supposed to have gone since the recent advent of civilized social ethics? Increasingly the disciplined urban environments of the technocracy restrict this side of our nature, forcing us into becoming mere spectators of competitive physical prowess on playing fields or television screens. When civilized men watch the abandoned rituals of some primitive societies, they tend not to see the outlet as healthy, but as savagely backward. But they may fail to register with any sense of horror the far more dangerous savagery that fills our highways, one of the few remaining arenas of predatory competition.

In Goodman's novels, human aggressiveness is always frankly given its place. Even when he allows the urge to turn destructively violent, Goodman handles it with an understanding receptivity. The effect is not sensationalistic, because Goodman never isolates the violence. He dignifies it by relating it convincingly to strong human need, even to high idealism. In *The Empire City*, the pacifist draft-dodger, Lothair, nearly mad with desperation, conjures up a plan to release the animals from the city zoo. Pacifist though he is, Lothair also needs to feel violence; but he cannot take satisfaction in the impersonal violence of world war. So he hits on a symbolic way of recreating the state of nature. He frees the lions and they half devour the infant son of one of the novel's heroines. At another point in the novel, the children of the city, evacuated during the war to the safety of the countryside, break out in a campaign of destruction and arson against the local farm properties. Goodman presents the episode indulgently as the unavoidable and ultimately beneficial response of urban kids to the sudden release of open country: "There is plenty of fuel for celebration for a long time when laborious people have for several generations been accumulating it in fences and houses."

More often in his novels, Goodman gives aggressiveness free expression in displays of athletic prowess. Episodes of raucous play can achieve an almost epic scale in the Goodman novels, as in the case of the boy-hero Horatio's great bicycle ride through New York in *The Empire City*.[10] It is a big moment, full of brash adolescent disruption, a bold street adventure expertly pulled off by a shrewd young cyclist willing to wager life and limb against his skill. Goodman's writing fairly glows with delight in such passages, when suddenly amid the claustrophobic congestion of the metropolis something of the old forest wilds opens up and the perfervid talents of the chase can be exercised again.

(4) Finally, there is the image of human nature which Gestalt offers when, at last, it must produce a therapeutic standard.

Now, every monistic system suffers for lack of a satanic principle—and Gestalt therapy is no exception. Sooner or later one must ask how it can come about that the natural and healthful unity of the organism/environment field becomes undone. Which is to ask how nature can produce an "unnatural" state of affairs. One must give Goodman credit for having the uncommon courage to unfold the theory of his school ambitiously and honestly enough to show up its ultimate conundrum. Yet the terms "natural" and "unnatural," derived from the Gestalt system, are the key words in his critical vocabulary—and one cannot help wanting some clearer understanding of their import than Goodman provides.

Take, for example, Goodman's style of pacifism, which oscillates delicately between the poles "natural-unnatural." He approves of fistfights "because that's natural." On the other hand, "war is unnatural violence," because it does not "liberate natural associations and release social inventiveness, but

10 Pp. 111–13.

on the contrary reinforces the coercive and authoritarian establishment." So too, Goodman finds that the non-violence of "doctrinal pacifists is unnatural and even somewhat wicked," because it is "a spiteful stalling to exacerbate guilt. Anger is at least contactful; and it seems false not to let anger follow through and strike."[11]

But even if these discriminations command one's sympathies, they are bound to be confusing. Since Gestalt begins by postulating a primal unity which is spontaneously self-regulating, it must of necessity defend the universality of nature. Nature must emerge always as the all-embracing whole that comprehends disease as well as health, destruction as well as creation, war as well as fistfights. Therefore, what can the terms "natural" and "unnatural" possibly mean?

When Goodman at last faces this central paradox in *Gestalt Therapy*, his response is startlingly blunt.

. . . "human nature" is a potentiality. It can be known only as it has been actualized in achievement and history, and as it makes itself today.

The question may quite seriously be asked, by what criterion does one prefer to regard "human nature" as what is actual in the spontaneity of children, in the works of heroes, the culture of classic eras, the community of simple folk, the feeling of lovers, the sharp awareness and miraculous skill of some people in emergencies? Neurosis is also a response of human nature and is now epidemic and normal, and perhaps has a viable social future.

We cannot answer the question.[12]

The evasion is strange, for the "criterion" is obvious enough. The behavior of children, heroes, lovers, "simple folk," and people in crisis is beautiful and ethically inspiring. It is,

[11] "The May Pamphlet," *Drawing the Line*, pp. 26–27.
[12] Perls, Hefferline, and Goodman, *Gestalt Therapy*, p. 319.

certainly for Goodman, the stuff of great art. The Gestalt criterion of health, like *every* criterion of health, is a moral-aesthetic one. Goodman the Gestalt therapist leads us back to Goodman the poet and novelist, searching for a notion of humanity around which he can weave the tensions of deep drama. That gives us a clear criterion; it is the sensibility of the artist. What it fails to give is an etiology of organic discord.

(There is a lengthy discussion in Goodman's well-known "May Pamphlet" of 1945 of natural and unnatural violence, in which all the distinctions are clear enough—and well argued. But, again, there is no etiology. We have no account of how primordial nature undoes and reverses itself so that some of its issue can legitimately be called "unnatural." The terms seem finally to come down to being Goodman's synonyms for "beautiful-ugly," "noble-base." Perhaps, in the face of so deep an issue, we must settle for that, and trust to the wisdom of a sensitive soul. If one objects that this lowers the terms to a non-scientific status, we should reply, I think, that it actually *raises* them to a moral-aesthetic status. For, after all, science is not everything, and in fact, is not very much at all when it comes to creating a creditable way of life for ourselves.)

At the root of Goodman's thinking, then, we find a mystical psychology whose conception of human nature sides aesthetically and ethically with the non-intellective spontaneity of children and primitives, artists and lovers, those who can lose themselves gracefully in the splendor of the moment. It is indeed one of the controversial glories of Gestalt that it has, against the entire psychiatric tradition since Freud, with its grim demand for conformity to a joyless conception of adulthood, asserted the nobility and healthiness of the child and the artist.

The childish feelings are important [Goodman tells us, and puts the observation in italics] *not as a past that must be undone, but as some of the most beautiful powers of adult life that must be recovered: spontaneity, imagination, directness of awareness and manipulation. . . .* "Maturity," precisely among those who claim to be concerned with "free personality", is conceived in the interest of an unnecessarily tight adjustment to a dubiously valuable workaday society, regimented to pay its debts and duties.[13]

Thus, well before either the beats or hippies had begun to sabotage the middle-class American "reality principle," Goodman the Gestalt therapist was laying the theoretical foundation of the great dropout.

* * * *

The life that Gestalt theory leads Goodman to consider healthy is clearly not livable in our existing social order. Far from it. The technocracy rejects spontaneity, self-regulation, animal impulsiveness as if they were so much poison in the body politic, preferring instead goals and behavior that can be expressed in vast, abstract magnitudes: national power (measured in units of overkill), high productivity and efficient mass marketing (measured as the GNP), the space race, the elaboration of administrative systems, etc. For the technocrat, more is always better. Wherever there is more input and more output—it does not matter what is being put in or put out—bombs, students, information, freeways, personnel, publications, goods, services—we have the sure sign of progress. The brutal incompatibility of such a fanatically quantitative ethos with the qualitative life-needs of the person is the basic theme of Goodman's novels. They are stories in which people who want to be people must continually

[13] *Gestalt Therapy*, p. 297.

"draw the line" against the depersonalized technocracy for the sake of defending their embattled humanity.

We see that in fact everybody who still has life and energy is continually manifesting some natural force and is today facing an unnatural coercion. And now, in some apparently trivial issue that nevertheless is a key, he *draws the line!* The next step for him to take is not obscure or difficult, it presents itself at once; it is even forcibly presented by Society! Modern society does not let one be—it is too total—it forces one's hand.[14]

The adamant defender of law and order, the "political realist," will seize upon such anarchist sentiments at once as evidence that Goodman harbors some impossibly rosy conception of human nature. Perhaps, with deep melancholy, he will quote Machiavelli, *If* men were all good . . . but as they are bad . . ."

Such bitter wisdom misses the point of the anarchist critique, however. Certainly it overlooks the complexity of Goodman's vision, which, as a novelist's vision must, spreads itself wide to grasp human character whole and without illusions. No one in a Goodman novel is ever easily set down as angel or devil, fool or wise man. Instead, Goodman continually plays off the splendors and follies of his people against one another. Elements of resourcefulness and nobility continually shine through the most unlikely characters; but conversely, all of Goodman's heroes turn out to be hopeless "fuck-ups," incapable of realizing their finest potentialities except for briefly splendid moments of love, sport, or sudden daring. It is for such fleeting glories that Goodman watches keenly; and then he cheers his people on exuberantly, but always with the underlying pathos of one who knows that the moment

[14] Goodman, *Drawing the Line*, pp. 8–9.

will pass into folly or even disaster. And yet, *what* a moment! Perhaps such moments are what life is all about.

It is out of this all-embracing conception of human nature that Goodman draws his communitarianism: not from the supposition that men are incarnate angels, but from the realization that only a social order built to the human scale permits the free play and variety out of which the unpredictable beauties of men emerge. But conversely (and here is the anarchist insight so frequently ignored) it is only a society possessing the elasticity of decentralized communities that can absorb the inevitable fallibilities of men. For where we have big systems run from the musclebound center, the blunders of the custodians will surely reverberate into total calamity. And *quis custodiet custodes?*

As Goodman has himself remarked, it is strange indeed that decentralist sentiments like these are usually rejected by the cautious as unthinkably "radical." The historical reference for his brand of anarchism harks back to the well-tested virtues of the neolithic village. "The 'conservatives,' on the other hand, want to stay with the oppressions of 1910 or perhaps Prince Metternich. It is only the anarchists who are really conservative, for they want to conserve sun and space, animal nature, primary community, experimenting inquiry."[15] So Goodman seeks, in his social criticism, the same end always: to scale down selectively our leviathan industrialism so that it can serve as handmaiden to the ethos of village or neighborhood.

It is Goodman's communitarianism which is, finally, his greatest and most directly appreciated contribution to contemporary youth culture. For the New Left he has functioned as the foremost theoretician of participative democracy, bringing back into lively discussion a tradition of anarchist thought that reaches back through Prince Kropotkin to Robert Owen.

[15] *Drawing the Line*, p. 16.

And so in spirit, if not in scholarly reference, it is anarchist politics that is being most hotly debated among the socially involved young—far more so than the Marxist tradition of socialism. Even the vices of the New Left and the Black Powerites—such as the current infatuation with guerrilla warfare—bear the anarchist imprint: war on a human scale with the chance for personal cunning, courage, and decision.

So too, the shape that beat-hip bohemianism has taken owes much to Goodman's influence. The pseudo-Indian tribes that now camp in our cities, the psychedelic communities in the California hinterlands or the wilds of Colorado, the Diggers with their hazy ideas about free stores and co-operative farms . . . whatever their failings, these are part of that Utopian anarchist tradition which has always bravely refused to knuckle under to the proposition that life must be a bad, sad compromise with Old Corruption.

. . . the "Utopian" socialists [Martin Buber reminds us] have aspired more and more to a restructuring of society; not, as the Marxist critic thinks, in any romantic attempt to revive the stages of development that are over and done with, but rather in alliance with the decentralist counter-tendencies which can be perceived underlying all economic and social evolution, and in alliance with something that is slowly evolving in the human soul: the most intimate of all resistances—resistance to mass or collective loneliness.[16]

The importance of this communitarian bent in our youth culture—especially at the bohemian fringe—is immense, though it is much misunderstood. How often have we heard old-line radicals condemn the bohemian young for the "irresponsibility" of their withdrawal into kooky communities of their own? Instead, they are advised to "grow up" and

[16] Martin Buber, *Paths in Utopia* (Boston: Beacon Press, 1960), p. 14.

"be responsible"—by which is meant, usually: "Give your energy to political action. Help organize the slums or the agricultural laborers; plan political coalitions; register voters in Mississippi; join the Peace Corps; find a project; agitate; sit-in; come to the demonstration; subscribe to *Dissent, Commentary, New Politics . . .*" The activities are noble enough. But they are, at best, only episodic commitments. Run them together as one may, they have not the continuity and comprehensiveness demanded by a way of life. And it is a way of life the young need to grow into, a maturity which may include political activity, but which *also* embraces more fundamental needs: love, family, subsistence, companionship. Political action and organizing cannot even provide a full-time career for more than a handful of apparatchiks, let alone a pattern of life for an entire generation. What, then, do the disaffiliated young have to grow toward? What ideal of adulthood has the world to offer them that will take the place of the middle-class debauch they instinctively reject?

An intelligent compromise, perhaps—which is what most of the old radicals have settled for. A teaching position, a civil service job, work with a journal, a newspaper, a trade union . . . something from eight to five that brings in an income for home and family and which leaves time for politicking outside. The trouble is: many of the young are just too alienated even for the intelligent compromise, with its inevitable disciplines, its taxed paycheck, its pinch of incense for the bourgeois conformities. The alienation has gone that far. The counter culture that began with Ginsberg's *Howl*: how can it finally comb its hair and set its alarm clock, take out a social security card and save its dissent for after hours? How can it make itself even that much beholden to Moloch?

And still . . . if you are twenty-five and have exhausted the dilatory possibilities of college and parental support, you *do* want to "grow up" and "be responsible." Which, of course, means you must put your hand to the political things that demand attention. But you must also "make do"—and SDS offers no long-term livelihood, nor does SNCC, nor CORE. And *damned* if you'll make that intelligent compromise! But you are twenty-five . . . and there are forty or fifty years ahead (if the bomb doesn't fall) and they must be shared with home and family, and be buoyed up by dependable subsistence, or that future will be a gray waste and the consciousness of life you want to expand will shrink and become bleak. So how *do* you grow up? Where is the life-sustaining receptacle that can nourish and protect good citizenship?

The answer is: you make up a community of those you love and respect, where there can be enduring friendships, children, and, by mutual aid, three meals a day scraped together by honorable and enjoyable labor. Nobody knows quite how it is to be done. There are not many reliable models. The old radicals are no help: they talked about socializing whole economies, or launching third parties, or strengthening the unions, but not about building communities.

It will take a deal of improvisation, using whatever examples one can find at hand: the life-way of Indian tribes, utopian precedents, the seventeenth-century Diggers, the French communities of work, the Israeli kibbutzim, the Hutterites. . . . Maybe none of them will work. But where else is there to turn? And where else can one any longer look for the beginnings of an honest revolution except in such "pre-revolutionary structure-making" (as Buber calls it)?[17]

Among all the urgent tasks that need to be done in the next month and the one after that, this especially needs doing for the next decade and the one after that: that the young who have greater expectations of life than their elders and who are more intolerably sensitive to corruptions should

[17] *Paths in Utopia*, pp. 44–45.

find an enduring mode of life that will safeguard those expectations and sensitivities. If the counter culture is to have a future that saves the best that is in it, these frenzied and often pathetic experiments in community will simply have to succeed. And who besides Goodman is offering much help in that direction?

From *Making Do*, the man considering the unhappy boy he loves:

. . . for him—and not only for him—there was in our society No Exit. When he had asked his germane question, and fifteen experts on the dais did not know an answer for him. But with ingenuity he had hit on a painfully American answer, *Do It Yourself*. If there is no community for you, young man, young man, make it yourself.

Chapter VII

THE MYTH OF OBJECTIVE CONSCIOUSNESS

If the preceding chapters have served their purpose, they will have shown how some of the leading mentors of our youthful counter culture have, in a variety of ways, called into question the validity of the conventional scientific world view, and in so doing have set about undermining the foundations of the technocracy. The object of these final chapters will be to summarize and, hopefully, give some comprehensive shape to this still embryonic critique of the dominant culture, in the hope that the thoughts offered here will help to sharpen what I take to be the most promising elements involved in the youthful dissent of our day.

If there is one especially striking feature of the new radicalism we have been surveying, it is the cleavage that exists between it and the radicalism of previous generations where the subjects of science and technology are concerned. To the older collectivist ideologies, which were as given to the value of industrial expansion as the capitalist class enemy, the connection between totalitarian control and science was not apparent. Science was almost invariably seen as an undisputed social good, because it had become so intimately related in the popular mind (though not often in ways clearly understood) to the technological progress that promised security and affluence. It was not foreseen even by gifted social critics that the impersonal, large-scale social processes to which technological progress gives rise—in economics, in politics, in education, in every aspect of life—generate their own characteristic problems. When the general public finds itself enmeshed in a gargantuan industrial apparatus which it admires to the point of idolization and yet cannot comprehend, it must of necessity defer to those who are experts or to those who own the experts; only they appear to know how the great cornucopia can be kept brimming over with the good things of life.

Centralized bigness breeds the regime of expertise, whether the big system is based on privatized or socialized economies. Even within the democratic socialist tradition with its stubborn emphasis on workers' control, it is far from apparent how the democratically governed units of an industrial economy will automatically produce a general system which is not dominated by co-ordinating experts. It is both ironic and ominous to hear the French Gaullists and the Wilson Labourites in Great Britain—governments that are heavily committed to an elitist managerialism—now talking seriously about increased workers' "participation" in industry. It would surely be a mistake to believe that the technocracy cannot find ways to placate and integrate the shop floor without compromising the continuation of super-scale social processes. "Participation" could easily become the god-word of our official politics within the next decade; but its reference will be to the sort of "responsible" collaboration that keeps the technocracy growing. We do well to remember that one of the great secrets of successful concentration camp administration under the Nazis was to enlist the "participation" of the inmates.

It is for this reason that the counter culture, which draws upon a profoundly personalist sense of community rather than upon technical and industrial values, comes closer to being a radical critique of the technocracy than any of the traditional ideologies. If one starts with a sense of the person that ventures to psychoanalytical depths, one may rapidly arrive at a viewpoint that rejects many of the hitherto undisputed values of industrialism itself. One soon begins talking about "standards of living" that transcend high productivity, efficiency, full employment, and the work-and-consumption ethic. Quality and not quantity becomes the touchstone of social value.

The critique is pushed even further when the counter culture begins to explore the modes of non-intellective consciousness. Along this line, questions arise which strike more deeply at technocratic assumptions. For if the technocracy is dependent on public deference to the experts, it must stand or fall by the reality of expertise. But what *is* expertise? What are the criteria which certify someone as an expert?

If we are foolishly willing to agree that experts are those whose role is legitimized by the fact that the technocratic system needs them in order to avoid falling apart at the seams, then of course the technocratic status quo generates its own internal justification: the technocracy is legitimized because it enjoys the approval of experts; the experts are legitimized because there could be no technocracy without them. This is the sort of circular argument student rebels meet when they challenge the necessity of administrative supremacy in the universities. They are invariably faced with the rhetorical question: but who will allocate room space, supervise registration, validate course requirements, coordinate the academic departments, police the parking lots and dormitories, discipline students, etc., if not the administration? Will the multiversity not collapse in chaos if the administrators are sent packing? The students are learning the answer: yes, the multiversity will collapse; but *education* will go on. Why? Because the administrators have nothing to do with the reality of education; their expertise is related to the illusory busywork that arises from administrative complexity itself. The multiversity creates the administrators and they, in turn, expand the multiversity so that it needs to make place for more administrators. One gets out of this squirrel cage only by digging deep into the root meaning of education itself.

The same radicalizing logic unfolds if, in confronting the technocracy, we begin looking for a conception of expertise which amounts to something more than the intimidating truism that tells us experts are those in the absence of whom the technocracy would collapse.

An expert, we say, is one to whom we turn because he is in control of reliable knowledge about that which concerns us. In the case of the technocracy, the experts are those who govern us because they know (reliably) about all things relevant to our survival and happiness: human needs, social engineering, economic planning, international relations, invention, education, etc. Very well, but what is "reliable knowledge"? How do we know it when we see it? The answer is: reliable knowledge is knowledge that is scientifically sound, since science is that to which modern man refers for the definitive explication of reality. And what in turn is it that characterizes scientific knowledge? The answer is: objectivity. Scientific knowledge is not just feeling or speculation or subjective ruminating. It is a verifiable description of reality that exists independent of any purely personal considerations. It is true . . . real . . . dependable. . . . It works. And that at last is how we define an expert: he is one who *really* knows what is what, because he cultivates an objective consciousness.

Thus, if we probe the technocracy in search of the peculiar power it holds over us, we arrive at the myth of objective consciousness. There is but one way of gaining access to reality— so the myth holds—and this is to cultivate a state of consciousness cleansed of all subjective distortion, all personal involvement. What flows from this state of consciousness qualifies as knowledge, and nothing else does. This is the bedrock on which the natural sciences have built; and under their spell all fields of knowledge strive to become scientific. The study of man in his social, political, economic, psychological, historical aspects—all this, too, must become objective: rigorously, painstakingly objective. At every level of human experience, would-be scientists come forward to endorse the myth of objective consciousness, thus certifying themselves as experts. And because they know and we do not, we yield to their guidance.[1]

* * * *

But to speak of "mythology" in connection with science would seem at first glance to be a contradiction in terms.

[1] In contrast to the line I take here, a young would-be revolutionary of considerable insight like Daniel Cohn-Bendit contends that "the monopoly of knowledge" on which the technocracy is based "is a capitalist myth" which will be dispelled once the workers realize that, by way of a true "people's university . . . knowledge is theirs for the asking." *Obsolete Communism: The Left-Wing Alternative* p. 109. But whatever kind of knowledge can he mean? Surely not the expertise which now characterizes the technocrat. For that is hard-won and esoterically specialized: the entrée to high-status professionalism. Those who acquire such knowledge, for the most part, are promoted to the level of functionaries within the existing industrial apparatus. I argue here that the important monopoly that must be broken is not at bottom a simple class privilege; it is, rather, the psychic monopoly of the objective consciousness. The dominant social status of expertise is founded on the dominant cultural status of this mode of consciousness: it is the "commanding height" of the technocracy. Where we deal with so integrative and so superficially democratic a social form as the technocracy, we must press beyond the class advantage to the cultural consensus that fosters it. What results from ignoring this level of analysis shows up in Cohn-Bendit's treatment of "communist bureaucracy," which he seems to blame on the sheer opportunistic bastardliness of Bolshevik leadership. The relationship of the technocracy—whether Stalinist, Gaullist, or American capitalist—to the universally honored mythos of high industrial society eludes him. The more subversive strategy for a "people's university" would be to show people that "knowledge" is theirs, not for "the asking," but for the debunking.

Science, after all, purports to be precisely that enterprise of the mind which strips life of its myths, substituting for fantasy and legend a relationship to reality based, in William James' phrase, on "irreducible and stubborn facts." Is not scientific knowledge, indeed, that residue which is left when all the myths have been filtered away? One might in fact argue that this is exactly what distinguishes the scientific revolution of the modern West from all previous cultural transitions. In the past, when one cultural epoch has displaced another, the change frequently involved little more than a process of mythological transformation: a *re*-mythologizing of men's thinking. So the figure of Christ stepped into the place prepared long since by the savior figures of various pagan mystery cults, and in time the Christian saints inherited their status from the deities of the Greco-Roman, Teutonic, or Celtic pantheons.

But science, we are to believe, does not re-mythologize life; it *de*-mythologizes it. This is supposedly what makes the scientific revolution a radically different, if not a final, cultural episode. For, with the advent of the scientific world view, indisputable truth takes the place of make-believe.

There is no doubting the radical novelty of science in contrast to all earlier mythological world views. What all non-scientific cultural systems have had in common is the tendency to mistake their mythologies for literal statements about history and the natural world—or at least the tendency to articulate mythological insights in what a scientific mind mistakes for propositional assertions. In this way, imaginative expressions rich in moral drama or psychic perception easily degenerate into fabulous conjectures about the exotic reaches of time and space. This is how we most often use the word "mythology" in our time: to designate the telling of unverifiable, if not downright false, tales about remote ages and places. The story of the Garden of Eden is a "myth" we say, because insofar as any believing Christian or Jew has ever tried to locate the story geographically and historically, skeptics have been able to call his evidence, if any, quite cogently into question.

Mythologies which are imaginative exaggerations of our ordinary perceptions or displacements of them to other times and places—let us call them in this sense temporal-physical mythologies—have always been vulnerable to critical inquiry. The doubting Thomas in the case need not even be a scientific skeptic. A devout Christian can practice an uncompromising skepticism toward the mythologies of other faiths and cultures, in the fashion of Charlemagne striking down the Saxon idols and defying their wrath, confident that no such heathen divinities existed. But a Christian's skepticism is necessarily partisan, sparing the believer any critical examination of his own dogmas. Even liberal Christian demythologizers like Rudolph Bultmann have had to stop short of extending their project to such essential teachings as the resurrection of Christ.

In contrast to such selective skepticism, the wholesale skepticism of science shows up to brilliant advantage. Science is the infidel to all gods in behalf of none. Thus there is no way around the painful dilemma in which the religious traditions of the world have found themselves trapped over the last two centuries. Every culture that has invested its convictions in a temporal-physical mythology is doomed before the onslaught of the scientific unbeliever. Any village atheist who persists in saying "show me" is in the position to hold up to ransom an entire religious culture, with little expectation that it will be able to find the price demanded. It would be difficult to say whether this situation partakes more of farce or of tragedy. Only a few generations ago, Clarence Darrow, no more than a skillful courtroom lawyer armed with a Sunday supplement knowledge of Darwin, was able to make laughingstock of a Judeo-Christian mythology that had served to inspire the finest philosophical and artistic minds of our culture over hundreds of generations. Yet, under unrelenting skeptical pressure, what choice have those who cling to temporal-physical mythologies but to undertake strategic retreat, conceding ever more ground to secular, reductionist styles of thought. The line of retreat falls back to interpretations of myth that are primarily ethical . . . or aesthetic . . . or, in some unspecified fashion, symbolic. Within the Christian tradition, this is a resort which is bound to weaken and confuse, since Christianity has had a uniquely significant commitment to the literal truth of its teachings. Indeed, the sweeping secularization of Western society that has come in the wake of scientific advance can be seen as a product of Christianity's peculiar reliance on a precarious, dogmatic literalism. Such a religious tradition need only prick its finger in order to bleed to death. And if the hard-pressed believer does turn to "symbolic" interpretations, even here the secular temperament tends to sweep the field by asserting reductionist psychological or sociological correlatives for the myth. The only other defense, that of standing fast in behalf of the literal truth, leads, as Kierkegaard recognized more than a century ago, to the crucifixion of the intellect.

The scientific world view is of course invulnerable to criticism at the same level as a temporal-physical mythology. It would be a ludicrous mistake to contend that the things and forces with which science fills time and space—electrons and galaxies, gravitational fields and natural selection, DNA and viruses—are the cultural equivalents of centaurs and Valhallas and angelic beings. What science deals in is not so poor in ordinary sensory verification—nor so rich in imaginative possibilities. Unlike the mythological traditions of the past, science is not in the first instance a body of supposed

knowledge about entities and events. Science would still be
science and very much in business if it encompassed no
knowledge at all other than the ruins of proven ignorance and
error. The scientific mind begins in the spirit of the Cartesian
zero, with the doubting away of all inherited knowledge in
favor of an entirely new *method* of knowing, which, whether it
proceeds on rationalist or empiricist lines, purports to begin
from scratch, free of all homage to authority.

What scientists know may therefore wax or wane, change
in part or whole as time goes on and as evidence accumulates.
If the Piltdown fossil proves to be a hoax, it can be discarded
without calling the science of physical anthropology into
question. If the telescopes of astronomers were to discover
angels in outer space, science as a method of knowing would
not be in any sense discredited; its theories would simply be
reformulated in the light of new discoveries. In contrast to
the way we use the phrase "world view" in other contexts,
science rests itself not in the *world* the scientist beholds at
any particular point in time, but in his mode of *viewing* that
world. A man is a scientist not because of what he sees, but
because of *how* he sees it.

At least, this is what has become the conventional way of
regarding scientific knowledge. Thomas Kuhn, who has
looked at the matter more carefully, has recently thrown
strong and significant doubt on this "incremental" conception of the history of science. His contention comes close to
suggesting that the progressive accumulation of "truth" in the
scientific community is something of an illusion, created by
the fact that each generation of scientists rewrites its textbooks in such a way as to select from the past what is still
considered valid and to suppress the multitude of errors and
false starts that are also a part of the history of science. As
for the all-important principles of validation that control this
natural selection of scientific truth from era to era—the so-

called "scientific method"—Kuhn is left unconvinced that they are quite as purely "rational" or "empirical" as scientists like to think.[2]

Yet the incremental conception of scientific knowledge is very much part of the mythology we are concerned with here. The capacity of science to progress stands as one of the principal validations of its objectivity. Knowledge progresses only when it is understood to survive the passing of particular minds or generations. Science, understood as the expanding application of a fixed method of knowing to ever more areas of experience, makes such a claim. A scientist, asked to explain why science progresses when other fields of thought do not, would doubtlessly refer us to the "objectivity" of his method of knowing. Objectivity, he would tell us, is what gives science its keen critical edge and its peculiarly cumulative character.

Are we using the word "mythology" illegitimately in applying it to objectivity as a state of consciousness? I think not. For the myth at its deepest level is that collectively created thing which crystallizes the great, central values of a culture. It is, so to speak, the intercommunications system of culture. If the culture of science locates its highest values not in mystic symbol or ritual or epic tales of faraway lands and times, but in a mode of consciousness, why should we hesitate to call this a myth? The myth has, after all, been identified as a universal phenomenon of human society, a constitutive factor so critical in importance that it is difficult to imagine a culture having any coherence at all if it lacked the mythological bond. Yet, in our society, myth as it is conventionally understood has become practically a synonym for falsehood. To be sure, we commonly hear discussion of various social and political myths these days (the myth of

[2] See Thomas Kuhn, *The Structure of Scientific Revolutions* (Chicago: The University of Chicago Press, 1962).

the American frontier, the myth of the Founding Fathers, etc.); the more enlightened clergy even talk freely of "the Christian myth." But myths so openly recognized as myths are precisely those that have lost much of their power. It is the myth we accept without question as truth that holds real influence over us. Is it possible that, in this sense, scientific culture is uniquely a-mythical? Or is it the case that we simply fail to look in the right place—in the deep personality structure of the ideal scientist—for the great controlling myth of our culture?

Such, at least, is what I propose here, though it would be pointless to press any further the purely semantic question of whether or not objective consciousness meets all the requirements of a "mythology." What is essential here is the contention that objective consciousness is emphatically *not* some manner of definitive, transcultural development whose cogency derives from the fact that it is uniquely in touch with the truth. Rather, like a mythology, it is an arbitrary construct in which a given society in a given historical situation has invested its sense of meaningfulness and value. And so, like any mythology, it can be gotten round and called into question by cultural movements which find meaning and value elsewhere. In the case of the counter culture, then, we have a movement which has turned from objective consciousness as if from a place inhabited by plague—and in the moment of that turning, one can just begin to see an entire episode of our cultural history, the great age of science and technology which began with the Enlightenment, standing revealed in all its quaintly arbitrary, often absurd, and all too painfully unbalanced aspects.

Perhaps, as Michael Polanyi has argued,[3] there is no such thing as objectivity, even in the physical sciences. Certainly

[3] Michael Polanyi, *Personal Knowledge: Towards a Post-Critical Philosophy* (Chicago: The University of Chicago Press, 1959).

his critique is a formidable challenge to scientific orthodoxy. But for our purposes here, this narrowly epistemological question is a subordinate consideration. Science, under the technocracy, has become a total culture dominating the lives of millions for whom discussions of the theory of knowledge are so much foreign language. Yet objectivity, whatever its epistemological status, has become the commanding life style of our society: the one most authoritative way of regarding the self, others, and the whole of our enveloping reality. Even if it is not, indeed, possible to be objective, it *is* possible so to shape the personality that it will feel and act *as if* one were an objective observer and to treat everything that experience presents to the person in accordance with what objectivity would seem to demand.

Objectivity as a state of being fills the very air we breathe in a scientific culture; it grips us subliminally in all we say, feel, and do. The mentality of the ideal scientist becomes the very soul of the society. We seek to adapt our lives to the dictates of that mentality, or at the very least we respond to it acquiescently in the myriad images and pronouncements in which it manifests itself about us during every waking hour. The Barbarella and James Bond who keep their clinical cool while dealing out prodigious sex or sadistic violence . . . the physiologist who persuades several score of couples to undertake coitus while wired to a powerhouse of electronic apparatus so that he can achieve a statistical measure of sexual normalcy . . . the characters of *Last Year At Marienbad* who face one another as impassively as empty mirrors . . . the Secretary of Defense who tells the public without blinking an eye that our country possesses the "overkill" capacity to destroy any given enemy ten times . . . the high-rise glass and aluminum slab that deprives of visual involvement by offering us only functional linearity and massive reflecting surfaces . . . the celebrated surgeon who assures us that his heart transplant was a "success" though of course the patient died . . . the computer technician who blithely suggests that we have to wage an "all-out war on sleep" in order to take advantage of the latest breakthrough in rapid communications . . . the modish expert who seeks (with phenomenal success) to convince us that the essence of communication lies not in the truth or falsehood, wisdom or folly of the message that person transfers to person, but rather in the technical characteristics of the intervening medium . . . the political scientist who settles for being a psephological virtuoso, pretending that the statistics of meaningless elections are the veritable substance of politics . . . all these (or so I would argue) are life under the sway of objective consciousness.

In short, as science elaborates itself into the dominant cultural influence of our age, it is the psychology and not the epistemology of science that urgently requires our critical attention; for it is primarily at this level that the most consequential deficiencies and imbalances of the technocracy are revealed.[4]

*   *   *   *

We can, I think, identify three major characteristics of the psychic style which follows from an intensive cultivation of objective consciousness. I have called them: (1) the alienative dichotomy; (2) the invidious hierarchy; (3) the mechanistic imperative.[5]

[4] This is the fascinating approach to science that Abraham Maslow has opened up in his *The Psychology of Science* (New York: Harper & Row, 1966). The study gains a deal of authority from Maslow's own experience in growing painfully away from a firm commitment to behavioral psychology.

[5] Rather than complicate the presentation with illustrations of the characteristics described here, I have gathered a small group of examples in the Appendix.

(1) Objective consciousness begins by dividing reality into two spheres, which would seem best described as "In-Here" and "Out-There." By In-Here is meant that place within the person to which consciousness withdraws when one wants to know without becoming involved in or committed to that which is being known. There are many kinds of operations that can be conducted by In-Here. In the natural sciences, the usual activities of In-Here would include those of observing, experimenting, measuring, classifying, and working out quantitative relationships of the most general kind. In the humanities and what we call the behavioral sciences, the operations are more various, but they include numerous activities that seek to imitate the natural sciences by way of tabulating, pigeonholing, applying information theory or game strategies to human affairs, etc. In-Here may be involved, however, in something as simple as the detached scrutiny of a document, a book, an *objet d'art*—meaning the study of this thing as if one's feelings were not aroused by it, or as if such feelings as might arise could be discounted or screened out.

Whatever the scientific method may or may not be, people think they are behaving scientifically whenever they create an In-Here within themselves which undertakes to know without an investment of the person in the act of knowing. The necessary effect of distancing, of estranging In-Here from Out-There may be achieved in any number of ways: by the intervention of various mechanical gadgets between observer and observed; by the elaboration of chilly jargons and technical terms that replace sensuous speech; by the invention of strange methodologies which reach out to the subject matter like a pair of mechanical hands; by the subordination of the particular and immediate experience to a statistical generalization; by appeal to a professional standard which excuses the observer from responsibility to anything other than a lofty abstraction—such as "the pursuit of truth," "pure research," etc. All these protective strategies are especially compatible with natures that are beset by timidity and fearfulness; but also with those that are characterized by plain insensitivity and whose habitual mode of contact with the world is a cool curiosity untouched by love, tenderness, or passionate wonder. Behind both such timidity and insensitivity there can easily lurk the spitefulness of a personality which feels distressingly remote from the rewards of warm engagement with life. It is revealing that whenever a scientific method of study is brought into play, we are supposed to regard it as irrelevant, if not downright unfair, to probe the many very different motivations that may underlie a man's desire to be purely objective. It is little wonder, then, that the ideal of objectivity can easily be invoked to cover a curiosity of callousness or hostility, as well as a curiosity of affectionate concern. In any event, when I convince myself that I can create a place within me that has been cleansed of all those murky passions, hostilities, joys, fears, and lusts which define my person, a place that is "Not-I," and when I believe that it is only from the vantage point of this Not-I that reality can be accurately perceived, then I have begun to honor the myth of objective consciousness.

The essential experience of being In-Here is that of being an unseen, unmoved spectator. Abraham Maslow characterizes the situation in this way:

It means looking at something that is not you, not human, not personal, something independent of you the perceiver. . . . You the observer are, then, really alien to it, uncomprehending and without sympathy or identification . . . You look through the microscope or the telescope as through a keyhole, peering, peeping, from a distance, from outside, not as one who has a right to be in the room being peeped into.[6]

[6] Maslow, *The Psychology of Science*, p. 49.

The spectating In-Here has been called by many names: ego, intelligence, self, subject, reason. . . . I avoid such designations here because they suggest some fixed faculty or psychic entity. What I prefer to emphasize is the *act* of contraction that takes place within the person, the sense of taking a step back, away from, and out of. Not only back and away from the natural world, but from the inarticulate feelings, physical urges, and wayward images that surge up from within the person. To these "irrationalities" Freud gave the revealing name, "the *it*": a something which is Not-I, but alien, incomprehensible, and only to be known reliably when it, too, is forced Out-There to become an object for analysis.

The ideal of the objective consciousness is that there should be as little as possible In-Here and, conversely, as much as possible Out-There. For only what is Out-There can be studied and known. Objectivity leads to such a great emptying-out operation: the progressive alienation of more and more of In-Here's personal contents in the effort to achieve the densest possible unit of observational concentration surrounded by the largest possible area of study. The very word "concentration" yields the interesting image of an identity contracted into a small, hard ball; hence a dense, diminished identity, something which is less than one otherwise might be. Yet the predilection of In-Here is to remain "concentrated" as long and as often as possible. Curiously, this great good called knowledge, the very guarantee of our survival, is taken to be something that is forthcoming only to this lesser, shriveled-up identity.

The scientific observer who comes to feel that Out-There has begun to implicate him personally—say, in the manner of a lover spellbinding one's sympathies so that one cannot tell clearly where one's self leaves off and the other begins —has begun to lose his objectivity. Therefore, he must fight back this irrational involvement of his personal feeling. Like Odysseus in the presence of the sirens' song, In-Here must be lashed to the mast, or its mission may never be completed. But if body, feelings, emotions, moral sentiment, sensuous enchantment are all to be located Out-There, then who is this In-Here that is so stalwartly struggling against the siren song? It is a weird identity indeed, this In-Here. More and more it looks like Kafka's castle: a stronghold well defended, but manned by . . . parties unknown.

It would be an interesting line of questioning to put to our experts, would it not? Who are "you" when you are being purely objective? How did you manage to bring this purely objective "you" into existence—and how can you be so sure you really pulled it off? Moreover, does this purely objective "you" prove to be an enjoyable identity? Or is that beside the point?

(2) The act of psychic contraction that creates In-Here simultaneously creates Out-There, which is whatever gets left behind in the wake of the contraction. The line which divides In-Here from Out-There now becomes a line between a place where it is desirable and secure to be (In-Here) and a place that is untrustworthy, perhaps downright dangerous (Out-There). In-Here is the center of reliable knowledge; it knows what it is doing; it learns, plans, controls, watches out cunningly for threats and opportunities. The alternative to being in a place of reliable knowledge is, obviously, to be in a place of drift, unpredictability, stupidity. Such is what Out-There becomes.

Now, in fact, anyone, even the most objective scientist, would fall into a state of total paralysis if he *really* believed that Out-There (beginning with his own organism and unconscious processes) was totally stupid. Nevertheless, In-Here is committed to studying Out-There *as if* it were completely stupid, meaning without intention or wisdom or purposeful pattern. In-Here cannot, if it is to be strictly objective, strive to empathize in any way with Out-There. It must not attribute to Out-There what cannot be observed, measured, and—ideally—formulated into articulate, demonstrable propositions for experimental verification. In-Here must maintain its alienative dichotomy at all times. And like the racist who cannot under Jim Crow conditions come to see the segregated black man as anything but a doltish and primitive nigger, so In-Here, as the unmoved spectator, cannot feel that Out-There has any ingenuity or dignity. Under this kind of scrutiny, even the other human beings who inhabit Out-There can be made stupid, for they were not made to function within laboratory conditions or according to the exacting needs of questionnaires and surveys. Under the eyes of an alien observer they also begin to lose their human purposefulness.

As soon as two human beings relate in detachment as observer to observed, as soon as the observer claims to be aware of nothing more than the behavioral surface of the observed, an invidious hierarchy is established which reduces the observed to a lower status. Of necessity he falls into the same category with all the stupid things of the world that fill Out-There. For consider the gross impertinence of this act of detached observation. Psychologist confronting his laboratory subject, anthropologist confronting tribal group, political scientist confronting voting public . . . in all such cases what the observer may very well be saying to the observed is the same: "I can perceive no more than your behavioral facade. I can grant you no more reality or psychic coherence than this perception allows. I shall observe this behavior of yours and record it. I shall not enter into your life, your task, your condition of existence. Do not turn to me or appeal to me or ask me to become involved with you. I am here only as a temporary observer whose role is to stand back and record and later to make my own sense of what you seem to be doing or intending. I assume that I can adequately understand what you are doing or intending without entering wholly into your life. I am not particularly interested in what *you* uniquely are; I am interested only in the general pattern to which you conform. I assume I have the right to use you to perform this process of classification. I assume I have the right to reduce all that you are to an integer in my science."

At the extreme, this alienated relationship is that of the Nazi physician experimenting upon his human victims, learning interesting new things about pain, suffering, privation. One cringes from the reference and protests, "*That* was an abnormal case. Normally, research involving human subjects stops short of inhumanity. And, in any event, whatever laboratory work is involved takes place in limited episodes; it is not a total way of life for experimenter or subject." Unhappily, however, the ethos of objectivity has gotten well beyond limited research episodes. Already legions of scientists and military men throughout the world, the products of careful training and selection, give themselves to whole lives of ultimate objectivity. They systematically detach themselves from any concern for those lives their inventions and weapons may someday do to death. They do their job as they are ordered to do it . . . objectively. For them the world at large has become a laboratory—in the same sense that when they enter upon their professional capacity, they leave their personal feelings behind. Perhaps they even take pride in their capacity to do so, for indeed it requires an act of iron will to ignore the claims that person makes upon person.

When In-Here observes Out-There, it is with the intention of giving order to what it perceives. The order can be understood to be that of "law," or statistical generalization, or classification. This orderliness is what sometimes leads scientists to speak of the "beauty of nature"—a notion to which we will return in the next chapter. But what is important about all these kinds of order is that they may concede no credit to Out-There for being autonomously clever or marvelous. The scientist's nature becomes "beautiful" when it has been tidied up and pigeonholed. The achievement lies in the scientist's "discovery" of this order; the credit belongs to the observing mind. It is a situation which reminds one of the quaint use of the term "discovery" in relationship to the European voyages of discovery. The phrase suggests that the Americas, Africa, and Asia, with all their indigenous peoples had been waiting eagerly to be found by the white man. We now recognize the comic ethnocentrism of that view; the cerebral anthropocentrism of scientific discovery is less obvious. But Abraham Maslow offers us one lovely example of the subliminal presumption. He mentions the scientist who praised a book on "the difficult problem of woman's sexuality" because it at last took up a subject "about which so little is known"! He goes on to comment on the psychology of the scientist's nomothetic project:

Organizing experience into meaningful patterns implies that experience itself has no meaningfulness, that the organizer creates or imposes or donates the meaning . . . that it is a gift from the knower to the known. In other words, "meaningfulness" of this kind is of the realm of classification and abstraction rather than of experience. . . . Frequently I sense also the implication that it is "human-created", i.e., that much of it would vanish if human beings disappeared.[7]

The relationship Maslow describes is obviously an hierarchical one. In-Here is the superior of Out-There. Out-There has no way to lay claim upon In-Here, to appeal for kindness, appreciation, adoration, etc., because it is In-Here that monopolizes meaning. Out-There is left without voice to speak

[7] Maslow, *The Psychology of Science*, pp. 56, 84.

in behalf of its sanctity or in its defense. Moreover, In-Here knows how Out-There works and therefore has power over Out-There. Since In-Here is the sole dispenser of meaning, who then can gainsay In-Here when it grants itself the unabridged right to use that power? The dead and the stupid are objects of contempt—or at best of condescension; they must submit to the scrutiny, experimentation, and exploitation of In-Here. The fact that Out-There seems not to recognize this hierarchical order only proves how dead or stupid it really is. Instead of making life secure for In-Here, Out-There blunders about producing disease, famine, death, riot, protest, and the many misfortunes of existence. Out-There is obviously unreliable. And the unreliability begins very close to home. It begins with those outbursts of fluid, imprecise, distractive imaginings that well up from the "irrational"; as well as with this troublesome body, which seems to do almost nothing properly.

If In-Here did not constantly intervene in the behavior of Out-There, what an impossible chaos would ensue! But fortunately In-Here, being vigilant and clever, is able to keep Out-There in line: to conquer it, to manipulate it, to improve upon it—beginning with the witless body, which is forever proving to be incompetent. In-Here must therefore devise forms of surgical and chemical intervention that will make sure the body sleeps, wakes, digests, excretes, grows, relaxes, feels gay, feels blue, has sex, etc., correctly, at the right time and place. In-Here may even devise ways to keep the body functioning indefinitely, so that it does not commit the ultimate incompetence of dying. Similarly, the natural environment must be conquered and subjected to forceful improvement. Climate and landscape must be redesigned. Waste space must be made livable, meaning covered over with an urban expansion into which nothing that is not man-made or man-arranged will intrude itself. Similarly, the social environment—the body politic—must be brought as completely under centralized, deliberative control as the physical body has been brought under the domination of the cerebrum. Unless the order of things is readily apparent to a command and control center—in the individual, it will be the forebrain; in the society, it will be the technocracy—and available for manipulation, it cannot be respected as order at all.

So, at last, Out-There emerges as a pitiful disappointment: an underdeveloped country awaiting the competent management of In-Here. As Joseph Wood Krutch comments, this reverses the age-old relationship of man to nature and rapidly leads to the unbridled assertion of human hubris: "Is there anything *we* can't do better?"

No age before ours would have made such an assumption. Man has always before thought of himself as puny by comparison with natural forces, and he was humble before them. But we have been so impressed by the achievement of technology that we are likely to think we can do more than nature herself. We dug the Panama Canal, didn't we? Why not the Grand Canyon?[8]

An objective, meaning an alienated, attitude toward the natural environment comes easily these days to a population largely born and raised in the almost totally man-made world of the metropolis. It would be difficult for anyone so raised, including a scientist, *not* to be objective toward a "nature" which he has only known in the form of tidy, if boring, artificialities arranged by the parks and gardens authorities. The flora, fauna, landscape, and increasingly the climate of the earth lie practically helpless at the feet of technological man, tragically vulnerable to his arrogance. Without ques-

[8] Joseph Wood Krutch, *Grand Canyon* (New York: William Sloane Associates, 1958), p. 25.

tion, we have triumphed over them . . . at least until the massive ecological consequences catch up with us.

(3) But there are other areas of nature which pose a more serious problem for the objective consciousness. They appear within the person.

No matter how strenuously In-Here strives to thrust out the "irrational," it continues to intrude itself with its claims in behalf of sensuous contact, fantasy, spontaneity, and concern for the person. From somewhere nearby, In-Here continues to feel the pressure of a strange need to moralize, to joke, to hate, to love, to lust, to fear. . . . Obviously the citadel of objectivity is a precarious place. This mysterious organism which In-Here pilots about is not a trustworthy machine. Therefore, In-Here, in search of impregnable objectivity, takes the final step. It sets about inventing a superior command and control center that will take over whenever In-Here's capacity to achieve perfect impersonality breaks down: an electronic nervous system! Such a device will never lose control of itself, never weaken, never turn unpredictably personal, for it will never have been a person in the first place.

Man's infatuation with the machine is frequently misunderstood as being a love affair with mere power. "Here I sell what all men crave: power!" So said Matthew Boulton, referring to the first steam-engine factory. But the great virtue of the machine lies not only in its power: many mechanisms —like timers or electric eyes or most cybernated systems—are not particularly powerful and yet are highly valued. Is it not the machine's capacity to be severely routinized that we admire quite as much as its sheer strength? Unlike the human organism, the machine can achieve perfect concentration, perfect self-control. It performs the one task to which it is assigned, with no possibility of being distracted. It acts without involvement in what it does. Indeed, the burden which industrialization lifted from men's backs was not physical labor so much as it was deadly routine, with its demand for unrelenting and exhaustive concentration. Thus, the archetypal machine in our society is not the gargantuan steam engine, but the lilliputian clock. For even the steam engine had no industrial significance until it became part of a regulated system of production, a system which ran like "clockwork." As Lewis Mumford reminds us, "the clock . . . is the paragon of automatons. . . . The automation of time, in the clock, is the pattern of all larger systems of automation."[9]

So then: if muscle power can be replaced by a mechanism, how much more desirable still to replace the mind behind the muscle with a mechanism! If In-Here cannot be entirely relied upon to remain objective, then why not design a machine whose In-Here is a totally controlled program which specifies unambiguous objectives and procedures? "Artificial intelligence" is the logical goal toward which objective consciousness moves. Again, it is the clock which anticipates the computer. True time (what Bergson called "duration") is properly the living experience of life itself and therefore radically intuitive. But for most of us, this true time has been hopelessly displaced by the rigid rhythm of clock time. What is fundamentally the vital flow of experience then becomes an arbitrarily segmented, external measuring rod imposed upon our existence—and to experience time in any other way becomes "mystical," or "mad."

If the experience of time can be thus objectified, then why not everything else? Why should we not invent machines that objectify thought, creativity, decision making, moral judgment . . . ? Let us have machines that play games, make poems, compose music, teach philosophy. To be sure, it was

[9] Mumford, *The Myth of the Machine*, p. 286. Mumford also calls our attention here to a similar insight on the part of Marx.

once thought that such things were to be done for the joy of the playing, the making, the composing, the teaching. But scientific culture makes no allowance for "joy," since that is an experience of intensive personal involvement. Joy is something that is known only to the person: it does not submit to objectification.

To a mournfully great extent, the progress of expertise, especially as it seeks to mechanize culture, is a waging of open warfare upon joy. It is a bewilderingly perverse effort to demonstrate that nothing, *absolutely nothing* is particularly special, unique, or marvelous, but can be lowered to the status of mechanized routine. More and more the spirit of "nothing but" hovers over advanced scientific research: the effort to degrade, disenchant, level down. Is it that the creative and the joyous embarrass the scientific mind to such an extent that it must try with might and main to degrade them? Consider the strange compulsion our biologists have to synthesize life in a test tube—and the seriousness with which this project is taken. Every dumb beast of the earth knows without thinking once about it how to create life: it does so by seeking delight where it shines most brightly. But, the biologist argues, once we have done it in a laboratory, *then* we shall really know what it is all about. Then we shall be able to *improve* upon it!

What a measure of our alienation it is that we do not regard that man as a fool who grimly devotes his life to devising routine laboratory procedures for that which is given to him like a magnificent gift in the immediacy of his own most natural desire. It is as if the organism could not be trusted with a single one of its natural functions, but this brain of ours must be brought forward to control and supervise and make sure everything is running along as efficiently as a well-programmed machine.

Neurology [Michael Polanyi reminds us] is based on the assumption that the nervous system—functioning automatically according to the known laws of physics and chemistry—determines all the workings which we normally attribute to the mind of the individual. The study of psychology shows a parallel tendency toward reducing its subject matter to explicit relationships between measurable variables; relationships which could always be represented by the performances of a mechanical artifact.[10]

Once conceive of human consciousness in this way, and the inevitable next step is to replace it with a machine just as good . . . or better. So we come to the ultimate irony: the machine which is a creature of the human being becomes —most fully in the form of the computerized process—its maker's ideal. The machine achieves the perfect state of objective consciousness and, hence, becomes the standard by which all things are to be gauged. It embodies the myth of objective consciousness as Jesus incarnated the Christian conception of divinity. Under its spell, a grand reductive process begins in which culture is redesigned to meet the needs of mechanization. If we discover that a computer cannot compose emotionally absorbing music, we insist that music *does* have an "objective" side, and we turn that into our definition of music. If we discover that computers cannot translate normal language, then we invent a special, more rudimentary language which they can translate. If we discover that computers cannot teach as teaching at its most ideal is done, then we redesign education so that the machine can qualify as a teacher. If we discover that computers cannot solve the basic problems of city planning—all of which are questions of social philosophy and aesthetics—then we redefine the meaning of "city," call it an "urban area," and assume that all the problems of this entity are quantitative. In this way man is

[10] Polanyi, *Personal Knowledge*, p. 262.

replaced in all areas by the machine, not because the machine can do things "better," but rather because all things have been reduced to what the machine is capable of doing.

It is unlikely that any single scientist, behavioral scientist, or technician would plead guilty to so sweeping a charge. None of them, as individuals, are involved in so global a project. But Jacques Ellul observes the key point:

. . . one important fact has escaped the notice of the technicians, the phenomenon of technical convergence. Our interest here is the convergence on man of a plurality, not of techniques, but of systems or complexes of techniques. . . . A plurality of them converge toward the human being, and each individual technician can assert in good faith that his technique leaves intact the integrity of its object. But the technician's opinion is of no importance, for the problem concerns not *his* technique, but the convergence of all techniques.[11]

There could be no better definition of the technocracy than to identify it as the center where, subtly, steadily, ingeniously, this convergence is brought into existence. Ellul, in his somber analysis, overlooks only one dismal possibility. The final convergence he predicts may not have to postpone its completion until the technocracy has acquired mechanisms and techniques that will replace the human being in all areas of our culture. Instead, we may only have to wait until our fellow humans have converted themselves into purely impersonal automatons capable of total objectivity in all their tasks. At that point, when the mechanistic imperative has been successfullly internalized as the prevailing life style of our society, we shall find ourselves moving through a world of perfected bureaucrats, managers, operations analysts, and social engineers who will be indistinguishable from the

[11] Jacques Ellul, *The Technological Society*, p. 391.

cybernated systems they assist. Already we find these images of internally deadened human beings appearing in our contemporary novels and films. Dispassionate lovers, dispassionate killers fill the movies of Godard, Truffaut, Antonioni, Fellini with their blank gaze and automatized reactions. So too in the absurdist plays of Harold Pinter and Samuel Beckett we find the logical—or rather psychological—conclusion of life dominated by ruthless depersonalization. Here we have the world of completely objectified human relations: people hopelessly locked off from one another, maneuvering their isolated In-Heres around and about each other, communicating only by their externalized behavior. Words become mere sounds, concealing more than they convey; gestures become mere physiological twitches; bodies touch without warmth. Each In-Here confronts the others Out-There with indifference, callousness, exploitive intention. Everyone has become a specimen under the other's microscope; no one can any longer be sure that anyone else is not perhaps a robot.

* * * *

We have C. P. Snow to thank for the notion of the "two cultures." But Snow, the scientific propagandist, scarcely grasps the terrible pathos that divides these two cultures; nor for that matter do most of our social scientists and scientistic humanists. While the art and literature of our time tell us with ever more desperation that the disease from which our age is dying is that of alienation, the sciences, in their relentless pursuit of objectivity, raise alienation to its apotheosis as our *only* means of achieving a valid relationship to reality. Objective consciousness *is* alienated life promoted to its most honorific status as the scientific method. Under its auspices we subordinate nature to our command only by estranging ourselves from more and more of what we experience, until the reality about which objectivity tells us so much finally becomes a universe of congealed alienation. It is totally within our intellectual and technical power . . . and it is a worthless possession. For "what does it profit a man that he should gain the whole world, but lose his soul?"

When, therefore, those of us who challenge the objective mode of consciousness are faced with the question "but is there any *other* way in which we can know the world?", I believe it is a mistake to seek an answer on a narrowly epistemological basis. Too often we will then find ourselves struggling to discover some alternative method to produce the same sort of knowledge we now derive from science. There is little else the word "knowledge" any longer means besides an accumulation of verifiable propositions. The only way we shall ever recapture the sort of knowledge Lao-tzu referred to in his dictum "those who know do not speak," is by subordinating the question "how shall we know?" to the more existentially vital question "how shall we live?"

To ask this question is to insist that the primary purpose of human existence is not to devise ways of piling up ever greater heaps of knowledge, but to discover ways to live from day to day that integrate the whole of our nature by way of yielding nobility of conduct, honest fellowship, and joy. And to achieve those ends, a man need perhaps "know" very little in the conventional, intellectual sense of the word. But what he does know and may only be able to express by eloquent silence, by the grace of his most commonplace daily gestures, will approach more closely to whatever reality is than the most dogged and disciplined intellectual endeavor. For if that elusive concept "reality" has any meaning, it must be that toward which the entire human being reaches out for satisfaction, and not simply some fact-and-theory-mongering fraction of the personality. What is important, therefore, is that our lives should be as *big* as possible, capable of embracing the vastness of those experiences which, though yielding no articulate, demonstrable propositions, nevertheless awake in us a sense of the world's majesty.

The existence of such experiences can hardly be denied without casting out of our lives the witness of those who have been in touch with such things as only music, drama, dance, the plastic arts, and rhapsodic utterance can express. How dare we set aside as a "nothing but," or a "merely," or a "just" the work of one artist, one poet, one visionary seer, without diminishing our nature? For these, as much as any scientist or technician, are our fellow human beings. And they cry out to us in song and story, in the demanding beauty of line, color, shape, and movement. We have their lives before us as testimony that men and women have lived—and lived magnificently—in communion with such things as the intellective consciousness can do no justice to. If their work could, after some fashion, be explained, or explained away, if it could be computerized—and there are those who see this as a sensible project—it would overlook the elemental fact that in the making of these glorious things, these images, these utterances, these gestures, there was a supreme joy, and that the achievement of that joy was the purpose of their work. In the making, the makers breathed an ecstatic air. The technical mind that by-passes the making in favor of the made has already missed the entire meaning of this thing we call "creativity."

When we challenge the finality of objective consciousness as a basis for culture, what is at issue is the size of man's life. We must insist that a culture which negates or subordinates or degrades visionary experience commits the sin of diminishing our existence. Which is precisely what happens when we insist that reality is limited to what objective consciousness can turn into the stuff of science and of technical manipulation. The fact and the dire cost of this diminishing is nothing that can be adequately proved by what I write here, for it is an experience which every man must find in his own life. He finds it as soon as he refuses to block, to screen out, to set aside, to discount the needs his own personality thrusts upon him in its fullness, often in its terrifying fullness. Then he sees that the task of life is to take this raw material of his total experience—its need for knowledge, for passion, for imaginative exuberance, for moral purity, for fellowship—and to shape it *all*, as laboriously and as cunningly as a sculptor shapes his stone, into a comprehensive style of life. It is not of supreme importance that a human being should be a good scientist, a good scholar, a good administrator, a good expert; it is not of supreme importance that he should be right, rational, knowledgeable, or even creatively productive of brilliantly finished objects as often as possible. Life is not what we are in our various professional capacities or in the practice of some special skill. What *is* of supreme importance is that each of us should become a person, a whole and integrated person in whom there is manifested a sense of the human variety genuinely experienced, a sense of having come to terms with a reality that is awesomely vast.

It is my own conviction that those who open themselves in this way and who allow what is Out-There to enter them and to shake them to their very foundations are not apt to finish by placing a particularly high value on scientific or technical progress. I believe they will finish by subordinating such pursuits to a distinctly marginal place in their lives, because they will realize that the objective mode of consciousness, useful as it is on occasion, cuts them off from too much that is valuable. They will therefore come to see the myth of objective consciousness as a poor mythology, one which diminishes life rather than expands it; and they will want to spend little of their time with it. That is only my hunch; I could be wrong.

But of this there can be no doubt: that in dealing with the reality our non-intellective powers grasp, *there are no experts.* The expansion of the personality is nothing that is achieved by special training, but by a naive openness to experience. Where and when the lightning will strike that unaccountably sets one's life on fire with imaginative aspirations is beyond prediction. Jakob Boehme found his moment when a stray beam of sunlight set a metal dinner dish flashing. Supposedly the Zen master Kensu achieved illumination upon biting into a shrimp he had just caught. Tolstoy was convinced that the moment came in the experience of self-sacrifice to one's fellows, no matter how inconsequential and obscure the act. The homely magic of such turning points waits for all of us and will find us if we let it. What befalls us then is an experience of the personality suddenly swelling beyond all that we had once thought to be "real," swelling to become a greater and nobler identity than we had previously believed possible. It is precisely this sense of the person we should look for in all those who purport to have something to teach us. We should ask: "Show us this person you have made of yourself. Let us see its full size. For how can we judge what you know, what you say, what you do, what you make, unless in the context of the whole person?" It is a matter of saying, perhaps, that truth ought not to be seen as the property of a proposition, but of the person.

This would mean that our appraisal of any course of personal or social action would not be determined simply by the degree to which the proposal before us squares with objectively demonstrable knowledge, but by the degree to which it enlarges our capacity to experience: to know ourselves and others more deeply, to feel more fully the awesomeness of our environment. This, in turn, means that we must be prepared to trust that the expanded personality becomes more beautiful, more creative, more humane than the search for objective correctness can make it. To take this attitude is, I think, far from eccentric. Is it not the attitude we feel spontaneously compelled to assume whenever we find ourselves in the presence of an authentically great soul? I, who do not share any of Tolstoy's religion or that of the prophets of Israel, and who do not believe that a single jot of Dante's or Blake's world view is "true" in any scientific sense, nevertheless realize that any carping I might do about the correctness of their convictions would be preposterously petty. Their words are the conduit of a power that one longs to share. One reads their words only with humility and remorse for having lived on a lesser scale than they, for having at any point foregone the opportunity to achieve the dimensions of their vision.

When a man has *seen* and has *spoken* as such men did, the criticisms of the objective consciousness fade into insignificance. What men of this kind invite us to do is to grow as great with experience as they have, and in so doing to find the nobility they have known. Compared with the visionary powers that moved in these souls, what is the value of all the minor exactitudes of all the experts on earth?

Were we prepared to accept the beauty of the fully illuminated personality as our standard of truth—or (if the word "truth" is too sacrosanctly the property of science) of ultimate meaningfulness—then we should have done with this idiocy of making fractional evaluations of men and of ourselves. We should stop hiding behind our various small-minded specializations and pretending that we have done all that is expected of us when we have flourished a tiny banner of expertise. We should be able to ask every man who desires to lead us that he step forward and show us what his talents have made of him as a whole person. And we should reject the small souls who know only how to be correct, and cleave to the great who know how to be wise.

Chapter VIII

EYES OF FLESH, EYES OF FIRE

"What," it will be Question'd, "When the Sun rises, do you not see a round disk of fire somewhat like a Guinea?" O no, no, I see an Innumerable company of the Heavenly host crying, "Holy, Holy is the Lord God Almighty."

—WILLIAM BLAKE

What are we to say of the man who fixes his eye on the sun and does not see the sun, but sees instead a chorus of flaming seraphim announcing the glory of God? Surely we shall have to set him down as mad . . . unless he can coin his queer vision into the legal tender of elegant verse. Then, perhaps, we shall see fit to assign him a special status, a pigeonhole: call him "poet" and allow him to validate his claim to intellectual respectability by way of metaphorical license. Then we can say, "He did not *really* see what he says he saw. No, not at all. He only put it that way to lend color to his speech . . . as poets are in the professional habit of doing. It is a lyrical turn of phrase, you see: just that and nothing more." And doubtless all the best, all the most objective scholarship on the subject would support us in our perfectly sensible interpretation. It would tell us, for example, that the poet Blake, under the influence of Swedenborgian mysticism, developed a style based on esoteric visionary correspondences and was, besides, a notorious, if gifted, eccentric. Etc. Etc. Footnote.

In such fashion, we confidently discount and denature the visionary experience, and the technocratic order of life rolls on undeterred, obedient to the scientific reality principle. From such militant rationality the technocracy must permit no appeal.

Yet, if there is to be an alternative to the technocracy, there *must* be an appeal from this reductive rationality which objective consciousness dictates. This, so I have argued, is the primary project of our counter culture: to proclaim a new heaven and a new earth so vast, so marvelous that the inordinate claims of technical expertise must of necessity withdraw in the presence of such splendor to a subordinate and marginal status in the lives of men. To create and broadcast such a consciousness of life entails nothing less than the willingness to open ourselves to the visionary imagination on its own demanding terms. We must be prepared to entertain the astonishing claim men like Blake lay before us: that here are eyes which see the world not as commonplace sight or scientific scrutiny sees it, but see it transformed, made lustrous beyond measure, and in seeing the world so, see it as it really is. Instead of rushing to downgrade the rhapsodic reports of our enchanted seers, to interpret them at the lowest and most conventional level, we must be prepared to consider the scandalous possibility that wherever the visionary imagination grows bright, magic, that old antagonist of science, renews itself, transmuting our workaday reality into something bigger, perhaps more frightening, certainly more adventurous than the lesser rationality of objective consciousness can ever countenance.

But to speak of magic is to summon up at once images of vaudeville prestidigitators and tongue-in-cheek nature-fakers: tricksters who belong to the tawdry world of the stage. We have learned in this enlightened age to tolerate magicians only as an adjunct of the entertainment industry, where it is strictly understood by performer and audience alike that a trick is no more than a trick, a practised effort to baffle us. When the impossible appears to happen on stage, we know better than to believe that it has really happened. What we applaud is the dexterity with which the illusion has been created. If the magician were to claim that his deed was more than an illusion, we would consider him a lunatic or a charlatan, for he would be asking us to violate our basic conception of reality; and this we would not tolerate. While there are many, surprisingly many, who remain willing to take spiritualists, faith healers, fortunetellers, and such seriously, the scientific skeptic is forced to discount all these phenomena as atavistic and to insist stubbornly on the primacy of a coherent world view. The skeptical mind argues doggedly that we live in the midst of a nature that has been explained and exploited by science. The vaccines we inject into our bodies, the electricity that goes to work for us at the flick of a switch, the airplanes and automobiles that transport us: these and the ten thousand more technological devices we live among and rely upon derive from the scientist's, not the charlatan's, conception of nature. How shall we, with intellectual conscience, enjoy so much of what science has with an abundance of empirical demonstration brought us, and then deny the essential truth of its world view?

It is a challenge before which even our clergy have had to yield ground. Reportedly, more than one hundred million Americans attend religious services every Sunday. But if the religion they found in their churches were anything more than such timid gestures, inspirational verbiage, and comfortable socializing as are compatible with the world of science and reason which they inhabit for the next six days, how many of them would continue to attend? The last place any respectable, right-thinking citizen or enlightened clergyman wants to find himself these days is on William Jennings Bryan's side of another monkey trial.

But magic has not always belonged to the province of the carnival or the vulgar occultist. Behind these debased versions there stretches a tradition which reaches back to a noble origin. The stage magician who calls for a drum roll to catch our skeptical attention is but our latter-day form of the old tribal shaman beating his animal skin tom-tom to invoke the communal spirits. It would perhaps seem strange to many in our society to refer to this as a "noble" exemplar of the magical arts. Witch doctor, medicine man, voodoo priest . . . the very names invite savage and comic stereotypes: bone rattles and macabre masks, mumbo jumbo and blood rituals, superstitious spells and charms and incantations that never work. In the classic Hollywood encounter, the tribal magician, a figure both sinister and absurd, quickly exhausts his inane bag of tricks; and then the great white hunter steps forward to cure the sick with wonder drugs or to amaze the bug-eyed natives with pocket watch or flashlight. The white man's magic wins because it is, after all, the product of science. It wins especially when it arrives in the form of gunpowder, armed colonization, and massive material investment, the standard vehicles of civilization.

But before we dismiss the ludicrous old shaman as readily as we do the side-show sleight-of-hand man, let us spend another moment contemplating some of his less comic features—if with no other attitude of mind than the noblesse oblige of the self-styled superior culture which is well on its way to forcing the shamans of the world into rapid extinction. Soon their drums will be silent forever, superseded in every quarter of the globe by the sonic boom and the chatter of ever more intelligent computers. Perhaps the old magician's image will be replaced even in our children's literature as the Merlins of the fairy stories give place to the heroes of science fiction and fact. If it means anything very interesting to be "civilized," it means to possess the willingness to consider as instructive examples all the human possibilities that lie within our intellectual horizon—including those that conventional wisdom tells us are hopelessly obsolescent.

When we look more closely at the shaman, we discover that the contribution this exotic character has made to human culture is nearly inestimable.[1] Indeed, the shaman might properly lay claim to being the culture hero *par excellence*, for through him creative forces that approach the superhuman seem to have been called into play. In the shaman, the first figure to have established himself in human society as an individual personality, several great talents were inextricably combined that have since become specialized professions. It is likely that men's first efforts at pictorial art —and brilliant efforts they were as they survive in the form of the great paleolithic cave paintings—were the work of shamans practising a strange, graphic magic. In the shaman's rhapsodic babbling we might once have heard the first rhythms and euphonics of poetic utterance. In his inspired taletelling we might find the beginnings of mythology, and so of literature; in his masked and painted impersonations, the origin of the drama; in his entranced gyrations, the first gestures of the dance. He was—besides being artist, poet, dramatist, dancer—his people's healer, moral counsellor, diviner, and cosmologer. Among his many skills, nearly the whole repertory of the modern circus entertainer could be found in its primordial form: ventriloquism, acrobatics, contortionism, juggling, fire eating, sword swallowing, sleight of

[1] For some especially sensitive discussions of the shamanistic world view I will be discussing here, see Mircea Eliade, *Shamanism* (Princeton, N. J.: Princeton University Press, 1964). Robert Redfield, *The Little Community and Peasant Society and Culture*; Géza Roheim, *Gates of the Dream* (New York: International Universities Press, 1952), pp. 154–258; and Dorothy Lee, *Freedom and Culture* (Englewood Cliffs, N.J.: Prentice-Hall, 1959), especially her final essay. For a fascinating treatment of a surviving contemporary shaman at work, see Carlos Casteneda, *The Teachings of Don Juan: A Yaqui Way of Knowledge* (Berkeley: University of California Press, 1968).

hand. Still today, we find, among surviving primitives, shamans who are proficient in most of these talents, combining in their ancient craft things we consider high art and religion with things we consider profane diversions.

Sorted out into its several surviving traditions, the shaman's craft speaks for itself as a human achievement. But if we look for the creative thrust that once unified these skills and arts, we find the most important thing the shaman has to teach us, which is the meaning of magic in its pristine form: magic not as a repertory of clever stunts, but as a form of experience, a way of addressing the world. Those who still find themselves confronted by something of the unaccountably marvelous in the talents of artists and performers have perhaps been touched by a faint, lingering spark of the ancient shamanistic world view and have, to that extent, glimpsed an alternative reality.

Magic, as the shaman practices it, is a matter of communing with the forces of nature as if they were mindful, intentional presences, as if they possessed a will that requires coaxing, argument, imprecation. When he conjures, divines, or casts spells, the shaman is addressing these presences as one addresses a person, playing the relationship by ear, watching out for the other's moods, passions, attitudes—but always respectful of the other's dignity. For the shaman, the world is a place alive with mighty, invisible personalities; these have their own purposes, which, like those of any person, are apt to be ultimately mysterious. The shaman is on intimate terms with the presences he addresses; he strives to find out their ways and to move with the grain of them. He speaks of them as "you," not "it."

Here, for example, is Sivoangnag, an Eskimo shaman, directing a weather incantation to the unseen forces behind wind and wave:

Come, he says, thou outside there; come, he says,
                                thou outside there.
Come, be says, thou outside there; come, he says,
                                thou outside there.
Thy Sivoangnag bids thou come,
Tells thou to enter into him.
Come, he says, thou outside there.[2]

What is this but an invitation extended respectfully to an old friend? Or here is a Wintu (California) Indian describing the contrasting relationship of her shamanistic culture and that of the white man to a common environment:

The white people never cared for land or deer or bear. When we Indians kill meat, we eat it all up. When we dig roots, we make little holes. . . . We shake down acorns and pinenuts. We don't chop down the trees. We only use dead wood. But the white people plow up the ground, pull up the trees, kill everything. The tree says, "Don't. I am sore. Don't hurt me." But they chop it down and cut it up. The spirit of the land hates them. . . . The Indians never hurt anything, but the white people destroy all. They blast rocks and scatter them on the ground. The rock says "Don't! You are hurting me." But the white people pay no attention. When the Indians use rocks, they take little round ones for their cooking. . . . How can the spirit of the earth like the white man? . . . Everywhere the white man has touched it, it is sore."[3]

"The tree says . . . ," "the rock says . . .": nothing could more easily express the difference between the scientific and the magical visions of nature. The Indian woman has been taught to hear the voices of plant and stone; we have been taught to "pay no attention." The essence of magic lies in just this sense that man and not-man can stand on communi-

[2] *Report of the Canadian Arctic Expedition, 1913–1918:* Vol. 14: "Eskimo Songs" (Ottawa, 1925), p. 486.
[3] Lee, *Freedom and Culture,* p. 163.

cable terms with one another. The relationship is not that of In-Here impassively observing Out-There, but of man carrying on a personal transaction with forces in his environment which are known to be turbulently, perhaps menacingly alive. The shaman enters into the field of these forces warmly, sensuously; and because he approaches with respect, they welcome him and permit him to strive and bargain with them.

It is not a relationship the presences accept with all comers. Unlike the scientific experiment, which is depersonalized and so should work for anyone who performs it, the magical relationship is available only to those chosen by the presences themselves. The shaman is ordinarily one who discovers his vocation upon being seized up by powers beyond his comprehension. He does not initially train for the position as for a prefabricated office; this is a development that ensues when the shaman's calling becomes routinized into the formal role of the priest. Rather, like the prophets of Israel to whom so much of the primitive tradition clings, the shaman is ambushed by the divine and called forth by surprise. The prophet Amos—protesting significantly in this case to the official temple priest—explains:

I was no prophet, neither was I a prophet's son; but I was an herdsman, and a gatherer of sycamore fruit; And the Lord took me as I followed the flock, and the Lord said unto me, Go, prophesy unto my people Israel. (Amos 7:14–15)

And prophesy he did, with an eloquence that defies explanation in one from so humble an origin.

Communion with the transcendent powers, then, is not a feat that can be achieved by anyone; it is a mystery peculiar to the one elected, and is therefore through and through personal in character. For this reason, the shaman ordinarily becomes one who stands apart from his people—not in a position of institutional authority, but in a position of talented uniqueness. The respect felt for him is the respect many of us still feel for the especially gifted person, the artist or performer whose uncanny influence over us does not lie in any office he holds but in his own manifest skill.

In order to heighten that skill, the shaman devotes himself to a life of severe discipline and solitude. He fasts, he prays, he meditates; he isolates himself in order that he may watch out for such signs as the presences make visible for his education. Above all, he becomes adept in cultivating those exotic states of awareness in which a submerged aspect of his personality seems to free itself from his surface consciousness to rove among the hidden powers of the universe. The techniques by which shamans undertake their psychic adventures are many; they may make use of narcotic substances, dizziness, starvation, smoke inhalation, suffocation, hypnotic drum and dance rhythms, or even the holding of one's breath. One recognizes at once in this trance-inducing repertory a number of practices which underlie the many mystical traditions of the world: the practices of oracles, dervishes, yogis, sibyls, prophets, druids, etc.—the whole heritage of mystagoguery toward which the beat-hip wing of our counter culture now gravitates.

By such techniques, the shaman cultivates his rapport with the non-intellective sources of the personality as assiduously as any scientist trains himself to objectivity, a mode of consciousness at the polar extreme from that of the shaman. Thus the shaman is able to diffuse his sensibilities through his environment, assimilating himself to the surrounding universe. He enters wholly into the grand symbiotic system of nature, letting its currents and nuances flow through him. He may become a keener student of his environment than any scientist. He may be able to taste rain or plague on the wind.

He may be able to sense the way the wild herds will move next or how the planting will go in the season to come.

The shaman, then, is one who knows that there is more to be seen of reality than the waking eye sees. Besides our eyes of flesh, there are eyes of fire that burn through the ordinariness of the world and perceive the wonders and terrors beyond. In the superconsciousness of the shaman, nothing is simply a dead object, a stupid creature; rather, all the things of this earth are swayed by sacred meanings. " 'Primitive man,' " Martin Buber observes, "is a naive pansacramentalist. Everything is to him full of sacramental substance, everything. Each thing and each function is ever ready to light up into a sacrament for him."[4]

This perception of the world is the outstanding characteristic of primitive song, a trait that reappears in the poetry our society most readily designates as Romantic or visionary —as if such poetry were only one of many equally valid styles, rather than being the style that remains truest to what would seem to be the original poetic impulse. The result is a rich symbolic brew that blends together the most diverse phenomena. Among the northern Australian aboriginals, for example, the coming of the monsoons, when the air is charged with thunder and lightning, introduces the community's courting season. The writhing lightning in the heavens takes on the aspect of mating snakes; in turn the serpentine atmosphere sets the stage for human love-making, with its attendant ceremonies. The magical perception unites the human, animal, and meteorological worlds in the lushly sensuous imagery of a communal love song:

> The tongues of the Lightning Snakes flicker and twist,
>   one to the other . . .

[4] Martin Buber, *Hasidism* (New York: Philosophical Library, 1948), p. 133.

They flash across the foliage of the cabbage palms . . .
Lightning flashes through the clouds; with the flickering
    tongues of the Snake . . .
All over the sky, their tongues flicker: at the place of the
    Two Sisters, the place of the Wauwalak
Lightning flashes through the clouds, flash the Lightning
    Snake . . .
Its blinding flash lights up the cabbage palm foliage . . .
Gleams on the cabbage palms and on the shining
    leaves . . .[5]

Now, to see the world in this way is precisely what our
culture is prone to call "superstition." We are forced to interpret the fact that the human race survived by such an understanding of nature for tens of thousands of years as so much
dumb luck. To believe that this magical vision is anything
but a bad mistake or, at best, a primitive adumbration of
science, is to commit heresy. And yet from such a vision of
the environment there flows a symbiotic relationship between
man and not-man in which there is a dignity, a gracefulness,
an intelligence that powerfully challenges our own strenuous
project of conquering and counterfeiting nature. From that
"superstitious" perception, there derives a sense of the world
as our house, in which we reside with the ease, if not always
the comfort, of creatures who trust the earth that raised them
up and nurtures them.

The trouble is, we *don't* trust to the way of the world.
We have learned—in part from the accelerating urbanization
of the race, in part from the objective mode of consciousness
so insistently promulgated by Western science, in part, too,
perhaps from the general Christian disparagement of nature[6]

[5] R. M. and C. H. Berndt, *World of the First Australians* (Chicago: University of Chicago Press, 1965), p. 315.
[6] On this point, see Lynn White's perceptive essay "Historical
Roots of Our Ecological Crisis," *Science*, March 10, 1967.

—to think of the earth as a pit of snares and sorrows. Nature is that which must be taken unsentimentally in hand and made livable by feverish effort, ideally by replacing more and more of it with man-made substitutes. So then, perhaps someday we shall inhabit a totally plastic world, clinically immaculate and wholly predictable. To live in such a completely programmed environment becomes more and more our conception of rational order, of security. Concomitantly, our biologists begin to think even of the genetic process as a kind of "programming" (though, to be sure, a faulty one that can be improved upon in a multitude of ways). The object almost seems to bear out the ideas of Otto Rank's return-to-the-womb psychology, with our goal being a world-wide, lifelong plastic womb. The perversely anti-scientific poet e. e. cummings would seem to be exactly right:

What does being born mean to mostpeople? Catastrophe unmitigated. Socialrevolution. The cultured aristocrat yanked out of his hyperexclusively utravoluptuous superpallazzo, and dumped into an incredibly vulgar detentioncamp swarming with every conceivable species of undesirable organism. Mostpeople fancy a guaranteed birthproof safetysuit of nondestructible selflessness. If mostpeople were to be born twice they'd improbably call it dying—[7]

As a culture, we have all but completely lost the eyes to see the world in any other way. In contrast to the hardedged, distinct focus of the scientist's impersonal eye, which studies this or that piece of the environment in order to pry its secrets from it, the sensuous, global awareness of the shaman seems like that sort of peripheral vision which is in-

[7] e. e. cummings, *Poems 1923–1954* (New York: Harcourt, Brace, 1954), p. 331.

tolerably imprecise. Our habit is to destroy this receptive peripheral vision in favor of particularistic scrutiny. We are convinced that we learn more in this way about the world. And, after a fashion, we do learn things by treating the world objectively. We learn what one learns by scrutinizing the trees and ignoring the forest, by scrutinizing the cells and ignoring the organism, by scrutinizing the detailed minutiae of experience and ignoring the whole that gives the constituent parts their greater meaning. In this way we become ever more learnedly stupid. Our experience dissolves into a congeries of isolated puzzles, losing its overall grandeur. We accumulate knowledge like the miser who interprets wealth as maniacal acquisition plus tenacious possession; but we bankrupt our capacity to be wonderstruck . . . perhaps even to survive.

Consider for a moment the admonition of the quaint old Wintu woman, who warns that the "spirit of the earth" hates us for what we have done to our environment. Of course we *know* there is no "spirit of the earth." But even now as I write and as you read, there reside in the bowels of the earth, in concrete silos throughout our advanced societies, genocidally destructive weapons capable of annihilating our safe and secure civilization. No doubt in her deeply poetic imagination the old woman would see in these dread instruments the vengeful furies of the earth poised to repay the white man for his overweening pride. A purely fanciful interpretation of our situation, we might say. But maybe there is more truth in the old woman's poetry than in our operations analysis. Maybe she realizes that the spirit of the earth moves in more mysterious ways than we dare let ourselves believe, borrowing from man himself its instruments of retribution.

* * * *

I have argued that the scientific consciousness depreciates our capacity for wonder by progressively estranging us from the magic of the environment. Is the charge unfair to science? Do not scientists, like the visionary poets, also teach us of the "beauties" and "wonders" of nature?

To be sure, they appropriate the words. But the experience behind the words is not the same as that of the shamanistic vision. The mode of objective consciousness does not expand man's original sense of wonder. Rather, it displaces one notion of beauty by another, and, in so doing, cuts us off from the magical sense of reality by purporting to supersede it. The beauty which objective consciousness discerns in nature is that of generalized orderliness, of formal relationships worked out by In-Here as it observes things and events. This is the beauty of the efficiently solved puzzle, of the neat classification. It is the beauty a chess player discovers in a well-played game or a mathematician in an elegant proof. Such nomothetic beauties are conveniently summed up and indeed certified by a formula or a diagram or a statistical generalization. They are the beauties of experience planed down to manageable and repeatable terms, packaged up, mastered, brought under control.[8] In accordance with the ideal of scientific progress, such beauties can be salted away in textbooks and passed onto posterity in summary form as established conclusions.

In contrast, the beauty of the magical vision is the beauty

[8] Cf. Jacob Bronowski's description of the scientific project: "Science is a way of ordering events: its search is for laws on which to base the single prediction. . . . The aim of science is to order the particular example by articulating it on a skeleton of general law." *The Common Sense of Science* (London: Pelican Books, 1960), p. 119. This leads him to speak of science as "a predictor mechanism in process of continual self-correction." (p. 117.) And in this he finds the beauty of science, since "We find the world regular as we find it beautiful, because we are in step with it." (p. 112.)

of the deeply sensed, sacramental presence. The perception is not one of order, but of power. Such experience yields no sense of accomplished and rounded-off knowledge, but, on the contrary, it may begin and end in an overwhelming sense of mystery. We are awed, not informed. The closest most of us are apt to come nowadays to recapturing this mode of experience would be in sharing the perception of the poet or painter in the presence of a landscape, of the lover in the presence of the beloved. In the sweep of such experience, we have no interest in finding out about, summing up, or solving. On the contrary, we settle for celebrating the sheer, amazing fact that this wondrous thing is self-sufficiently there before us. We lose ourselves in the splendor or the terror of the moment and ask no more. We leave what we experience—this mountain, this sky, this place filled with forbidding shadows, this remarkable person—to be what it is, for its being alone is enough.

The scientist studies, sums up, and has done with his puzzle; the painter paints the same landscape, the same vase of flowers, the same person over and over again, content to re-experience the inexhaustible power of this presence interminably. The scientist reduces the perception of colored light to a meteorological generalization; the intoxicated poet announces, "My heart leaps up when I behold a rainbow in the sky," and then goes on to find a hundred ways to say the same thing over again without depleting the next poet's capacity to proclaim the same vision still again. What conceivable similarity is there between two such different modes of experience? None whatsoever. One clichéd argument suggests that the work of the scientist *begins* with the poet's sense of wonder (a dubious hypothesis at best) but then goes *beyond* it armed with spectroscope and light meter. The argument misses the key point: the poet's experience is defined precisely by the fact that the poet does *not* go beyond it. He begins and ends with it. Why? Because it is sufficient. Or rather, it is inexhaustible. What he has seen (and what the scientist has *not* seen) is not improved upon by being pressed into the form of knowledge. Or are we to believe it was by failure of intelligence that Wordsworth never graduated into the status of weatherman?

If we are to use the word "beauty" for both the aesthetic of orderly relations and the aesthetic of empowered presence, let us be aware that these refer to radically different experiences. Abraham Maslow believes that a harmonious relationship might be achieved between the two modes of consciousness on the basis of "hierarchical integration," the poetic perception taking precedence in the hierarchy over the objective perception.[9] Perhaps . . . but we must also consider the real possibility that in many individuals and in any one culture as a whole the two modes will approach mutual exclusion. Wordsworth suggests as much when he warns:

> Sweet is the lore which Nature brings;
> Our meddling intellect
> Mis-shapes the beauteous forms of things:
> We murder to dissect.

And if we cannot bring ourselves to murder, then we shall not be able to dissect.

To be sure, a single man may be capable at different times of both experiences, and this possibility leads us into serious errors. The physicist Max Born once reported, for example, what deep satisfaction he found in translating German lyric poetry and what delight his scientist colleagues took in their musicianship. So too, Einstein was an avid violinist and the economist Keynes, a great patron of the ballet.

[9] "Hierarchical integration" is the major proposal of Maslow's *The Psychology of Science*, a program of reform which Maslow believes will "enlarge science, not destroy it," p. xvi.

But one is reminded by such examples of the pathetic banker in T. S. Eliot's play *The Confidential Clerk*, who found greater rewards in his secret avocation as a potter than in his public position as a financier. Of necessity, however, his two worlds of ceramic art and high finance had to remain strictly compartmentalized; there was no basis on which they could interpenetrate. The world does not evaluate the talents of a financier by reference to his potting any more than one scientist evaluates another's work by reference to his artistic tastes. The expert's work must be judged on its purely objective merits; which means it must be cleansed of all personal eccentricities, no matter how delightful. That is what it means to be a specialist. A private passion for lyric poetry or the violin is no more than a quaint biographical detail in the career of an expert. When we are informed, as no doubt we shall be someday soon, that a clever young biologist has finally synthesized protoplasm in a test tube, we are not apt to suspend judgment on his achievement until we know how well developed his appreciation of Rilke is. The discovery will stand and the Nobel prize will accordingly be rewarded, though the man is the worst of philistines. And it would be news indeed to discover that the scientific and technical communities held any doubts that the worst of philistines could be a decently productive member of the guild and to see that doubt reflected in the curriculum through which the apprentices pass.

At best, the artistically inclined person within a predominantly scientific culture lives a schizoid existence, finding an out-of-the-way corner of his life in which to pursue some creative use of leisure time. In the technocratic society such a schizoid strategy is fast becoming standard practice. Men build careers and shape their worlds in their public roles as technicians and specialists. They keep their creative gestures to themselves as private and irrelevant pleasures. Such ges-

tures are a personal therapy; they help keep us a little more
sane and resilient in this grim world; but men do not let
such hobbies define their professional or social identity. We
value our little creative outlets, but we learn how to keep
them in their proper, marginal place. Or perhaps we make a
neat career as academic specialists in the official and approved
category of expertise called "the humanities." We ignore or
are never acquainted with the fact that what are interesting
concerns and exhilarating diversions for us were all-consuming
passions for the great souls who created the raw materials of
our exercises in culture appreciation.

How easily we deceive ourselves in these matters! How
marvelously the assimilative capacities of the technocracy be-
guile and mislead! As the educational level of the Great
Society rises, we all assume a veneer of eclectic cultural
polish. We decorate our lives with good music stations and
expensive reproductions of the old masters, with shelves of
paperback classics and extension courses in comparative religions. Perhaps we go on to dabble in watercolors or the classical guitar, flower arranging or a bit of amateur yoga. Higher
education, tamed and integrated into the needs of the
technocracy, treats us to magisterial surveys of great art and
thought in order that we might learn how not to be boors—as
befits a society of imperial affluence. The senatorial classes of
ancient Rome sent their scions touring the schools of Athens;
the American middle class processes its young through the
multiversity. Another generation and surely our corridors of
power will sparkle with the best conversation in the land. We
have already had the taste of a President who could festoon
his every speech with learned allusions, a Secretary of Defense
who could quote Aristotle.

But these adventures in sophistication are viciously subversive. They allow us to throw off flurries of intellectual
sparks, but short-circuit any deeper level of the personality.

They teach us appreciative gestures, but avoid the white-hot experience of authentic vision that might transform our lives and, in so doing, set us at warlike odds with the dominant culture. To achieve such a shattering transformation of the personality *one* poem by Blake, *one* canvas by Rembrandt, *one* Buddhist sutra might be enough . . . were we but opened to the power of the word, the image, the presence before us. When such an upheaval of the personality happens, our dissenting young show us the result. They drop out! The multiversity loses them . . . the society loses them. They go over to the counter culture. And then the concerned parents, the administrators, the technocrats wag their heads dolefully and ask, "Where have we failed our youth?" Meaning: "How have we made the mistake of producing children who take with such desperate seriousness what was only intended as a little cultural savvy?"

It would be one of the bleakest errors we could commit to believe that occasional private excursions into some surviving remnant of the magical vision of life—something in the nature of a psychic holiday from the dominant mode of consciousness—can be sufficient to achieve a kind of suave cultural synthesis combining the best of both worlds. Such dilettantism would be a typically sleazy technocratic solution to the problem posed by our unfulfilled psychic needs; but it would be a deception from start to finish. We have either known the magical powers of the personality or we have not. And if we have felt them move within us, then we shall have no choice in the matter but to liberate them and live by the reality they illuminate. One does not free such forces on a part-time basis any more than one falls madly in love or repents of sin on a part-time basis. To suggest that there may be some halfway house between the magical and the objective consciousness in which our culture can reside is quite simply to confess that one does not know what it is to see with the eyes of fire. In which case, we shall never achieve the personal, transactive relationship with the reality that envelops us which is the essence of the magical world view. Accordingly, whatever our degree of intellectual sophistication, we shall as a culture continue to deal with our natural environment as lovingly, as reverently as a butcher deals with the carcass of a dead beast.

* * * *

Yet, if we have lost touch with the shamanistic world view by which men have lived since the paleolithic beginnings of human culture, there is one sense in which magic has not lost its power over us with the progress of civilization. It is not only the dumfounded populations of so-called underdeveloped societies that perceive and yield to the white man's science and technology as a form of superior magic. The same is true of the white man's own society—though we, as enlightened folk, have learned to take the magic for granted and to verbalize various non-supernatural explanations for its activity. True enough: science possesses theory, methodology, epistemology to support its discoveries and inventions. But, alas! most of us have no better understanding of these things than the bewildered savages of the jungle. Even if we have acquired the skill to manipulate vacuum tubes and electrical circuits and balky carburetors, few of us could articulate one commendable sentence about the basic principles of electricity or internal combustion, let alone jet propulsion, nuclear energy, deoxyribonucleic acid, or even statistical sampling, which is supposedly the key to understanding our own collective opinions these days.

It is remarkable how nonchalantly we carry off our gross ignorance of the technical expertise our very lives depend upon. We live off the surface of our culture and pretend we know enough. If we are cured of disease, we explain the matter by saying a pill or a serum did it—as if that were to say anything at all. If the economy behaves erratically, we mouth what we hear about inflationary pressures . . . the balance of payments . . . the gold shortage . . . down-turns and up-swings. Beyond manipulating such superficial notions, we work by faith. We believe that somewhere behind the pills and the economic graphs there are experts who understand whatever else there is to understand. We know they are experts, because, after all, they talk like experts and besides possess degrees, licenses, titles, and certificates. Are we any better off than the savage who believes his fever has been cured because an evil spirit has been driven out of his system?

For most of us the jargon and mathematical elaborations of the experts are so much mumbo jumbo. But, we feel certain, it is all mumbo jumbo that *works*—or at least seems to work, after some fashion that the same experts tell us should be satisfactory. If those who know best tell us that progress consists in computerizing the making of political and military decisions, who are we to say this is not the best way to run our politics? If enough experts told us that strontium 90 and smog were good for us, doubtless most of us would take their word for it. We push a button and something called the engine starts; we press a pedal and the vehicle moves; we press the pedal more and it moves faster. If we believe there is someplace to get and if we believe it is important to get there very, very fast—despite the dangers, despite the discomforts, despite the expense, despite the smog—then the automobile is an impressive piece of magic. That is the sort of magic science can bring about and which shamanistic incantations never will. Push another button and the missile blasts off; aim it correctly and it will blow up a whole city . . . maybe, if the hardware is sophisticated enough, the whole planet. If blowing up the planet is deemed worth doing (under certain well-considered conditions, to be sure), then science is what we want. Incantations will never do the job.

But if the role of the technical expert in our society is analogous to that of the old tribal shaman—in the sense that both are deferred to by the populace at large as figures who conjure with mysterious forces in mysterious ways—what significant difference is there between cultures based on scientific and visionary experience? The difference is real and it is critical. It requires that we make a distinction between good and bad magic—a line that can be crossed in any culture, primitive or civilized, and which has been crossed in ours with the advent of the technocracy.

The essence of good magic—magic as it is practised by the shaman and the artist—is that it seeks always to make available to all the full power of the magician's experience. While the shaman may be one especially elected and empowered, his role is to introduce his people to the sacramental presences that have found him out and transformed him into their agent. His peculiar gift confers responsibility, not privilege. Similarly, the artist lays his work before the community in the hope that through it, as through a window, the reality he has fathomed will be witnessed by all who give attention. For the shaman, ritual performs the same function. By participating in the ritual, the community comes to know what the shaman has discovered. Ritual is the shaman's way of broadcasting his vision; it is his instructive offering. If the artist's work is successful, if the shaman's ritual is effective, the community's sense of reality will become expansive; something of the dark powers will penetrate its experience.

To take but one example, here is how the great Wanapum Indian shaman Smohalla, one of the forerunners of the nineteenth-century Amerindian Ghost Dance tradition, led his people in ceremonies designed to introduce them to the dream world he had discovered:

The procession started from the old "Salmon House," once used to store dried fish and now transformed into Smohalla's church, where the religious ceremony was held. The responsive recitation of the litany, choral singing to the accompaniment of tomtoms, and dancing with a great variety of rhythms—the tempo being underscored by appropriate mimicry—constituted the ritual, which took place on Sunday, according to Christian practice. . . . Ritual excitement was heightened by singing, dancing, and the rhythmic beating of the drums, which gradually hypnotized the participants and sent most of them into trance, or dreams, as they were called in this cult. Visions were publicly narrated according to traditional custom, the Dream Dance being regarded as the cure for every ill introduced by the white man.[10]

In this way, realms that Smohalla had explored were opened to the entire community, not simply by report but by way of personal awareness.

Good magic opens the mysteries to all; bad magic seeks simply to mystify. The object of the bad magician is to monopolize knowledge of the hidden reality (or simply to counterfeit it) and to use the monopoly to befuddle or cow. The bad magician—in the form of the priest or the expert —strives to achieve the selfish advantage of status or reward precisely by restricting access to the great powers he purports to control. Something of the distinction I am making survives in the Catholic Church's concept of simony, the sin against the Holy Ghost. The simoniac priest who uses his privileged control of the sacraments for personal gain is, by the teaching of the Church, committing the blackest of sins. He is betraying what lingers in his profession of the old shamanistic

[10] Vittorio Lanternari, *The Religions of the Oppressed* (New York: Mentor Books, 1963), pp. 112–13.

calling, which is to make the sacramental presence available to everyone.

It was exactly this tendency of institutionalized religion to indulge in self-seeking obscurantism and authoritarian manipulation which led to the series of great revolts against the churches of the West that culminated in the militant secularism of the Enlightenment. But in the process of throwing off the obscurantists, the very idea of mystery was radically altered. Mystery, as it was known in primordial rite and ritual, as it was experienced in the sacraments of the mystery cults, had stood as a boundary defining man's proper station in the world. It was that which was sacred and taught man wise limitations. The existence of mystery in this sense—as the non-human dimension of reality which was not to be tampered with but to be revered—served to enrich the lives of men by confronting them with a realm of inexhaustible wonder. With the appearance of scientific skepticism, however, the mysterious came to be either a tricky puzzle to be solved or a guilty secret to be exposed. In either case, the mystery came to be seen as an intolerable barrier to reason and justice. Since the sacred had become the mask of scoundrels and frauds, away then with the sacred! *Écrasez l'infâme!*

As Alfred North Whitehead observes, "the common sense of the eighteenth century . . . acted on the world like a bath of moral cleansing." But what the heroic skeptics and principled agnostics of that age did not anticipate was the fact that "if men cannot live on bread alone, still less can they do so on disinfectants."[11] Even more tragically, they did not foresee the possibility, indeed the inevitability, that the scientific world view might well be corrupted by the same kind of bad magic that had turned Christianity into the bul-

[11] Alfred North Whitehead, *Science and the Modern World* (New York: Mentor Books, 1925), p. 59.

wark of exploitive privilege. Yet science and technology, with
their relentless insistence on specialization and expertise, were
themselves to come full circle and be transformed into as
closed a priesthood as any in history. Where the shaman
looked to communal ritual to validate his vision of reality,
scientific experts have had to look more and more to professional approval by self-selected authorities to validate their
ever more esoteric knowledge.[12] The general public has had
to content itself with accepting the decision of experts that
what the scientists say is true, that what the technicians
design is beneficial. All that remained to be done to turn
such an authoritative professionalism into a new regime of
bad magicians was for ruling political and economic elites to
begin buying up the experts and using them for their own
purposes. It is in this fashion that the technocracy has been
consolidated. We arrive, at last, at a social order where everything from outer space to psychic health, from public opinion
to sexual behavior is staked out as the province of expertise.
The community dares not eat a peach or spank a baby without looking to a certified specialist for approval—lest it seem
to trespass against reason.

Even the experts who hold out gamely against this system,
challenging the certification authority of state, corporation,

[12] The idea that scientific knowledge is "public knowledge" must
be severely qualified as the work of scientists grows more esoteric,
even with respect to colleagues pursuing research in other scientific
fields. On this point, see Thomas Kuhn's remarks on the role of the
"uniquely competent professional group" as the "exclusive arbiter of
professional achievement" in a scientific culture. The group to whom
the scientist addresses himself (and this becomes true as time goes
on of scholarship in the social sciences and humanities as well) "may
not . . . be drawn at random from society as a whole, but is rather
the well-defined community of the scientist's professional compeers.
. . . The group's members, as individuals and by virtue of their
shared training and experience, must be seen as the sole possessors of
the rules of the game or of some equivalent basis for unequivocal
judgements." *The Structure of Scientific Revolutions*, p. 167.

university, or party, can do no more than ask the community to accept *their* authority on trust. For the reality which scientific knowledge examines cannot be translated into either art or ritual which the community can participate in experiencing. The research of experts can be popularized or vulgarized as a body of information—and inevitably distorted in the process. It cannot be democratized as a form of vital experience. Such is the price we pay for replacing the immediacy of the personal vision with the aloofness of objective knowledge. The old magic that could illuminate the sacramental presence in a tree, a pond, a rock, a totem is derided as a form of superstition unworthy of civilized men. Nothing we come upon in the world can any longer speak to us in its own right. Things, events, even the person of our fellow human beings have been deprived of the voice with which they once declared their mystery to men. They can be known now only by the mediation of experts who, in turn, must rely upon the mediation of formulas and theories, statistical measures and strange methodologies. But for us there is no other reality, unless we are willing to let ourselves be set down as incorrigibly irrational, the allies of sinister and reactionary forces.

* * * *

In harking back to the shamanistic world view, a cultural stage buried in the primitive past of our society, I may seem to have strayed a long way from the problems of our contemporary dissenting youth. But that is hardly the case. The young radicalism of our day gropes toward a critique that embraces ambitious historical and comparative cultural perspectives. The New Left that rebels against technocratic manipulation in the name of participative democracy draws, often without realizing it, upon an anarchist tradition which has always championed the virtues of the primitive band, the tribe, the village. The spirit of Prince Kropotkin, who learned the anti-statist values of mutual aid from villagers and nomads little removed from the neolithic or even paleolithic level, breathes through all the young say about community. Our beatniks and hippies press the critique even further. Their instinctive fascination with magic and ritual, tribal lore, and psychedelic experience attempts to resuscitate the defunct shamanism of the distant past. In doing so, they wisely recognize that participative democracy cannot settle for being a matter of political-economic decentralism—only that and nothing more. As long as the spell of the objective consciousness grips our society, the regime of experts can never be far off; the community is bound to remain beholden to the high priests of the citadel who control access to reality. It is, at last, reality itself that must be participated in, must be seen, touched, breathed with the conviction that *here* is the ultimate ground of our existence, available to all, capable of ennobling by its majesty the life of every man who opens himself. It is participation of this order—experiential and not merely political—that alone can guarantee the dignity and autonomy of the individual citizen. The strange young oters who don cowbells and primitive talismans and who take to the public parks or wilderness to improvise outlandish communal ceremonies are in reality seeking to ground democracy safely beyond the culture of expertise. They give us back the image of the paleolithic band, where the community during its rituals stood in the presence of the sacred in a rude equality that predated class, state, status. It is a strange brand of radicalism we have here that turns to prehistoric precedent for its inspiration.

To be sure, there is no revolutionizing the present by mere reversion to what is for our society a remote past. Prehistoric or contemporary primitive cultures may serve as models to guide us; but they can scarcely be duplicated by us. As Martin

Buber warns us in his discussion of the magical world view of primitive man, "he who attempts a return ends in madness or mere literature."[13] It is, as he says, a "*new* pansacramentalism" we need, one which works within and expands the interstices of the technocracy, responding wherever possible to the thwarted longings of men. There will have to be experiments—in education, in communitarianism—which will seek not coexistence with the technocracy and less still the treacherous satisfactions of quick publicity; but which aim instead at subverting and seducing by the force of innocence, generosity, and manifest happiness in a world where those qualities are cynically abandoned in favor of bad substitutes. To the end that there shall be more and more of our fellows who cease to live by the declared necessities of the technocracy; who refuse to settle for a mere after-hours outlet for the magical potentialities of their personalities; who become as if deaf and blind to the blandishments of career, affluence, the mania of consumption, power politics, technological progress; who can at last find only a sad smile for the low comedy of these values and pass them by.

But further, to the end that men may come to view much that goes by the name of social justice with a critical eye, recognizing the way in which even the most principled politics —the struggle against racial oppression, the struggle against world-wide poverty and backwardness—can easily become the lever of the technocracy in its great project of integrating ever more of the world into a well-oiled, totally rationalized managerialism. In a sense, the true political radicalism of our day begins with a vivid realization of how much in the way of high principle, free expression, justice, reason, and humane intention the technocratic order can adapt to the purpose of entrenching itself ever more deeply in the uncoerced alle-

[13] Buber, *Hasidism*, p. 134.

giance of men. This is the sort of insight our angriest dissenters tend to miss when, in the course of heroic confrontation, they open themselves to the most obvious kinds of police and military violence. They quickly draw the conclusion that the status quo is supported by nothing more than bayonets, overlooking the fact that these bayonets enjoy the support of a vast consensus which has been won for the status quo by means far more subtle and enduring than armed force.

For this reason, the process of weening men away from the technocracy can never be carried through by way of a grim, hard-bitten, and self congratulatory militancy, which at best belongs to tasks of ad hoc resistance. Beyond the tactics of resistance, but shaping them at all times, there must be a stance of life which seeks not simply to muster power against the misdeeds of society, but to transform the very sense men have of reality. This may mean that, like George Fox, one must often be prepared not to act, but to "stand still in the light," confident that only such a stillness possesses the eloquence to draw men away from lives we must believe they inwardly loathe, but which misplaced pride will goad them to defend under aggressive pressure to the very death—their death and ours.

A political end sought by no political means . . . it is as Chuang-tzu tells us:

The wise man, when he must govern, knows how to do nothing. Letting things alone, he rests in his original nature. If he loves his own person enough to let it rest in its original truth, he will govern others without hurting them. Let him keep the deep drives in his own guts from going into action. Let him keep still, not looking, not hearing. Let him sit like a corpse, with the dragon power alive all around him. In complete silence, his voice will be like thunder. His movements will be invisible, like those of a spirit, but the powers of heaven will go with them. Unconcerned, doing nothing, he will see all things grow ripe around him. Where will he find time to govern?[14]

Perhaps only in this fashion do we make visible the submerged magic of the earth and bring closer that culture in which power, knowledge, achievement recede before the great purpose of life. Which is, as an old Pawnee shaman taught: to approach with song every object we meet.

[14] Thomas Merton, trans. *The Way of Chuang Tzu* (New York: New Directions, 1965), p. 71.

Appendix

OBJECTIVITY UNLIMITED

The items contained in this appendix are meant to give at least a minimal illustration of the psychology of objective consciousness as characterized in Chapter VII. The examples offered are few in number; but they could be multiplied many times over.

It is likely that some readers will protest that these items do not give a "balanced" picture of science and technology, but unfairly emphasize certain enormities and absurdities. Let me therefore make three points in explanation of why and how the examples of objectivity below were selected.

(1) Often, when one enters into a discussion of the less encouraging aspects of scientific research and technical innovation, the cases brought forward for consideration are either obviously extreme examples that are universally condemned (like that of the Nazi physicians who experimented on human specimens), or they are images conjured up from science fiction, which are easily waved aside precisely because they *are* fictitious. The items in this appendix are not drawn from either of these sources. Rather, they derive from what I believe can fairly be called mainstream science (I include the behavioral sciences in the term) and technology. I have tried to offer reports, examples, and statements from thoroughly reputable sources which can pass muster as possessing professional respectability. My object is to present items that have a routine, if not an almost casual, character and can therefore stand as the voice of normal, day-to-day science and technology as they are practiced in our society with a sense of complete innocence and orthodoxy—and often with the massive subsidization of public funds. Indeed, I sus-

pect that many scientists and technicians would find nothing whatever to object to in the remarks and projects referred to here, but would view them as perfectly legitimate, if not extremely interesting, lines of research to which only a perversely anti-scientific mentality would object.

(2) Further, I would contend that the material presented here typifies what the technocracy is most eager to reward and support. These are the kinds of projects and the kinds of men we can expect to see becoming ever more prominent as the technocratic society consolidates its power. Whatever enlightening and beneficial "spin-off" the universal research explosion of our time produces, the major interest of those who lavishly finance that research will continue to be in weapons, in techniques of social control, in commercial gadgetry, in market manipulation, and in the subversion of democratic processes by way of information monopoly and engineered consensus. What the technocracy requires, therefore, is men of unquestioning objectivity who can apply themselves to any assignment and deliver the goods, with few qualms regarding the ultimate application of their work.

As time goes on, it may well be that gifted and sensitive talents will find it more and more difficult to serve the technocratic system. But such conscience-stricken types—the potential Norbert Wieners and Otto Hahns and Leo Szilards—will be easily replaced by acquiescent routineers who will do what is expected of them, who will play dumb as they continue grinding out the research, and who will be able to convince themselves that the high status they receive is, in truth, the just and happy reward their idealistic quest for knowledge deserves. One would think that a man who had been hired by pyromaniacs to perfect better matches would begin to sense, at some point, how much of a culprit he was. But fame and cash can do wonders to bolster one's sense of innocence.

Not long before his death, the greatest scientific mind since Newton confessed to the world that, if he had to choose over again, he would rather have been a good shoemaker. I have often felt that, long before he learns a single thing about mesons or information theory or DNA, every aspiring young scientist and technician in our schools should be confronted with that heartbroken admission and forced to fathom its implications. But alas, I suspect there is in the great man's lament a pathos too deep any longer to be appreciated by the sorcerer's apprentices who crowd forward in disconcerting numbers to book passage on the technocratic gravy train. And where the scientists and technicians lead, the pseudo-scientists and social engineers are quick to follow. Given the dazzling temptations of a sky's-the-limit research circus, what time is there to dally over traditional wisdom or moral doubt? It distracts from the bright, hard, monomaniacal focus that pays off for the expert—especially if one bears in mind that in the technical fields these days apprentices make their mark early . . . or perhaps never. So the sweaty quest for quick, stunning success goes off in all directions. If only one can find a way to graft the head of a baboon on to a blue jay (after all, why not?) . . . if only one can synthesize a virus lethal enough to wipe out a whole nation (after all, why not?) . . . if only one can invent a Greek-tragedy writing machine (after all, why not?) . . . if only one can dope out a way to condition the public into believing that War is Peace and that the fallout shelter is our home away from home (after all, why not?) . . . if only one can devise a way to program dreams so that perhaps commercial announcements can be inserted (after all, why not?) . . . if only one can find out how to scramble DNA so that parents can order their progeny tailor-made as guaranteed-or-money-back Mozarts, Napoleons, or Jesus Christs (after all, why not?) . . . if only one can invent a method of shooting passengers like bullets from Chicago to Istanbul (after all, why not?) . . . if only one can develop a computer that will simulate the mind of God (after all, why not?) . . . one's name is made!

It is, once again, the key strategy of the technocracy. It

monopolizes the cultural ground; it sponges up and anticipates all possibilities. Where science and technology are concerned, its concern is to keep its magician's hat filled with
every conceivable form of research and development, the
better to confound and stupefy the populace. Thus it must
stand prepared to subvene every minor intellectual seizure
that lays claim to being or pursuing some form of scientific
knowledge. For after all, one never can tell what may come
of pure research. Best buy it all up, so that one can be in
the position to pick and choose what to exploit and
develop.

(3) The notion of "balance," as applied to the evaluation
of scientific and technical work, implies the existence of
well-defined values which can be brought to bear to distin-
guish a desirable from an undesirable achievement. The
supposition that such values exist in our culture is misleading
in the extreme; but that supposition plays a critically important part in the politics of the technocracy and is, indeed,
one of its stoutest bulwarks.

To begin with, we must understand that there exists no
way whatever, on strictly scientific grounds, to invalidate
any objective quest for knowledge, regardless of where it may
lead or how it may proceed. The particular project may be
unpalatable to the more squeamish among us—for "purely
personal reasons"; but it does not thereby cease to be a
legitimate exercise of objectivity. After all, knowledge is
knowledge; and the more of it, the better. Just as Leigh-
Mallory set out to climb Everest simply because it was *there*,
so the scientific mind sets out to solve puzzles and unravel
mysteries because it perceives them as being *there*. What
further justification need there be?

Once an area of experience has been identified as an
object of study or experimental interference, there is no
rational way in which to deny the inquiring mind its right to
know, without calling into question the entire scientific

enterprise. In order to do so, one would have to invoke some notion of the "sacred" or the "sacrosanct" to designate an area of life that must be closed to inquiry and manipulation. But since the entire career of the objective consciousness has been one long running battle against such suspiciously nebulous ideas, these concepts survive in our society only as part of an atavistic vocabulary. They are withered roses we come upon, crushed in the diaries of a prescientific age.

We are sadly deceived by the old cliché which mournfully tells us that morality has failed to "keep up with" technical progress (as if indeed morality were a "field of knowledge" in the charge of unidentified, but presumably rather incompetent, experts). The expansion of objective consciousness must, of necessity, be undertaken at the expense of moral sensibility. Science deracinates the experience of sacredness wherever it abides, and does so unapologetically, if not with fanatic fervor. And lacking a warm and lively sense of the sacred, there can be no ethical commitment that is anything more than superficial humanist rhetoric. We are left with, at best, good intentions and well-meaning gestures that have no relationship to authoritative experience, and which therefore collapse into embarrassed confusion as soon as a more hard-headed, more objective inquirer comes along and asks, "But why not?" Having used the keen blade of scientific skepticism to clear our cultural ground of all irrational barriers to inquiry and manipulation, the objective consciousness is free to range in all directions. And so it does.

It is only when we recognize the essentially no-holds-barred character of the objective consciousness—its illimitable thrust toward knowledge and technical mastery of every kind —that the demand for a balanced appreciation of its achievements becomes irrelevant, as well as sleazy in the extreme. The defense of science and technology by reference to balance is, in fact, the worst vice of our culture, betraying an ethical superficiality that is truly appalling. For the balance that is called for is *not* something the scientific community itself provides, or in any sense employs as a control upon its activities. Rather, it is *we* the public who are expected to supply the balance by way of our private assessments of what the objective consciousness lays before us. The scientists and technicians enjoy the freedom—indeed they demand the freedom—to do *absolutely anything* to which curiosity or a research contract draws them. And while they undertake their completely indiscriminate activities, the technocracy which sponsors them provides the public with a scorecard. On this scorecard we can, on the basis of our personal predilections, chalk up the pluses and minuses in any way we see fit. It is all admirably pluralistic: the technocracy can afford to be pluralistic in the matter, because it knows that over the long run there will be achievements and discoveries a-plenty to meet everybody's tastes. After all, if one keeps reaching into a grab bag filled with an infinite number of things, sooner or later one is bound to pluck out enough nice things to offset the undesirable things one has acquired. But the balance involved is hardly guaranteed by those who fill the bag; it is based entirely on chance and personal evaluation.

So we arrive at the lowest conceivable level of moral discourse: ex post facto tabulation and averaging within a context of randomized human conduct. The balance that emerges from such a situation might just as well be gained if our society were to agree to subsidize every whim that arose within a community of certified lunatics, on the assumption that a certain amount of what such a procedure eventually produced would meet any standard of worthwhileness one cared to name. Where moral discrimination is concerned, the scientific and technical mandarins of the technocracy operate not very differently from the composer of chance music who offers us a chaos of sound: if we do not like what we hear, we need only wait a little longer. Eventually . . . eventually . . . there will come a concatenation of noises that charms our taste. At that point, presumably, the score as a whole is vindicated.

The demand for a balanced view of science and technology amounts, then, to something rather like a con game which the technocracy plays with the general public. Since balance is in no sense an ethical discipline the technocracy imposes upon itself by reference to a pre-established moral end, we have absolutely no guarantee that the future of scientific and technical work has anything to offer us but more of everything. All we can be sure of is that the objective consciousness will expand into more areas of life militantly and inexorably, entrenching its alienative dichotomy, invidious hierarchy, and mechanistic imperative ever more deeply in our experience. As that happens, the dreams of reason are bound to become more and more a nightmare of depersonalization. If one wonders how the world will then look to men, one need scarcely turn to the inventions of science fiction; we need only examine the activities and sentiments of those whose capacity for experience has already been raped by the ethos of objectivity. And that is what the items offered here are meant to illustrate.

(1) The first item dates back nearly a century; but it is cited without criticism in a recent survey of psychology as a significant example of pioneering neurological research. It concerns the work of Dr. Roberts Bartholow of the Medical College of Ohio. In 1874 Dr. Bartholow conducted a number of experiments on a "rather feeble-minded" woman of thirty named Mary Rafferty. The experiments involved passing an electric current into the young woman's brain through a portion of the skull that had eroded away. Here is a selection from the records of Dr. Bartholow, who introduces his findings by saying, "It has seemed to me most desirable to present the facts as I observed them, without comment."

Observation 3. Passed an insulated needle into the left posterior lobe. . . . Mary complained of a very strong and unpleasant feeling of tingling in both right extremities. In order to develop more decided reactions, the strength of the current was increased. . . . her countenance exhibited great distress, and she began to cry. . . . left hand was extended . . . the arms agitated with clonic spasms, her eyes became fixed, with pupils widely dilated, lips were blue and she frothed at the mouth. (Quoted in David Krech, "Cortical Localization of Function," in Leo Postman, ed., *Psychology in the Making* [New York: A. A. Knopf, 1962], pp. 62–63.)

Three days after this experiment, Mary Rafferty was dead. Those who think such experimentation on human specimens —especially on imprisoned persons like Mary Rafferty—is uncommon, should see M. H. Pappworth's *Human Guinea Pigs: Experimentation on Man* (London: Routledge & Kegan Paul, 1967).

(2) To spare a sigh for the fate of animals undergoing laboratory experimentation is generally considered cranky in the extreme. The reasons for this no doubt include the layman's inability to gain a clear picture of what is happening to the animals through the technical terminology of such accounts as appear in the many journals of physiology, psychology, and medical research, as well as the prevailing assumption that such research is directly related to human benefit and is therefore necessary. The following is a fairly comprehensible report of research done for the British Ministry of Supply during World War II on the effects of poison gases. If the account detours into too many technicalities, the situation is simply this: the experimenter has forced a large dose of Lewisite gas into the eye of a rabbit and is recording over the next two weeks precisely how the animal's eye rots away. But note how the terminology and the reportorial style distance us from the reality of the matter. As in the case of Mary Rafferty above, it is impossible to focus on the fact that the event is happening before a human observer.

Very severe lesions ending in loss of the eye: . . . In two eyes of the 12 in the series of very severe lesions the destructive action of the

Lewisite produced necrosis [decay] of the cornea before the blood vessels had extended into it. Both lesions were produced by a large droplet. In one case the rabbit was anaesthetized, in the other it was not anaesthetized and was allowed to close the eye at once, thus spreading the Lewisite all over the conjunctival sac [eyeball]. The sequence of events in this eye begins with instantaneous spasm of the lids followed by lacrimation in 20 seconds (at first clear tears and in one minute 20 seconds milky Harderian secretion). In six minutes the third lid is becoming oedematous [swollen] and in 10 minutes the lids themselves start to swell. The eye is kept closed with occasional blinks. In 20 minutes the oedema [swelling] is so great that the eye can hardly be kept closed as the lids are lifted off the globe. In three hours it is not possible to see the cornea and there are conjunctival petechiae [minute hemorrhages]. Lacrimation continues.

In 24 hours the oedema is beginning to subside and the eye is discharging muco-pus. There is a violent iritis [inflammation] and the cornea is oedematous all over in the superficial third. . . . On the third day there is much discharge and the lids are still swollen. On the fourth day the lids are stuck together with discharge. There is severe iritis. The corneae are not very swollen. . . . On the eighth day there is hypopyon [pus], the lids are brawny and contracting down on the globe so that the eye cannot be fully opened. . . . In 10 days the cornea is still avascular, very opaque and covered with pus. On the 14th day the center of the cornea appears to liquify and melt away, leaving a Descemetocoele [a membrane over the cornea], which remains intact till the 28th day, when it ruptures leaving only the remains of an eye in a mass of pus. (Ida Mann, A. Pirie, B. D. Pullinger, "An Experimental and Clinical Study of the Reaction of the Anterior Segment of the Eye to Chemical Injury, With Special Reference to Chemical Warfare Agents," *British Journal of Ophthalmology*, Monograph Supplement XIII, 1948, pp. 146–47.)

By way of explaining the methodological validity of such research, P. B. Medawar offers the following hard-headed observation:

For all its crudities, Behaviorism, conceived as a methodology rather than as a psychological system, taught psychology with brutal emphasis that "the dog is whining" and "the dog is sad" are statements of altogether different empirical standing, and heaven help psychology if it ever again overlooks the distinction. (P. B. Medawar, *The Art of the Soluble* [London: Methuen, 1967], p. 89.)

Professor Medawar does not make clear, however, on whom the "brutal emphasis" of this distinction has fallen: the experimenter or the experimental subject. Does it, for example, make any difference to the methodology if the subject is capable of saying, "I am sad," "I am hurt"?

For a wise discussion of the ethics and psychology of animal experimentation (as well as a few more ghastly examples of the practice), see Catherine Roberts, "Animals in Medical Research" in her *The Scientific Conscience* (New York: Braziller, 1967).

(3) The following comes from a study of the effects of wartime bombing on civilian society, with special reference to the probable results of thermonuclear bombardment. The research was done under grants from the U. S. Air Force and the Office of the Surgeon General at the Columbia University Bureau of Applied Social Research, and published with the aid of a Ford Foundation subsidy. It should be mentioned that the scholar's conclusions are generally optimistic about the possibilities of rapid recovery from a nuclear war. He even speculates that the widespread destruction of cultural artifacts in such a war might have the same long-term effect as the barbarian devastation of Greco-Roman art and architecture: namely, a liberation from the dead hand of the artistic past such as that which prepared the way for the Italian Renaissance.

We have deliberately avoided arousing emotions. In this area, which so strongly evokes horror, fear, or hope, a scientist is seriously tempted to relax his standards of objectivity and to give vent to his own subjective feelings. No one can fail to be deeply aroused and disturbed by the facts of nuclear weapons. These sentiments are certainly necessary to motivate actions, but they should not distort an investigation of the truth or factual predictions.

This book deals with the social consequences of actual bombing, starting with different types of destruction as given physical events, tracing step by step the effects upon urban populations—their size, composition, and activities—and finally investigating the repercussions upon national populations and whole countries. . . . While we are deeply concerned with the moral and humanitarian implications of bomb destruction, we excluded them from this book, not because we judged them to be of secondary importance, but because they are better dealt with separately and in a different context.

This "different context," however, has not to date been explored by the author. But he does turn to considering "the effect upon morale" of wholesale carnage. Note how the use of phrases like "apparently" and "it appears" and "it can be argued" and "there is evidence of" neatly denature the horror of the matters under discussion.

The impact of casualties upon morale stems mainly from actually seeing dead or injured persons and from the emotional shock resulting from the death of family and friends. . . . No other aspect of an air raid causes as severe an emotional disturbance as the actual witnessing of death and agony. Interviews with persons who have experienced an atomic explosion reveal that ⅓ of them were emotionally upset because of the casualties they saw, while only 5 percent or fewer experienced fear or some other form of emotional disturbance on account of the flash of the explosion, the noise, the blast, the devastation, and the fires.

An atomic bombing raid causes more emotional reactions than a conventional raid. Janis declares:
"Apparently it was not simply the large number of casualties but also the specific character of the injuries, particularly the grossly altered physical appearance of persons who suffered severe burns, that had a powerful effect upon those who witnessed them. Hence, it appears to be highly probable that, as a correlate of the exceptional casualty-inflicting properties of the atomic weapon, there was an unusually intense emotional impact among the uninjured evoked by the perception of those who were casualties."

The strong emotional disturbance that results from the sight of mangled bodies has also been reported from lesser peacetime disasters such as a plant explosion.

We are interested here in this emotional agitation only as it affects the overt behavior of city dwellers. Two contradictory reactions could be suggested as short-range effects. It can be argued that apathy and disorganization will prevail. On the other hand, it is conceivable that the emotional disturbance from casualties will intensify rescue or defense activities. While there is evidence of both forms of reactions after a disaster, the latter is encouraged by effective leadership which directs survivors toward useful activities. (Fred C. Iklé, *The Social Impact of Bomb Destruction* [Norman, Okla.: University of Oklahoma Press, 1958], pp. vii–viii; 27–29.)

(4) As the selection above suggests, the new social science of operations analysis has done an impressively ambitious job of opening up hitherto neglected avenues of research. Here, for example, are some suggested research subjects for which the RAND Corporation received government grants totaling several million dollars during 1958 as part of its civilian defense studies:

A study should be made of the survival of populations in environments similar to overcrowded shelters (concentration camps, Russian and German use of crowded freight cars, troopships, crowded prisons, crowded lifeboats, submarines, etc.). Some useful guiding principles might be found and adapted to the shelter program.

The object of such research would be to "act as reassurance that the more unpleasant parts of the experience had been foreseen and judged to be bearable by a peacetime government." (Herman Kahn, "Some Specific Suggestions for Achieving Early Non-Military Defense Capabilities and Initiating Long-Range Programs," RAND Corporation Research Memorandum RM-2206-RC, 1959, pp. 47–48.)

And to give but one more example of the truly Faustian élan of our military-oriented rescarch, we have this prognosis from a naval engineer:

Weather and climate are never neutral. They are either formidable enemies or mighty allies. Try to imagine the fantastic possibilities of one nation possessing the capability to arrange over large areas, or perhaps the entire globe, the distribution of heat and cold, rain and sunshine, flood and drought, to the advantage of itself and its allies and to the detriment of its enemies. We *must* think about it—*now* —for this is the direction in which technology is leading us. . . .

The question is no longer: "Will mankind be able to modify the weather on a large scale and control the climate?" Rather, the question is: "Which scientists will do it first, American or Russian?" . . . (Commander William J. Kotsch, USN, "Weather Control and National Strategy," *United States Naval Institute Proceedings*, July 1960, p. 76.)

(5) The classic justification for technological progress has been that it steadily frees men from the burdens of existence and provides them with the leisure in which to make "truly human uses" of their lives. The following selections would suggest, however, that by the time we arrive at this high plateau of creative leisure, we may very well find it already thickly inhabited by an even more beneficent species of inventions which will have objectified creativity itself. It is quite unclear what the justification for this form of progress is, other than the technocratic imperative: "What can be done must be done."

I would like to teach a machine how to write a limerick, and I suspect I can do it. I am quite sure that in the first batch it will be easy for anybody to pick out from a random array those limericks created by an IBM machine. But perhaps in a little while the distinctions will not be so clear. The moment we can do that we will have carried out a psychological experiment in new terms which for the first time may give a sharp definition of what is meant by a joke. (Edward Teller, "Progress in the Nuclear Age," *Mayo Clinic Proceedings*, January 1965.)

Can a computer be used to compose a symphony? As one who has been engaged in programming a large digital computer to program original musical compositions, I can testify that the very idea excites incredulity and indignation in many quarters. Such response in part reflects the extreme view of the nineteenth-century romantic tradition that regards music as direct communication of emotion from composer to listener—"from heart to heart," as Wagner said. In deference to this view it must be conceded that we do not *yet* understand the subjective aspect of musical communication well enough to study it in precise terms. . . . On the other hand, music does have its objective side. The information encoded there relates to such quantitative entities as pitch and time, and is therefore accessible to rational and ultimately mathematical analysis. . . . it is possible, at least in theory, to construct tables of probabilities describing a musical style, such as Baroque, Classical or Romantic, and perhaps even the style of an individual composer. Given such tables, one could then reverse the process and compose music in a given style. (Lejaren A. Hiller, Jr., in *Scientific American*, December 1959. Italics added.)

The most ominous aspect of such statements is the ever-present "yet" that appears in them. To offer another example: "No technology as *yet* promises to duplicate human creativity, especially in the artistic sense, if only because we do not *yet* understand the conditions and functioning of creativity. (This is not to deny that computers can be useful aids to creative activity.)" (Emmanuel G. Mesthene, *How Technology Will Shape the Future*, Harvard University Program on Technology and Society, Reprint Number 5, pp. 14–15.) The presumption involved in such statements is almost comic. For the man who thinks that creativity might *yet* become a technology is the man who stands no chance of ever understanding what creativity is. But we can be sure the technicians will eventually find us a bad mechanized substitute and persuade themselves that it is the real thing.

(6) The literature of our society dealing with imprisonment and capital punishment is extensive, including contributions by Tolstoy, Camus, Dostoyevsky, Sartre, and Koestler. Since, however, these men offer us only imaginative fiction, their work is obviously of little scientific value. What follows is

an attempt by two psychiatrists to gain, at long last, some hard data on the experience of awaiting execution. The sample population is nineteen people in the Sing Sing death house. "One might expect them," the researchers state, "to show severe depression and devastating anxiety, yet neither symptom was conspicuous among these 19 doomed persons. By what mechanisms did they avoid these expected reactions to such overwhelming stress? Do their emotional patterns change during a year or two in a death cell? And do these defenses function to the moment of execution—or do they crumble towards the end?"

Here are the psychiatrists' thumbnail sketches of their specimens—all of whom, they observe, come from "deprived backgrounds," with extensive experience of institutional confinement, and none of whom had long premeditated the killings they were convicted of. Notice how effectively the terminology and the data provided screen out the observer so that we have no sense of the character of the human presence with which these pathetic prisoners were interacting—surely a key factor in the situation. Note, too, how the concluding table of findings turns the life-and-death matter into a statistical abstraction.

This inmate is the only woman in this series. She is of dull intelligence, acts in a playful and flirtatious manner. She was usually euphoric, but became transiently depressed when she thought her case was going badly. She frequently complained of insomnia and restlessness. These symptoms quickly disappeared when she was visited by a psychiatrist whom she enjoyed seeing and talking to in a self-justifying and self-pitying manner. Psychological tests showed pervasive feelings of insecurity, repressive defenses, and an inability to handle angry and aggressive feelings in an effectual manner.

This inmate is an illiterate, inadequate individual who was convicted as an accomplice to a robbery-murder. He had an overall IQ of 51. He showed primarily depression, withdrawal, and obsessive rumination over the details of his crime and conviction. He eventually evolved a poorly elaborated paranoid system whereby he supposedly was betrayed and framed by his girl friend and one of the codefendants. Despite the looseness of his persecutory thinking, it was accompanied by a clear-cut elevation in his mood and reduction of anxiety.

He is one of the two inmates in this series who uses religious preoccupation as his major defense mechanism. He repeatedly in an almost word for word way stated his situation as follows. "No one can understand how I feel unless it happened to you. Christ came to me and I know He died for my sins. It doesn't matter if I am electrocuted or not. I am going to another world after this and I am prepared for it." As his stay progresses he becomes increasingly more hostile and antagonistic, and his behavior progressively out of keeping with his professed religious ideas. In addition to obsessive rumination, projection and withdrawal are employed to ward off feelings of anxiety and depression.

The researchers summarize their findings as follows:

Psychological defense mechanisms used
(Totals more than 19; some used more than one)
Denial by isolation of affect 7
Denial by minimizing the predicament 4
Denial by delusion formation 1
Denial by living only in the present 4
Projection 7
Obsessive rumination in connection with appeals 3
Obsessive preoccupation with religion 2
Obsessive preoccupation with intellectual or philosophical
    matters 5

(Harvey Bluestone and Carl L. McGahee, "Reaction to Extreme Stress: Impending Death by Execution," *The American Journal of Psychiatry*, November 1962, pp. 393–96.)

(7) Reportedly, within the last decade, the most promising scientific brains have been drifting away from physics to biology and medical science, where the frontiers of research

have begun to reveal more intriguing prospects. Some of them, like that which follows, vie with the ingenuity of H. G. Wells' Dr. Moreau.

Dr. Vladimir Demikhov, an eminent Soviet experimental surgeon whose grafting of additional or different heads and limbs on to dogs has drawn considerable attention, has come up with a new suggestion for the advancement of transplantation surgery.

According to "Soviet Weekly," Dr. Demikhov believes that it would be simple to store organs for spare-part surgery—not by developing techniques for banks of particular organs or tissues but by temporarily grafting the stored organ on to the exterior of human "vegetables."

A human "vegetable" is a human being who, through accident or disease, has lost all intelligent life, but is otherwise functioning normally. The surgeon's "bank" would consist of technically living bodies, each supporting externally a number of additional organs. (Anthony Tucker, science correspondent, *The Guardian* [London], January 20, 1968.)

For a popularized survey of recent work in the biological sciences, see Gordon Rattray Taylor, *The Biological Time-Bomb* (New York: World, 1968). Among other breathtaking possibilities the biologists have in store for us, there will be the capacity to produce carbon-copy human beings with interchangeable parts and faultless collective co-ordination. We shall then have, we are told, "exceptional human beings in unlimited numbers," as well as ideal basketball teams . . . and (no doubt) armies.

(8) The following are two examples of scientists doing their utmost to defend the dignity of pure research against any moralizing encroachments.

In December 1967, Dr. Arthur Kornberg, a Nobel prize winning geneticist, announced the first successful synthesis of viral DNA, an important step toward the creation of test-tube life. After the announcement Dr. Kornberg was interviewed by the press.

At the end, the moral problem was posed. "Dr. Kornberg, do you see the time when your work will come into conflict with traditional morality?" Again he took off his glasses and looked down and meditated. Very gently, he replied: "We can never predict the benefits that will flow from advancements in our fundamental knowledge. There is no knowledge that cannot be abused, but I hope that our improved knowledge of genetic chemistry will make us better able to cope with hereditary disease. I see no possibility of conflict in a decent society which uses scientific knowledge for human improvement." . . . He left it to us to define, or redefine, a decent society. (Alistair Cooke, reporting in *The Guardian* [London], December 17, 1967.)

In the summer of 1968, a controversy blew up in Great Britain over the part played by academic scientists in the activities of the Ministry of Defence Microbiological Establishment at Porton, one of the world's most richly productive centers of chemical and biological warfare research. (Porton, for example, developed some of the gases most extensively used by American forces in Vietnam.) Professor E. B. Chain of Imperial College protested this "irresponsible scoop hunting" in a lengthy letter to *The Observer*, detailing the many worthwhile lines of research that had come out of the work done at Porton.

What is wrong with accepting research grants from the Ministry of Defence? As is well known, thousands of scientists have, for many years, accepted such grants from the US Navy, the US Air Force, NATO, and similar national and international organisations for fundamental research in many branches of the physical and biological sciences: this does not mean that such work involved them in research on military technology. One can only be grateful for the wisdom and foresight shown by those responsible for formulating and deciding the policies of these organisations in allowing their funds to be made available for sponsoring fundamental university research which bears no immediate, and usually not even a remote, relation to problems of warfare technology.

Of course, almost any kind of research, however academic, and almost any invention, however beneficial to mankind, from the knife to atomic energy, from anaesthetics to plant hormones, can be used for war and other destructive purposes, but it is, of course, not the scientist and inventor who carries the responsibility for how the results of his research or his inventions are used. (*The Observer* [London], June 1, 1968.)

It is actually a dubious proposition that any scientist worth his salt cannot make a pretty accurate prediction of how his findings might be used. But even if one were to grant the point, there is one kind of result which is completely predictable and which is bound never to be far from the awareness of the researcher. Productive research results in a handsomely rewarded career, in acclaim and wide recognition. Is it too cynical to suggest that this all-too-predictable result frequently makes it ever so much harder to foresee the probable abuses of one's research?

(9) C. Wright Mills once called the middle class citizenry of our polity a collection of "cheerful robots." Perhaps it is because the human original has fallen so far short of authenticity that our behavioral scientists can place such easy confidence in the simulated caricatures of humanity upon which their research ever more heavily comes to bear. One begins to wonder how much of what our society comes to accept as humanly normal, legitimate, and appropriate in years to come will be patterned upon the behavior of such electronic homunculi as those described below.

A pioneering demonstration of the feasibility of computer simulation appeared in 1957 when Newell, Shaw, and Simon published a description of their Logic Theorist program, which proved theorems in elementary symbolic logic—a feat previously accomplished only by humans. Among subsequent applications of information processing programs to classical problems of psychological theory are Feigen-baum's Elementary Perceiver and Memorizer, a computer model of verbal rote memorization; Feldman's simulation of the behavior of subjects in a binary-choice experiment, and Hovland and Hunt's model of human concept formulation. Lindsay explores another facet of cognitive activity in his computer processing of syntactic and semantic information to analyze communications in Basic English, and Bert Green and associates have programmed a machine to respond to questions phrased in ordinary English. Still another aspect of human decision-making appears in Clarkson's model of the trust investment process. At a more general level, Newell, Shaw, and Simon have programmed an information processing theory of human problem solving, a model whose output has been compared systematically with that of human problem solvers. Reitman has incorporated elements of this general problem-solving system in simulating the complex creative activity involved in musical composition.

While early applications of information processing models focus on relatively logical aspects of human behavior, recent simulation models incorporate emotional responses. Concerned by the singlemindedness of cognitive activity programmed in the Newell, Shaw, and Simon General Problem Solver, Reitman and associates recently have programmed a Hebbian-type model of human thinking that is not in complete control of what it remembers and forgets, being subject to interruptions and to conflict. Kenneth Colby, a psychiatrist, has developed a computer model for simulating therapeutic manipulation of emotions as well as a patient's responses. In HOMUNCULUS, our computer model of elementary social behavior, simulated subjects may at times emit anger or guilt reactions, or they may suppress aggression and later vent it against a less threatening figure than the one who violated norms regarding distributive justice.

. . . Among other computer applications involving considerations of emotional behavior are Coe's simulation of responses to frustration and conflict, Loehlin's simulation of socialization, and Abelson's design for computer simulation of "hot," affect-laden cognition. Imaginative computer simulations of voting behavior have been done by Robert Abelson, William McPhee, and their associates. Using the fluoridation controversies as a case in point, Abelson and Bernstein blend theories from several disciplines and from both field and experimental phenomena in constructing their model. Simulated individuals are assigned characteristics known to be relevant, and the programmed model specifies the processes by which they may change during the fluoridation campaign. . . .

In another study . . . Raymond Breton has simulated a restriction-of-output situation. According to this model, under most conditions pressures from fellow workmen result in a more homogeneous output, presumably in conformity with the norm. When motivation for monetary reward is intensified, however, some simulated workers develop negative sentiments toward those attempting to apply constraints, and variability of output increases.

(J. T. and J. E. Gullahorn, "Some Computer Applications in Social Science," *American Sociological Review*, vol. 30, June 1965, pp. 353–365.)

Who borrows the Medusa's eye
Resigns to the empirical lie.
The knower petrifies the known:
The subtle dancer turns to stone.

BIBLIOGRAPHICAL NOTES

Chapter I: Technocracy's Children and *Chapter II:* An Invasion of Centaurs

Much of what is most valuable in the counter culture does not find its way into literate expression—a fact well worth bearing in mind if one wants to achieve any decent understanding especially of what the more hip-bohemian young are up to. One is apt to find out more about their ways by paying attention to posters, buttons, fashions of dress and dance—and especially to the pop music, which now knits together the whole thirteen to thirty age group. Timothy Leary is probably correct in identifying the pop and rock groups as the real "prophets" of the rising generation. Unfortunately, I find this music difficult to take, though I recognize that one probably hears the most vivid and timely expression of young dissent not only in the lyrics of the songs but in the whole raucous style of their sound and performance. While one cannot avoid being impressed with the innovation and dazzling sophistication of the best pop music, I fear I tend to find much of it too brutally loud and/or too electronically gimmicked up. I am not particularly in favor of turning musicianship and the human voice into the raw material of acoustical engineering. I also feel that the pop music scene lends itself to a great deal of commercial sensationalizing: the heated search for startling new tricks and shocks. However . . .

In the way of reading matter, the most timely sources are the innumerable and often ephemeral underground newspapers. (Is anyone anywhere collecting a decent file of this material?) It is a measure of how contagious the counter culture is that even medium-sized towns (Spokane, Northampton, Massachusetts, Dallas . . .) are now producing these journals of militant irreverence. The major papers include *The Berkeley Barb, The East Village Other,* the San Francisco and Southern California *Oracles,* the Los Angeles and New York *Free Presses,* and, in London, *The International Times, Peace News,* and *Oz.* There has been an effort to anthologize this scattered material in the *Underground Digest*, published by Underground Communications, Inc. (PO Box 211, Village Station, New York, N.Y.).

The vice of these papers is that they easily slide off into the bizarrely salacious or the psychedelically mushy. Worse still, some of the more militant examples seem to be fabricated out of a crude and frenetic contempt for everybody but the editorial staff. However, amid the sheer smut and windy anger one often finds some wry wit (especially in the comic art), a cry of the heart that is gentle and innocent, and even a reliable piece of reporting.

At the national level, *The Realist* appears to do the best job of keeping up with the more wild and woolly dissent of the day. One of the pioneer efforts of the underground press was the one-shot *Journal for the Protection of All Beings* (San Francisco: City Lights, 1961), a fantastic and delightful collection of essays which must now be a collector's item.

The catalogues of the various free and experimental universities provide another convenient way of keeping abreast of counter cultural interests.

Norman Mailer's eccentric essay *The White Negro* (San Francisco: City Lights Pocket Poets Series, 1957) is still one of the best early evaluations of youthful dissent. More currently there is *Revolution for the Hell of It* (New York: Dial Press, 1969) by Abbie Hoffman, who has become androgynous (apparently) and now goes by the name of Free. Hoffman, a leader of the Youth International Party (of Battle of Chicago fame) conveys the foul-mouthed whimsy of hip a-politics.

The New Left offers more articulate materials. Its periodicals include *The New University Conference Newsletter* (Chicago), *Liberation* (New York), and at the slick mass-circulation level, *Ramparts*. Mitchell Cohen and Dennis Hale, eds., *The New Student Left*, rev. ed. (Boston: Beacon Press, 1967) is a good anthology. Paul Jacobs and Saul Landau, *The New Radicals: A Report with Documents* (New York: Vintage Books, 1966) provides a knowledgeable handbook especially on historical background and the distinctions between the many left-wing student groups.

On some of the more important student insurrections, see Hal Draper, *The New Student Revolt*, with an introduction by Mario Savio (New York: Grove Press, 1966); S. M. Lipset and S. S. Wolin, eds., *The Berkeley Student Revolt: Facts and Interpretations* (New

York: Anchor Books, 1966); Jerry Avorn, et al, *Up Against the Ivy Wall: A History of the Columbia Crisis* (New York: Atheneum, 1968); Hervé Bourges, ed., *The French Student Revolt: The Leaders Speak* (New York: Hill & Wang, 1968). If revolutionaries must still wait for history to vindicate them, American publishers are clearly making sure that history gets down in black and white no more than nine months after the event.

Daniel and Gabriel Cohn-Bendit's *Obsolete Communism: The Left-Wing Alternative* (New York: McGraw-Hill, 1969) is a shrewd and brightly phrased analysis of the May '68 Paris insurrection by its most prominent anarchist spokesmen. The Cohn-Bendits display a marvelous libertarian sensitivity to managerial manipulation of both the technocratic economy and its would-be revolutionary opposition movements. "The real meaning of revolution is not a change in management," the authors argue, "but a change in man. . . . the revolution must be born of joy and not of sacrifice." But I fear they overestimate the potentialities of what the "spontaneous resistance" of "insurrectional cells" can accomplish in the absence of a deep and pervasive critique of the mythos of the technocracy. Lacking that, I doubt that their strategy of ad hoc agitation in the streets can lead to more than temporarily therapeutic outbursts of frustration.

A thoughtful discussion of "The New Left and the Old" appears in *The American Scholar* for Autumn 1967. The participants are Dwight MacDonald, Richard Rovere, Ivanhoe Donaldson, and Tom Hayden.

There are searching studies of the problems of achieving adulthood these days in Kenneth Keniston, *Young Radicals* (New York: Harcourt, Brace & World, 1968); Edgar Friedenberg, *The Dignity of the Young and Other Atavisms* (Boston: Beacon Press, 1965); and of course, Paul Goodman, *Growing up Absurd* (New York: Random House, 1960). Goodman's book is flawed by the quaint idea that females have no special problems about growing up. No doubt because they have the option of passing into a prefabricated social subordination—something our own black youth seem to have decided is no great favor.

For some reflections on how the ethos of dissent affects the learned professions, see Theodore Roszak, ed., *The Dissenting Academy* (New York: Pantheon, 1968).

On the technocracy, the best theoretical statement is Jacques Ellul,

The Technological Society, trans. John W. Wilkinson (New York: A. A. Knopf, 1964). The book suffers from being far too verbose and crushingly pessimistic. Just as pessimistic, but less verbose is Roderick Seidenberg, *Posthistoric Man* (Chapel Hill, N.C.: University of North Carolina Press, 1950), which attempts an evolutionary explanation of our technological obsessions. The best attempt so far to work out a full socioeconomic anatomy of our burgeoning American technocracy is John Kenneth Galbraith, *The New Industrial State* (Boston: Houghton Mifflin, 1967). The thesis of the work is that "the imperatives of technology and organization, not the images of ideology, are what determine the shape of economic society." Lacking the inclination to step outside the mystique of scientific knowledge, Galbraith fails to see that "the imperatives of technology and organization" comprise a very definite ideology, but one which cannot be challenged without calling into question the myth of objective consciousness. For this reason, too, his proposed reforms are pallid, especially where he laments the philistinism of the "techno-structure." Strange that Galbraith does not recognize how magnificently cultivated a society we are fast becoming. I have little doubt myself that within another generation our National Security Council will hold its deliberations while performing string quartets. We shall indeed be a society of warrior and industrial humanists. Galbraith's proposals for expanding the "aesthetic dimension" of higher education (by which he seems to mean good taste) should be checked against some important articles on the denaturing of the humanities: Louis Kampf, "The Humanities and the Inhumanities," *The Nation,* September 30, 1968; and William Arrowsmith, "The Future of Teaching," *The Public Interest,* Winter 1967.

Norbert Wiener's *The Human Use of Human Beings* (Boston: Houghton Mifflin, 1950) established the concept of "cybernetics" and worked out one of the key propositions of technocratic managerialism: namely, that man and social life generally are so much communications apparatus. Along the lines of this unfortunate metaphor we arrive at all sorts of commonplace contemporary idiocies which small minds are now busily elaborating into a *Weltanschauung,* such as that a photoelectric cell is a "sense organ," that feedback is "proprioception," that computers have "memories," can "learn," "teach," "make decisions," and "create." Despite Wiener's intelligent forebodings about the potential abuses of cybernation (see his tenth chapter), the book is a painful example of how a scientist of great conscience contributes in spite of himself to the degradation of human personality. For some healthy doubts about the purely technical capabilities of computers, see Mortimer Taube, *Computers and Common Sense* (New York: McGraw-Hill, 1961).

For a recent expression of the technocratic mentality at work, see Robert McNamara, The Essence of Security (New York: Harper & Row, 1968). Two further voices of technocratic orthodoxy are James R. Killian, Jr., "Toward a Research-Reliant Society," and Jerome B. Weisner, "Technology and Society," both essays in Harry Woolf, ed., *Science as a Cultural Force* (Baltimore, Md.: The Johns Hopkins Press, 1964). With respect to research, development, expertise, and government support thereof, the invincible argument of these essays is as follows: more, more, more, MORE. Against such mighty logic, no public authority can or wants to stand.

Beyond this, simply give attention to anything that derives from past, present, and future presidential policy advisors on defense, economics, or foreign affairs: McGeorge Bundy, A. A. Berle, Edward Teller, W. W. Rostow, Henry Kissinger, and such. Anything by Herman Kahn will also serve as an authoritative sample of the technocratic style, as will whatever publications one comes across from RAND, the Harvard University Program on Technology and Science, Kahn's own Hudson Institute, the Stanford Research Institute, Technical Operations Incorporated . . . and ever so many other military-industrial-university think-tanks.

For a fictional presentation of utopian social engineering, there is B. F. Skinner's *Walden Two* (New York: Macmillan, 1948).

John Wilkinson, ed., *Technology and Human Values* (Santa Barbara, Calif.: Center for the Study of Democratic Institutions, 1967) contains several interesting essays relating to the Ellul thesis.

Stanley Kubrick's *Dr. Strangelove* is the strongest comment on the obscenity of it all. Unhappily, such satire of absurd exaggeration is pretty nearly defunct in an age whose so-called reality exceeds the insanities of the satirical imagination. Not even Jonathan Swift could have invented such pernicious lunacy as the balance of terror or thermonuclear civil defense.

Much of the best thought on technocratic social forms and practices appears throughout the works of Herbert Marcuse and Paul Goodman, as listed below.

Chapter III: The Dialectics of Liberation

Herbert Marcuse's major works are: *Reason and Revolution: Hegel and The Rise of Social Theory* (Oxford: Oxford University Press, 1941); *Soviet Marxism: A Critical Analysis* (London: Routledge & Kegan Paul, 1958); *Eros and Civilization,* for which one should see the Vintage Books edition of 1962 with its important "new preface"; *One-Dimensional Man* (Boston: Beacon Press, 1964).

Marcuse's essay, "Socialism in the Developed Countries," *International Socialist Journal,* April 1965, pp. 139–51, is a good, brief exposition of his social theory, free of much of the Germanic ponderousness of his longer works.

One of Marcuse's most widely read essays, especially among the European young, is "Repressive Tolerance," which appears in Robert Wolff, Barrington Moore, Jr., and H. Marcuse, *A Critique of Pure Tolerance* (Boston: Beacon Press, 1965). The unhappy thesis of this piece seems to be that tolerance ought to be withdrawn from repressive right-wing spokesmen and extended to progressive left-wing spokesmen—if necessary (and how else?) by invoking the "natural right" of "oppressed and overpowered minorities to use extralegal means . . ." Ideas of this vintage hardly require the heady philosophical justification Marcuse offers them. Their legitimacy tends to be generated spontaneously whenever righteous indignation and revolutionary power are compounded. I am more inclined to agree with Tolstoy, who, when asked if he did not see a difference between reactionary repression and revolutionary repression, replied that there was, of course, a difference: "the difference between cat shit and dog shit."

A number of essays dealing with Marcuse's thought appear in Kurt H. Wolff and Barrington Moore, Jr., eds. *The Critical Spirit: Essays in Honor of Herbert Marcuse* (Boston: Beacon Press, 1967).

Marcuse's interpretation of Freud should be compared with the doctrinaire Marxist reading of Paul Baran in "Marxism and Psychoanalysis," *Monthly Review,* October 1959.

On Marxist Humanism, see Daniel Bell, "In Search of Marxist Humanism: The Debate on Alienation," *Soviet Survey,* No. 32, April–June 1960 and its bibliographical notes. Erich Fromm's *Marx's*

Concept of Man (New York: Ungar, 1961), is a good, if often too adulatory, essay on the subject. The book contains translated excerpts from Marx's *Economic and Philosophical Manuscripts*, the whole of which has been published by the Foreign Languages Publishing House, Moscow, 1959. Some interesting remarks by Marcuse on Marxist Humanism appear in "Varieties of Humanism," *Center Magazine* (Center for the Study of Democratic Institutions, Santa Barbara), June 1968.

Norman O. Brown's major works are *Life against Death: The Psychoanalytical Meaning of History* (Middletown, Conn.: Wesleyan University Press, 1959) and *Love's Body* (New York: Random House, 1966). His essay, "Apocalypse: The Place of Mystery in the Life of the Mind" in *Harper's*, May 1961, is vital to the understanding of *Love's Body*. So too is the exchange between Marcuse and Brown in *Commentary* for February and March 1967.

Chapter IV: Journey to the East . . .

Allen Ginsberg's poetry has appeared in too many places to be listed here. Collections of his work are easily located. A statement on his poetics appears in Donald M. Allen, ed., *The New American Poetry 1945–1960* (New York: Grove Press, 1960). His collection of early poems, *Empty Mirror* (New York: Totem Press, 1961), with its preface by William Carlos Williams, makes an important contribution to the understanding of his later poems. While Ginsberg's work is one of the best and most visible weather vanes of the times, and while it is always charmingly big-hearted, I cannot think very highly of it as poetry, except for *jolie laide* passages here and there which invariably come across better when he reads them aloud than they do in print. Ginsberg says all the right things, but I prefer the way poets like Gary Snyder, Robert Bly, and Denise Levertov (among the poets of the 1950s and 1960s) say them. Lawrence Ferlinghetti seems to me a marvelous comic poet. His wise and wry *Coney Island of the Mind* (New York: New Directions, 1958) is probably the most widely read book of verse among the college-age young of this century. Michael McClure's poetry also appeals to me; but his much-praised play *The Beard* is a sad example of how easily the counter culture weakens toward pretentious (and commercially advantageous) pornography—and with such unabashed self-congratulations it weakens!

At some point along the way, one must mention Kenneth Rexroth, whose influence on our youth culture has been subtle, pervasive, and entirely healthy. His poetry, which I find superior to anything his younger colleagues have produced, makes it obvious that he was there before the counter culture arrived.

Jack Kerouac's latest book, *Satori in Paris* (New York: Grove Press, 1966), only makes one wonder if he was ever worth taking seriously, alas!

Of Alan Watts' many books, those I have liked most are *The Way of Zen* (New York: Pantheon, 1957) and *Psychotherapy East and West* (New York: Pantheon, 1961). *This Is It* (New York: Collier Books, 1967) contains the essay "Beat Zen, Square Zen, and Zen." *The Book: On the Taboo against Knowing Who You Are* (New York: Collier Books, 1967) is a good example of Watts playing "philosophical entertainer"—in this case primarily to college audiences.

D. T. Suzuki's *Zen Buddhism*, edited by William Barrett (New York: Doubleday, 1956) carries his most widely read essays.

My own slender knowledge of Zen and Taoism owes much to all the standard Arthur Waley translations; to Nyogen Senzaki and R. S. McCandless, eds., *The Iron Flute* (Tokyo: Tuttle, 1961); and to Thomas Merton's translations in The Way of Chuang Tzu (New York: New Directions, 1965). Also to the music of John Cage . . . which may be questionable *as* music, but is, I think, delightful nonsense.

Chapter V: The Counterfeit Infinity

Robert S. DeRopp, *Drugs and the Mind* (London: Gollancz, 1958) is a good survey of the psychedelics and the influence they have had on cultural expression since the time of De Quincey. William James, *The Varieties of Religious Experience* (New York: Modern Library, 1936) is still the most comprehensive attempt to bring the states of transnormal consciousness into the philosophical mainstream—though not one that has had much impact on academic thought. The most influential recent books are Aldous Huxley's *Doors of Perception* (New York: Harper, 1954) and Alan Watts, *The Joyous Cosmology: Adventures in the Chemistry of Consciousness*, foreword by Timothy Leary and Richard Alpert (New York: Pantheon, 1962).

Timothy Leary's contribution is summed up in *High Priest* (New York: World, 1968) and *The Politics of Ecstasy* (New York: Putnam, 1968). The former, the first of a projected four-volume autobiography, is a perfect caricature of most of the counter cultural themes discussed in this book, well larded with a most unbecoming egotism.

Ralph Metzner, ed., *The Ecstatic Adventure* (New York: Macmillan, 1968) anthologizes about forty accounts of psychedelic experiments. It strikes me that those interested enough in the subject to wade through this much reportage should probably stop reading and start doing it themselves. There is also Jane Dunlap (pseud.), *Exploring Inner-Space: Personal Experiences under LSD-25* (London: Gollancz, 1961), a small sampling of which should be enough to scale down anyone's evaluation of the psychedelic promise.

Carlos Casteneda's *The Teachings of Don Juan: A Yaqui Way of Knowledge* (Berkeley: University of California Press, 1968) places the psychedelic experience in the context of an Amerindian shamanistic world view and is therefore a distinctive contribution to the literature on the subject.

Chapter VI: Exploring Utopia

Paul Goodman's works are too numerous and by now too well known to be listed here. I would, however, emphasize the importance of *The Empire City*, (New York: Macmillan, 1964) and *Gestalt Therapy* (New York: Delta Books, 1951), coauthored by Frederick Perls and Ralph Hefferline, in the understanding of Goodman. His *Persons or Personnel: Decentralizing and the Mixed System* (New York: Random House, 1965) offers important reflections on the technocracy and its alternatives. Goodman's essay "The Diggers in 1984," in *Ramparts*, September 1967, is a nice example of his visionary sociology.

Goodman's short stories, some of which are fine pieces of writing, have been collected in the volume *Adam and His Works* (New York: Vintage Books, 1968). Some of these stories capture the essential Goodman in a few pages' space: the anarchist social theory, the athleticism, the Reichian sexuality, the Taoist-Gestalt mysticism.

On anarchism generally, George Woodcock's *Anarchism* (Cleveland, Ohio: Meridian Books, 1962) is a good basic summary of the movement's history and the classical theoretical works. Alex Comfort, *Authority and Delinquency in the Modern State: A Criminological Approach to the Problem of Power* (London: Routledge & Kegan Paul, 1950) is a classic analysis of the corruptions of power, by a leading English anarchist theorist (and physician, and poet, and novelist, and critic . . .) whose work is remarkably similar to Goodman's. The English periodical *Anarchy* (London) offers the best continuing coverage of anarchist thought on current problems. Prince Kropotkin is, I think, the most winning of the tradition's great ideologues.

On communitarianism, I would suggest Arthur Morgan, *The Small Community* (New York: Harper, 1942), and Clare Huchet Bishop, *All Things Common* (New York: Harper, 1950), which deals with the Boimondau community of work in France, in whose image we ought to have more experiments. Above all, there is Martin Buber's absolutely superb *Paths in Utopia* (Boston: Beacon Press, 1960).

Finally, I think one must mention Aldous Huxley's novel *Island* (New York: Harper & Row, 1962), which is cluttered with brilliant communitarian ideas and insights, and which has had great influence among its young readers.

Chapter VII: The Myth of Objective Consciousness

The recent literature dedicated to celebrating the virtues of the scientific world view is extensive. Jacob Bronowski is among the most cultivated of the science boosters. See his *The Common Sense of Science* (London: Pelican Books, 1960) and *Science and Human Values*, rev. ed. (New York: Harper Torchbooks, 1965). I find it interesting how Bronowski's views (e.g., " . . . men have asked for freedom, justice, and respect precisely as the scientific spirit has spread among them") parallel those of the right-wing "objectivist" ideologue, Ayn Rand. Julian Huxley's *Religion Without Revelation* (London: Max Parrish, 1959) advocates the transmutation of science into a secular religion.

See also P. B. Medawar, *The Art of the Soluble* (London: Methuen, 1967) and the widely cited (and cheerfully technocratic) C. P. Snow, *The Two Cultures and the Scientific Revolution* (Cambridge: Cambridge University Press, 1963). C. C. Gillespie, *The Edge of Objectivity* (Princeton, N.J.: Princeton University Press, 1960) is a strong, stoical presentation of the alienative trend of scientific thought—though it frankly mystifies me how anyone can settle for such a grimly masochistic conception of what the pursuit of truth leads us to.

Marshall McLuhan's *Understanding Media* (New York: McGraw-Hill, 1964), along with his other writings, carries to a revealing extreme the subordination of personality to technology. I rather feel that the young who have taken to McLuhan fail to understand the full implications of what the man is saying. My thoughts on McLuhan appear in "The Summa Popologica of Marshall McLuhan" in *McLuhan Pro and Con*, edited by Raymond Rosenthal (New York: Funk & Wagnalls, 1968).

The fullest and most exuberant recent survey of technological art is Jasia Reichardt, ed., *Cybernetic Serendipity: The Computer and the Arts* (New York and London: Studio International, 1968).

The following are the works I have found helpful in one degree or another in taking issue with the conventional scientific world view: Alfred North Whitehead, *Science and the Modern World* (New York: Mentor Books, 1925); Suzanne Langer, *Philosophy in a New Key*, 2d ed. (New York: Mentor Books, 1962); Michael Polanyi, *Personal Knowledge* (Chicago: University of Chicago Press, 1959)—an outstanding critique of scientific objectivity; René Dubos, *The Dreams of Reason* (New York: Columbia University Press, 1961) and *The Mirage of Health* (New York: Harper, 1959). The latter raises some startling questions about our most commonplace assumptions regarding the progress of medical science. Jacques Barzun, *Science: The Glorious Entertainment* (New York: Harper & Row, 1964); Arthur Koestler, *The Ghost in the Machine* (New York: Macmillan, 1967) is especially good for its forceful criticism of behavioral psychology; Barry Commoner, *Science and Survival* (New York: Viking Press, 1966); Catherine Roberts, *The Scientific Conscience* (New York: Braziller, 1967).

Of the many wise contributions of Lewis Mumford, I find the following the most important for the purposes of my discussion here: *The Conduct of Life* (New York: Harcourt, Brace & World, 1951); *The Transformations of Man* (New York: Collier Books, 1956); *The Myth of the Machine* (New York: Harcourt, Brace & World, 1967).

The latter develops a highly significant conception of the origins of machine technology and its relevance to civilization.

Abraham Maslow, *The Psychology of Science* (New York: Harper & Row, 1966) is absolutely essential to an intelligent evaluation of scientific objectivity.

Lynn White's "Historical Roots of Our Ecological Crisis," *Science*, March 10, 1967, attempts to assess Christianity's contribution to our misconception of nature.

The Society for Social Responsibility in Science Newsletter (published in Bala-Cynwyd, Pa.) carries on an admirable discussion of the professional ethics of science. S. P. R. Charter's periodical *Man on Earth* (published in Olema, Calif.) is an ambitious effort to criticize the bad ecological habits of our society.

By far the most searching, on-going discussions of science I know of appear in the remarkable publication, *Manas* (POB 32112, El Sereno Station, Los Angeles, Calif.)

I will also mention Bertrand Russell's *Autobiography*, 2 vols. (Boston: Little, Brown, 1967–68), which offers some heartrending expressions of the spiritual inadequacy of the scientific world view on the part of one of its greatest investigators and promoters.

Chapter VIII: Eyes of Flesh, Eyes of Fire

Much of what is said in this chapter derives generally from the Romantic sensibility. Anything Blake ever wrote seems supremely relevant to the search for alternative realities. Shelley's, *"Defence of Poetry"* is surely a key statement. From an earlier period, the poetry of Thomas Traherne also seems to me especially important to renewing our capacity for experience. Henri Bergson's *Two Sources of Morality and Religion* (Garden City, N.Y.: Anchor Books, 1954) taught me a basic distinction in the discussion of religion which is invariably overlooked by the secularized humanism of our time.

Among more recent works that impinge on this chapter are John Beer, *Blake's Humanism* (New York: Barnes & Noble, 1968); Ernst Lehrs, *Man or Matter: Introduction to a Spiritual Understanding of Nature Based on Goethe's Method*, rev. ed. (New York: Harper, 1958); R. D. Laing, *The Politics of Experience and the Bird of Paradise* (London: Penguin Books, 1967). Everything I have ever read by Martin Buber, but especially his *Hasidism* (New York:

Philosophical Library, 1948), speaks with beautiful cogency to the problem of cleansing the doors of perception.

The anthropological notions contained in the chapter are probably eccentric from the viewpoint of professional orthodoxy. I am inclined, however, to agree with Paul Goodman's contention (in *Gestalt Therapy*, p. 307) that the great task of anthropology is "to show what of human nature has been 'lost' and, practically, to devise experiments for its recovery."

I draw principally upon: Mircea Eliade, *Shamanism* (Princeton, N.J.: Princeton University Press, 1964)—an indispensable survey and analysis—and *Myths, Dreams and Mysteries* (New York: Harper, 1961); Joseph Campbell, *Hero with a Thousand Faces* (New York: Pantheon, 1949); Dorothy Lee, *Freedom and Culture* (Englewood Cliffs, N.J.: Prentice-Hall, 1959); Robert Redfield, *The Primitive World and its Transformations* (Ithaca, N.Y.: Cornell University Press, 1953) and *The Little Community and Peasant Society and Culture* (Chicago: The University of Chicago Press, 1960); Géza Roheim, *Gates of the Dream* (New York: International Universities Press, 1952); R. H. Lowie, *Primitive Religion* (New York: Boni & Liveright, 1924). The latter makes the critical point that the essence of religion (and magic) is the sense of "the Extraordinary." On this primitive awareness of the sacred, now being so relentlessly driven toward inadequate secular substitutes ("bad magic" as I term it), see also B. Malinowski, *Magic, Science and Religion* (New York: Doubleday-Anchor, 1948) and Roger Callois, *Man and the Sacred* (Glencoe, Ill.: Free Press, 1959). The latter is rather lightweight as anthropology, but like Rudolph Otto's classic *The Idea of the Holy* (New York: Galaxy Books, 1958), it is stimulating philosophical speculation.

Kaj Birket-Smith, *The Eskimos* (London: Methuen, 1936) is an excellent study of the world view of one primitive culture and of the role of the shaman. C. M. Bowra, *Primitive Song* (New York: Mentor Books, 1963) examines the magical vision as it is expressed in the songs of surviving primitives. Along the same lines, see Jerome Rothenberg, ed., *Technicians of the Sacred* (New York: Doubleday, 1968), a very fine anthology of primitive poetry, equipped with brilliant commentaries by the editor.